ART WITHOUT FRONTIERS

Annebella Pollen

ART WITHOUT FRONTIERS

THE STORY OF THE BRITISH COUNCIL, VISUAL ARTS, AND A CHANGING WORLD

ART/BOOKS

ENDPAPERS Ed Hall, *British Council Collection Banner*, 2012, cotton drill, fabric paint, 194 × 358 cm (P8393) (detail)

PAGE 2 Albert Richards, *Take Off and Landing Field*, 1943, oil on cardboard, 62.2 × 75.5 cm (P161) (detail)

First published in the United Kingdom in 2023 by Art Books Publishing Ltd

Art Books Publishing Ltd
77 Oriel Road
London E9 5SG
Tel: +44 (0)20 8533 5835
info@artbookspublishing.co.uk
www.artbookspublishing.co.uk

ISBN 978-1-908970-52-7

British Library Cataloguing-in-Publication Data
A catalogue record for this book is available from the British Library

Designed by Art / Books
Printed and bound in Latvia by Livonia Print

Distributed outside North America by
Thames & Hudson
181a High Holborn
London WC1V 7QX
United Kingdom
Tel: +44 (0)20 7845 5000
Fax: +44 (0)20 7845 5055
sales@thameshudson.co.uk

Available in North America through
ARTBOOK | D.A.P.
75 Broad Street, Suite 630
New York, N.Y. 10004
www.artbook.com

CONTENTS

PREFACE

In late 2018, the British Council put out an open call for a historian to tell the story of its visual arts work in international cultural relations. With more than eighty years of exhibition-making under its belt, and a body of nearly nine thousand works by some of the biggest names in British art history – now known as the British Council Collection – this was an incredible opportunity to research an important untold story of art in Britain and its role in the wider world. I leapt at the chance and was awarded the commission.

I soon realized the scale of the task. The British Council works in more than one hundred countries. Its purposes and practices have developed and flexed over time and in different places. Not only has the organization changed shape and style, but so too have social attitudes, cultural tastes, and political contexts shifted fundamentally during the turbulent transformations of the twentieth and twenty-first centuries. I mapped these movements through an extensive array of art works and archives, exhibition catalogues and news coverage, letters and ledgers held in public and private hands. With free access to all British Council resources, fleshed out with further additions of my own, I listened to artists and administrators, exhibition attendees and ambassadors, and learned from current and former staff. Through these abundant materials, I gained a personal perspective on an ambitious enterprise, full of surprises and success stories, with art and its international audiences at its heart. Several years in the making, the book you hold in your hands is not an official history, nor a definitive interpretation, but an independent outsider's assessment of an ongoing story of art in a global context.

Suki Dhanda, *Untitled*, 2002, C-type print mounted on aluminium, 125 × 125 cm (P8509) (detail)

INTRODUCTION

Establishing the Collection

The British Committee for Relations with Other Countries was first established in 1934. 'Committee' became 'Council' the following year, and by 1936 the eight-word description had been abbreviated to the British Council, which still stands today. These two words formed a more manageable moniker, but the abbreviation concealed the core purpose contained in the extended name. In part because of its opaque title and the fact that its work largely takes place outside the country, too few Britons know what the British Council does and what it has achieved. This book looks at the organization's practices and objectives by exploring how it has purchased, collected, and displayed visual art and crafts in international cultural relations from its founding to the present day. It tells a chronological series of stories that focus on its global exhibition programme and its acquisition, development, and use of the group of art works now known as the British Council Collection.

Art Without Frontiers asks several core questions: what is the value of art in international cultural exchange, and how does that change over time? What do exhibitions of British art and crafts communicate as they travel overseas? How do the collecting, exhibiting, and touring activities of the British Council reflect and even shape Britain's standing in the world? The answers to these and other questions that emerge in the following pages come from an immer-

Frances Hodgkins, *Arrangement of Jugs*, 1938, lithograph, 44.7 × 60.5 cm (P2459) (detail)

sive investigation of institutional papers, archival photographs, art works and exhibition ephemera, government documents, news reports, internal correspondence, and personal interviews. The book maps the interrelation between the policies of the wider organization and the practices of what is today called the Visual Arts department. Through the discussion of a number of key objects, personalities, and exhibitions, and by following the British Council Collection as it moves across the years and around the globe, it explores the department's historic intentions and achievements, but also its disruptions and controversies.

Definitions and purposes

The British Council's definition and purpose was reflected upon and refined repeatedly in its early years, and the self-scrutiny continues nine decades later as the meaning of international relationships and cultural exchange continues to shift and flex. Nonetheless, despite the passing generations and the rapidly changing world, the Council still describes itself as 'the United Kingdom's international organization for cultural relations and educational opportunities'.[1] Across the twentieth and twenty-first centuries, continuities prevail.

Terminology was always a thorny issue for the British Council, not only in what it was called, but also in what it did and does. Its core emphasis was and remains the building of overseas relations through cultural practices, separated, inasmuch as they can be, from economics and politics. The organization's annual report for 1942–3 characterized these relations as the 'exchange between this and other countries of information about the work of scientists, doctors, engineers, teachers, lawyers, architects, trade unionists, scholars, musicians and artists'. Such relations were variously called 'ordinary' and 'popular' in the Council's early days. But, as the report reflected, 'Few Englishmen at home ever understood what these popular relations might be, and looked darkly upon any effort to create them as a form of propaganda – that word so displeasing to the British ear.'[2] At least since the First World War, propaganda had been seen in Britain as a practice of persuasion utilized by totalitarian governments; the British Council recognized that any official body engaged in related or similar activities would be viewed as ideologically suspect.

In part because of this unease, Britain was a relative latecomer in the establishment of an institution for cultural relations overseas, particularly in comparison with France, Germany, and Italy. As the author and Labour politician Harold Nicolson claimed in 1955, on the occasion of the British Council's twenty-first birthday, this disposition – of being backwards-in-coming-forwards – was the result of national characteristics that were simultaneously modest and arrogant. He stated, mockingly, 'It pleases us to imagine that we are bad at self-advertisement and even at self-explanation. The Americans, we are assured, are born with the gift of salesmanship and go through life lauding the size, the novelty and the excellence of their wares.' By contrast, the British had been 'trained to regard as obnoxious all forms of self-display'. As a consequence, then, a haughty non-communicative attitude became entrenched. Nicolson playfully encapsulated the nationally exceptionalist state of mind: 'If foreigners failed to appreciate, or even to notice, our gifts of invention or our splendid adaptability, then there was nothing that we could or should do to mitigate their obtuseness. The genius of England, unlike that of lesser countries, spoke for itself.'[3]

The first attempts to establish a British organization to develop formal international relationships had been made in the 1920s by George Curzon, 1st Marquess Curzon of Kedleston, at the time the secretary of state for foreign affairs. At this point, the intention was to support British expatriates, to establish British libraries overseas, and to promote 'political or commercial propaganda in foreign countries'. The political propaganda element of Lord Curzon's scheme was summarily dismissed; only trade relations were allowed to stand.[4] Ambivalent attitudes to national self-promotion were fundamentally shifted, however, by what Nicolson described as the 'devastating efficiency' of 'our enemies' in the same area.[5] The rise of fascism across Europe in the 1930s sharpened the collective mind, and the British Council was put in place, at least in part, to counter this growing threat. Notably, for the newly instituted body, 'propaganda' was usually perceived as what was done by other countries; Britain's own activities were framed as the propagation of 'truth', hence the authoritative certainty of its founding motto: 'Truth will Triumph'.

English wood and stone engraver and typographer Reynolds Stone designed several early logos and coats of arms for the British Council, each bearing the new organization's motto 'Truth Will Triumph', including this bookplate from 1938.

Nonetheless, the softer-sounding qualification of 'cultural propaganda' – another early British Council term – was allowed and it provided a more modified descriptor of its early practices. But, it admitted, this was a 'double horror of a phrase'. It paired political messaging with the complications of culture, that most contested of terms, replete with its 'implications of priggish precocity' to British minds suspicious of such a thing.[6] Cultural diplomacy or, as is currently preferred, 'cultural relations', may best encapsulate the British Council's mission, but words such as 'information' or 'projection' were also used at the outset, especially in regard to the dissemination of a British national identity, whatever that might be understood to be. These terms had their own issues; for instance, they implied a one-way communication strategy rather than any form of exchange. As the Council's 1945 annual report surmised, a focus on projection also presumed 'a concentration on the difference between one national "way of life" and others at a time when the concentration should be upon likeness, in other words upon common interests that exist almost everywhere to an extent not usually realised'. In the British Council's early ambitions, cultural relations were 'not competitive but reciprocal'.[7] At best, it aimed to develop 'the non-political, non-economic relations between peoples' as 'an instrument of peace'.[8]

How one perceives the connections between culture, economics, and politics depends on how one views the relationship of the British Council to the Foreign, Commonwealth and Development Office (to give the department its current formulation). Initially wholly dependent for its funding on this part of government, but now receiving only around fourteen percent of funds in the form of a grant-in-aid, the British Council has sometimes been characterized as the Foreign Office's cultural wing, its chief ally, or, in a less-than-lovely phrase, the 'lubricant to the everyday workings of British foreign policy'.[9] While there is no doubt that the British Council's practices are informed by the agendas of its funders, a core principle is that the organization stands at arm's length from government. This was the intention from the outset. In Nicolson's appraisal, 'although general policy must remain under the distant supervision of the Government, it would be an error to render the Council the subsidiary of any Whitehall Department. It was felt that, on the analogy of the British Broadcasting Corporation, better results would be secured if the Council, in its administration and functioning, were to be accorded the greatest possible autonomy.'[10]

The ambition for political and cultural independence for the Council was outlined in its annual report of 1947: 'In Literature, in the Arts, in Science and in Education, no attempt is made by the Government of the day to impose its authority for the propagation of partisan political or philosophical doctrines. The British Council can rightly claim that it is divorced from politics and political theories and can spread the knowledge of British culture in foreign countries free from suspicion of any political objective.'[11] Within the Council, too, from the beginning, each specialist department was expected to have its own decision-making autonomy. In practice, separating politics and economics from culture is not always as neat as in this claim. Nonetheless, the policy of independence is one that the British Council has continued to exercise as a core principle. It can be measured and tested, to a greater or lesser extent, in all the examples that follow.

The shifting interrelationships between politics and culture – and often the tensions between them – form one of the leitmotifs of this book. On one

First chair of the Fine Arts Committee, Sir Lionel Lawson Faudel-Phillips (second left) with artist Fred Roe (far left) and industrialist Charles Cheers Wakefield, 1st Viscount Wakefield (second right), c. 1933

level, government expectations about the function of art overseas may align or be at odds with the ambitions and outcomes of the British Council. On another, while the objectives of the Council as a whole and the interests of its individual departments have often dovetailed, on some occasions they have pulled in different directions. Contributing artists and receiving audiences, too, have their own distinct ideas about what forms of culture may be wanted and what is accepted – and what is acceptable. Art changes its meaning as it crosses borders, and its status as a non-political form can be put to political use, potentially creating conflict as well as opportunities. Through the dynamic intersections between policy and practice, ideals and expectations, cultural relations play out. And through these encounters, myriad issues of autonomy and authority, dialogue and dissent, projection and partnership can be evaluated and explored. As will be discussed, these meanings and values take tangible form in the nearly nine thousand art works of the British Council Collection.

Fine Arts foundations

With its philosophical aims still in formation, in its first year the new British Council began to develop an organizational method. This included the creation of specialist departments focused on science, education – particularly the teaching of English – and the arts. The latter department was initially divided into Music, Theatre, and Fine Arts; to each strand was appointed a committee of advisors responsible for the strategic direction and delivery of activities appropriate to the Council's agenda.

The seventeen members of the Fine Arts Committee met for the first time on 7 November 1935, with Sir Lionel Faudel-Phillips as chairman. Its early membership, like that of the British Council itself, was an esteemed parade of knights, professors, and peers of the realm. Among those with substantial reputations stood Sir Kenneth Clark, director of the National Gallery, and Sir Eric Maclagan, director of the Victoria and Albert Museum; other members included from the beginning or soon added held senior managerial or trustee

Sir Kenneth Clark, photographed by Howard Coster, 1937

Sir Eric Maclagan, photographed by Howard Coster, 1937

The British Pavilion at the 1938 Venice Biennale. The Council's Fine Arts Committee had taken over responsibility for the pavilion the previous year. One of the seven artists on show, Blair Hughes-Stanton won the International Prize for Engraving.

roles at major national art institutions, such as the British Museum, the Tate Gallery, and the Wallace Collection. The professional profile of the committee brought together the very highest level of art-historical expertise, and established its authority as the pre-eminent decision-making body for British art on the international stage.

The minutes of the first meeting – like many of those recorded over subsequent decades – concerned matters practical, political, and aesthetic. Committee members were tastemakers, translating parliamentary policy into public outcomes, managing budgets – always deemed too small – and mediating diplomatic messages to be artistically meaningful as well as internationally ambassadorial. Initially, the British Council had no art collection of its own; the Fine Arts Committee's principal function was the selection of works from national museums, private lenders, dealers and artists for exhibitions in which Britain's creative output, especially in modern art, could be showcased. Money was modest – beginning with around £700 per year – and consequently the Fine Arts section's early ambitions were small-scale too, as finances seemed to permit only one major exhibition every two years.[12] From the outset, the committee fielded requests for exhibitions from across the globe. These were split between requests from countries with British Council offices and 'representatives' (that is, overseas-based coordinators); international events where a national presence was expected, and where the Fine Arts team managed the British selection (including the Venice Biennale); and Foreign Office-directed diplomatic activities that required arts input to achieve their ends.

New York World's Fair

An early example of the latter activity was the contribution of contemporary prints, drawings, paintings, and sculptures to the British Pavilion at the New York World's Fair in 1939. As part of a broader cultural offensive designed to build alliances with the United States in the case of war, and following a long-standing model of national representation at international exhibitions dating back to the Great Exhibition of 1851, the British government invested in a pavilion in New York. Here was displayed a spectacular range of exhibits, including commissioned film documentaries on British life; music from

The British Pavilion at the World's Fair of 1939, alongside the artificial lake named the Lagoon of Nations. The tower of the Italian Pavilion can be seen in the background.

Robert Hudson on board the RMS *Queen Mary* at Southampton docks on 3 May 1939, shortly before leaving for the New York World's Fair, which opened four days earlier.

leading British composers including Ralph Vaughan Williams; replicas of the Crown Jewels; and a copy of the Magna Carta displayed in a carefully named 'Hall of Democracy'.

The contribution that the Fine Arts section could make to this endeavour was seen as sufficiently significant for Robert Hudson, 1st Viscount Hudson, the secretary for overseas trade, to be described as 'extremely anxious' to see a British art display as part of the proceedings. Separate from the committee's existing budget, the Department for Overseas Trade provided a grant of £500 and bore all expenses, including sending out the British Council's exhibitions officer to New York.[13] Newly flush with funds, the Fine Arts department designed and populated the *Exhibition of Contemporary British Art* in the British Pavilion, featuring works by artists such as Graham Sutherland, Augustus John, and Walter Sickert, and one of the earliest showings of a Henry Moore sculpture in the United States.

Although it has been argued by British historian Nicholas J. Cull that 'the individual exhibits aimed to show Britain's artistic vitality and not to make any political point', the broader purpose of the exhibition was undoubtedly politically motivated, both implicitly and explicitly.[14] By 1936, amidst the escalating European crisis, it was evident that Britain would not be able to win a war without American support. A year later, against this backdrop, and in the knowledge that the United States operated a strict 'No Propaganda' rule, the

Contemporary postcards show two views of the British Pavilion and adjoining pavilion, which also housed the exhibits of Australia, New Zealand, and the British Colonial Empire section.

Huge portraits of Queen Elizabeth and King George VI and large crowds greeted the royal couple when they visited the British Pavilion on 10 June 1939.

A set of commemorative postcards was produced by the World's Fair to mark the occasion and to extend the hand of 'peace and friendship' more widely.

The cover of the official guide to the British Pavilion of the World's Fair in New York

foreign secretary, Anthony Eden, asked the British ambassador to Washington to advise on alternative tactics that might be utilized to drum up an American alliance. The advice was that psychological and emotional appeals were best made through culture; British literature, film, and theatre, for example, were said to move American people in a way that political propaganda did not.[15] 'Goodwill' was the preferred term to describe the strategic relationship-building that was planned in earnest to shift the United States out of its isolationist position. The British Pavilion constituted a kind of performative pact; it aimed to produce what it proclaimed. This was outlined in its dedication, writ large on the imposing entrance to the building, to 'lasting peace and friendship between the peoples of the United States of America and the British Empire'. The significance of the message was secured through the high status of the Pavilion's loaned exhibits. Finally, it was hammered home by a visit by the new King George VI and the Queen Consort.

By the time war broke out in September 1939, the art exhibition in the British Pavilion in New York had been seen by eleven million visitors.[16] Lenders of works – including the Royal Collection – were persuaded by the pressing

Daily---1,950,000
Sunday--3,500,000

DAILY NEWS

NEW YORK'S PICTURE NEWSPAPER

FINAL

Vol. 22. No. 9 New York, Friday, July 5, 1940 44 Pages 2 Cents

BOMB AT FAIR KILLS TWO

PLANTED IN SUITCASE AT BRITISH PAVILION

Story on Page 3

Victims of Fair Bomb. Bodies of two detectives, killed when bomb exploded near British Pavilion at World's Fair, lie where they were thrown by force of blast. The bomb, contained in canvas suitcase, was being carried from British Pavilion when it went off in rear of Polish Building.

The New York *Daily News* from 5 July 1940 reports on the bomb attack at the British Pavilion the previous day. The bomb was removed to a remote location but exploded and killed the two policemen who were attempting to defuse it.

new context to continue with their loans for a 1940 iteration of the exhibition that was more explicitly propagandist, including newsreels of British life during wartime from the Ministry of Information.[17] By this time, the purpose was more pointed; the support of the United States was wanted not just for aid and trade, but for fighting on the ground. Its goodwill – and more – was essential to Britain's survival.

The most dramatic event of the Fair took place in July 1940 when an abandoned suitcase in the British Pavilion was identified to security staff as suspicious. Taken outside for checking by the New York Police Department, it was found to be packed with dynamite and a timer; the bomb blew a five-foot-wide crater in the ground, killing two detectives.[18] The British Pavilion remained intact, but this incident removed any doubt that it was a politicized location. It had been recognized as such by those who saw it as a prime site for attack – a Nazi banner was found hidden in the British Pavilion but the perpetrators were never found. It became a focal point for hatred as well as for friendship.[19]

The Pavilion was a conscious act of political alignment and met a national need to warm hearts and change minds. The urgency that underpinned its exhibits was grounded in legitimate threat. Britain's artistic contributions to the New York World's Fair may not be mapped precisely onto social consequences and material effects, but the overall effort appears well spent. By the end of 1941, the United States joined the Allies; political anxieties were vindicated and cultural connections consolidated.

The Wakefield Collection

While the membership of senior museum directors on the Fine Arts Committee enabled privileged access to high-quality exhibition material from national collections, in order to act quickly and to meet growing requests from across the globe without abusing the generosity of lenders, the committee needed a collection of its own. It took its first steps in this direction in 1937, when a special reserve of funds – initially £1,000 a year for three years – was gifted to the Fine Arts department by the industrialist Charles Cheers Wakefield, 1st Viscount Wakefield. The committee elected to use Lord Wakefield's donation to build a collection of twentieth-century graphic art, that is, to gather 250 to 300 works, at a cost of around £5 a time, to be 'used for making up one or more exhibitions, with or without the addition of borrowed paintings'.[20] A further purpose of the Collection was to decorate British Council offices overseas; its broad early remit meant that Fine Arts Committee advised not only on travelling exhibitions, but also on the use of art in such institutional interiors. These were sites where important connections were enabled and performed between, for example, ministers and arts professionals, as well as between British government representatives and foreign officials and dignitaries; an appropriate aesthetic message was part and parcel of conveying British cultural authority.

The resulting purchases, initially known as the Wakefield Collection, comprised original drawings and watercolours alongside engravings, woodcuts, lithographs, aquatints, and etchings. Their acquisition, mostly concentrated in the years 1938 to 1948, took place first under the directorship of Campbell Dodgson, keeper of prints and drawings at the British Museum,

LEFT H. Andrew Freeth, *Campbell Dodgson, Esq.*, 1938, etching, 25 × 18.6 cm (P2449). One of the first Wakefield works bought, this portrait of the committee member responsible for the purchases was sent to the New York exhibit in 1939.

OPPOSITE John Austen, *The Old Plough*, undated, woodcut, 24 × 30.1 cm (P2333). This bucolic countryside scene was typical of the works on show in New York.

and later under James Laver, keeper of prints, drawings, and paintings at the Victoria and Albert Museum. Early Wakefield buys supplemented the loans to the New York World's Fair exhibit in 1939, while the Wakefield Collection as a whole, which amounts to 450 or so works, has toured extensively in the intervening years in dedicated exhibitions in its own right and alongside other objects from the British Council Collection. The Wakefield works have also provided the backdrop for countless cultural agreements and events across the British Council's worldwide estate.

As with all art bought for British Council purposes, the Wakefield acquisitions were pragmatic, not least in relation to form. Graphic arts were relatively cheap to buy in comparison with original paintings; by their nature, prints tend to be produced in multiples. As Andrea Rose, director of the Visual Arts department from 1994 to 2014, has noted of the works on paper in the British Council Collection, 'their modest scale and flat packing guaranteed that they would fit inside the hold of an aircraft or guard's van worldwide, and that they could be assembled and installed by almost anyone'.[21] As I will show, prints' portability and reproducibility made them relatively low-risk materials to send overseas to places without museum infrastructures and to which national collections would not otherwise lend; but they also conveyed particular cultural values as they travelled. British woodcuts, engravings, and lithographs variously communicated historical tradition, technical accomplishment, and technological innovation. Their subject matter also carried a parallel set of codes.

Graphic art sent to the New York World's Fair from the Wakefield Collection offers a case in point. At first glance, the selection seems to represent a rather academic body of material, offering a backward-looking nostalgia for an old country rather than a contemporary view; subjects include cricket-bat and hurdle makers, agricultural reapers and binders, milkmaids and rustic ploughs. The English landscape tradition is reproduced in prints that take fenland and woodland, millponds and country lanes as central subjects. Mythic imagery of satyrs and St George seem far removed from life in Britain in the late 1930s. Given that items in the Wakefield Collection were purchased in part to provide office decoration, the works could be dismissed as comforting scenes

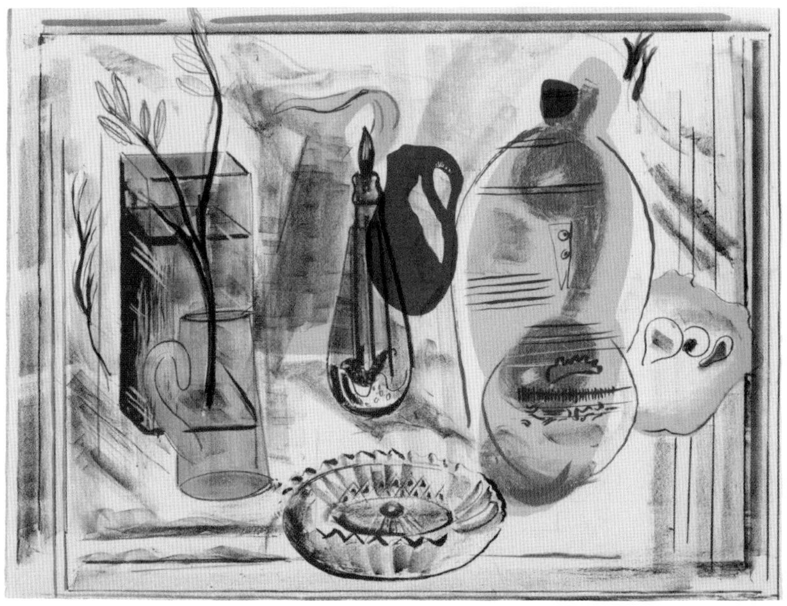

ABOVE Frances Hodgkins, *Arrangement of Jugs*, 1938, lithograph, 44.7 × 60.5 cm (P2459)

OPPOSITE Eric Gill, *Eve*, 1926, wood engraving with hand colouring, 23.7 × 118 cm (P2392)

for homesick diplomats. Across the Collection as a whole, however, in treatment and in message, the themes are more complex. Even pastoral scenes and seemingly innocuous still lifes can be rendered in non-naturalistic, modernist revisions that disrupt any straightforward depiction.

Arrangement of Jugs by Frances Hodgkins, for example, provides splashes of colour onto disorientating floating forms; sketchy pitchers, vases, and other vessels are layered impressionistically in an arresting lithograph designed to democratize art collecting and communicate contemporary culture to schools. Biblical themes, as handled by Eric Gill in *Eve*, are radical remodellings of familiar motifs. His erotic black-inked nude was a challenging image in its own time and even more so now; in 1989, Gill's sexual abuse of two of his daughters became public knowledge.[22] He is a figure at the centre of debates about

10/50
ERIC G

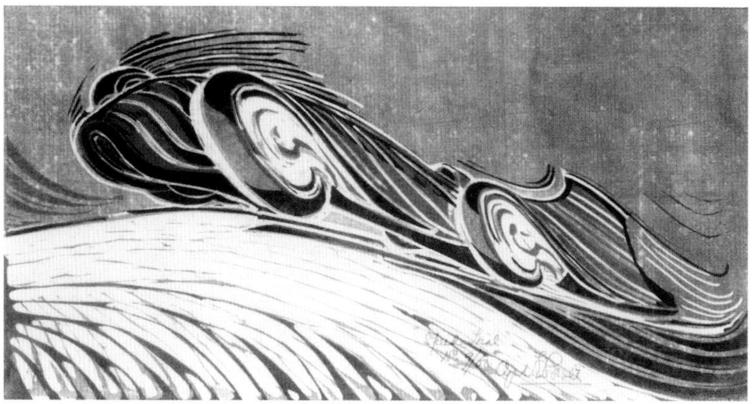

whether it is possible, or desirable, to separate the art work from the actions of the artist. Cyril Power's *Speed Trial* linocut of *c.* 1935 shows a Vorticist-inspired love of the machine in its subject matter and in its vibrating, fractured aesthetic; his *Air Raid* of the same year is even more Futurist in style with swirling forms and vivid colours embodying visual noise. Informed by his role in the Royal Flying Corps in the First World War, it was produced on the brink of the Second with a haunting prescience. Blair Hughes-Stanton's semi-abstract woodcuts are wild fantasies inspired by metaphysical poetry and utopian lifestyles. By the time the United States entered the fray, Hughes-Stanton was interned as a prisoner of war, where he received a bullet in the face from a camp guard.[23] The visions of the Wakefield Collection are not so cosy.

OPPOSITE TOP Cyril Power, *Air Raid*, *c.* 1935, linocut, 32.5 × 30 cm (P2375)

OPPOSITE BOTTOM Cyril Power, *Speed Trial*, *c.* 1935, linocut, 19.6 × 37.5 cm (P2376)

RIGHT Blair Hughes-Stanton, *The Rock*, 1935, coloured wood engraving, 22 × 16 cm (P2334)

Blair Hughes-Stanton, *Horizon*, 1935, coloured wood engraving, 55 × 40.6 cm (P2832)

Establishing the template

The early years of the British Council, and the Fine Arts department within it, were a developmental period for devising a philosophy of purpose and a mode of operation. The first committee brought together a panel of national significance. Its purchases and exhibitions tested out ways of communicating British culture through various forms, in pursuit of projection and propaganda, friendship and freedom, underwritten by art-historical authority and diplomatic need.

En masse and piece by piece, in the service of a range of international contexts and agendas, the first acquisitions under the Wakefield donation have travelled far and wide, carrying multiple messages. The war work performed in New York was replicated across further cities in the United States in the early 1940s, before they moved on to Canada, Australia, New Zealand, and Fiji. Beyond this, in an illustration of the utility and versatility of the Collection, Wakefield prints have circulated in exhibitions in Austria, Brazil, Chile, Colombia, Cyprus, Egypt, Finland, Germany, India, Japan, Kenya, Malaysia, Mexico, Pakistan, Palestine, Peru, Philippines, Poland, Portugal, Slovakia, Soviet Union, Spain, Sri Lanka, Switzerland, Turkey, Uruguay, Venezuela, Zambia, and Zimbabwe. To provide just one measure of the impact of these shows, the display in Ankara in 1942–3 was visited by the Turkish prime minister, the minister of education, the minister of economy, the foreign minister, and others; it was seen by 6,500 visitors in one day.[24] The modest ambition to purchase prints at £5 a time in the late 1930s has proven to be an investment of enormous and enduring cultural value – and its services are far from exhausted. As such, it established the template for the British Council Collection as a whole.

Over nearly ninety years and spanning most of the globe, the Council's activities have taken a wide range of forms and served several functions. There are clearly many possible tales to tell. In examining visual art, this book offers a distinctive point of view. In its focus on the Collection, it offers tangible evidence for the mostly intangible work of cultural relations. Following its development and use, its varied ambitions and purposes, and not least, its public performance through exhibitions that reach millions of people each year, *Art Without Frontiers* is as much a narrative of geopolitical encounters as it is an art history.

CHAPTER 1

Crafts at war and at peace

In 1942, in the midst of the Battle of the Atlantic, across waters riddled with U-boats, the British Council sent six tons of handmade objects for the *Exhibition of Modern British Crafts* at the Metropolitan Museum of Art, New York. Teapots and table mats, ashtrays and armoires, corn dollies and cushion covers travelled 3,500 miles by sea, and then, over the next three years, took in fifteen cities across the United States and Canada. Under conditions of total war, what could an exhibition of crafts achieve? Its contents were mostly modest and homely, and split between the decorative and the utilitarian. Against the complex machinery of modern conflict, such handicrafts might seem rather rudimentary and weak. Beside the everyday reality of life-or-death situations, the exhibition and the objects within it could appear trivial. And yet, the British Council invested significant time and effort in the project, supported by King George VI, who offered the Royal Library at Windsor Castle as a space to assemble exhibits while London was under attack in the Blitz. As Major Alfred A. Longden, the then director of the Fine Arts department put it, 'The Council regards this exhibition as one of the greatest importance.'[1] It did so because it recognized that craft's embodiments of the rural, the domestic, and the handmade could carry particular messages about British tradition, modernity and industry, and even war and peace to wide audiences overseas.

Eric Ravilious, *Garden Implements Jug*, 1939, earthenware with printed design and lustre, height 19.6 cm (C189) (detail)

Front cover of the catalogue of the *Exhibition of Modern British Crafts*, 1942–3

Consequently, this major wartime undertaking in North America – soon followed by a second, postwar exhibition of rural crafts in Australia and New Zealand – was the Council's earliest effort to communicate globally ideas of British national identity through the prism of craft and vernacular design. It was the first, but not the last, occasion that craft in its different forms played a significant role in Britain's international cultural relations. As I will show, however, craft has held an unstable place in the British Council Collection, falling in and out of favour over time. Through studying the shifts in values visible in the Collection's emphases and gaps, the broader uses and expectations of craft in cultural relations are revealed.

Repairing the broken world

The *Exhibition of Modern British Crafts* was a product of 'conditions of peculiar difficulty', as Sir Eric Maclagan, the member of the Fine Arts Committee tasked with writing the introduction to the catalogue, reflected. 'Everybody who can use his hands, or hers, is using them for another purpose. Silk means parachutes, not embroidery; the guns can spare no iron; and the potteries are too busy with insulators to supply decorative tea services.'[2] As a result of these

Muriel Rose, photographed in the 1920s

conditions, Maclagan suggested, craftspeople had been undervalued. 'We may be too busy with other things to pay much attention to them. There is temptation enough to brush aside their activities as of no real importance whatever.' He set the scene for the exhibition's ambitions by quoting from Ecclesiasticus in praise of those who work with their hands: 'They shall not be sought for in public counsel, nor sit high in the congregation. ... But they will maintain the state of the world.' Maclagan asked in conclusion, 'And has that state ever found itself in greater need of being maintained?'[3]

Those who would repair and maintain the broken world included weavers and potters, book illustrators and wallpaper printers, silversmiths and glass-blowers, toy makers and embroiderers, among many more, all brought together under the careful aesthetic and administrative eye of Muriel Rose, the exhibition's organizing secretary and the former proprietor of the Little Gallery. Established in Sloane Street, Chelsea, in 1928 as a space 'to enable craftsmen to hold exhibitions of their work in the same way as painters and sculptors', Rose's gallery played a key role in the British interwar crafts revival, showing the work of leading makers, including pottery by Bernard Leach and Michael Cardew, textiles by Phyllis Barron and Dorothy Larcher, and printed wallpapers by Edward Bawden and John Aldridge.[4] Through Rose, the Little Gallery's contacts and contents directly informed the shape and style of the *Exhibition of Modern British Crafts*.

In a series of interlocking rooms, staged as three-sided sets, with tables laid for dinner and musical instruments strewn on the sofa, the exhibition was styled as an ideal home. Every item, from bookshelf to table mat, was an exhibit, including the paper on the walls and the rugs on the floor. The photographs of the unpopulated installations in the Metropolitan Museum of Art have a slightly eerie air, evoking an abandoned house. Given the conditions under which the exhibit was produced – the catalogue notes, for example, that all of Britain's young silversmiths had left to join the Royal Air Force – there is a temptation to read the display as a living project rudely interrupted by war. This chilling interpretation was not how the exhibition was experienced by the tens of thousands who flocked to see it on its multi-city tour, however. It was perceived as warm and familiar, and visitors felt completely at home.

By 1942, the British Council's Fine Arts department had been organizing overseas exhibitions for several years; what made this show different and exceptionally valuable was 'its appeal to a much wider cross-section of the public than those reached by exhibitions of paintings'. Rose observed, 'showing domestic objects, pottery and glass, chairs and tables, books and textiles, particularly when grouped in arrangements suggesting rooms, does not present the barrier of strangeness many feel in regard to modern painting, and a collection of this kind is at once closely related to the daily life of visitors of every sort'. Many of the host museums noted that the record-breaking numbers of attendees were also not the audiences they usually attracted, that is, those who were highly cultured in a conventional sense. Rose argued that the person who is less well-informed about art and culture is also the 'type of person who is likely to be the least informed and possibly the most prejudiced against Great Britain'.[5]

Two pages from Muriel Rose's personal scrapbook showing a pair of the 'rooms' in the *Exhibition of Modern British Crafts* at the Metropolitan Museum of Art, New York

Music Room

Country Dining Room

Singing, crying, and drinking tea

While objections can be made about mapping the appreciation of art onto social enlightenment more broadly, these ideas that underpinned the exhibition, as well as its broad reach – to craftspeople, educators, trade groups, occupational therapists and their patients, and particularly to 'the formidable body of Women's Clubs' – shifted the usual register of museum displays, and made it an emotive site for transatlantic community-building.[6] Arrangements were made for groups to handle exhibits in ways that are not usually possible in galleries. Textiles were turned over and cabinet drawers were opened as part of the inspection of workmanship. Opening-night parties were held where displayed ceramics were used to sup tea.

In contrast to the grey, empty spaces suggested by the unpopulated photographs, the exhibition was busy with people and sensual engagement. Gramophone records played modern composers behind the scenes of the music room; children in groups massed in their hundreds. Rose notes the attendance of 'various societies of persons of British ancestry' who attended in costume, played bagpipes, or sang Welsh songs. Her reports are full of emotional encounters. A visiting Ukrainian migrant, a 'candidate for American citizenship' who could 'only speak a few words of English', for example, apparently broke down in tears at the sight of a spinning wheel, which took him back to his mother, his childhood, and his home. Rose surmised, 'the sight of these familiar household objects gave him the uttermost joy'. Another 'human element' that she observed was 'the number of people who now have boys in Britain and who felt the show to be a link with them'.[7] This was a deliberately affective exhibition; the goods were homely and the galleries were made familial; objects were felt, songs were sung, and tears were shed.

This emotional tempo was also reported in official appraisals. Many warmly appreciated the show in the light of its circumstances, as Allan Eaton, director of the Arts Department of the Russell Sage Foundation in New York,

More pages from Muriel Rose's personal scrapbook, showing photographs of some of the younger visitors to the *Exhibition of Modern British Crafts*

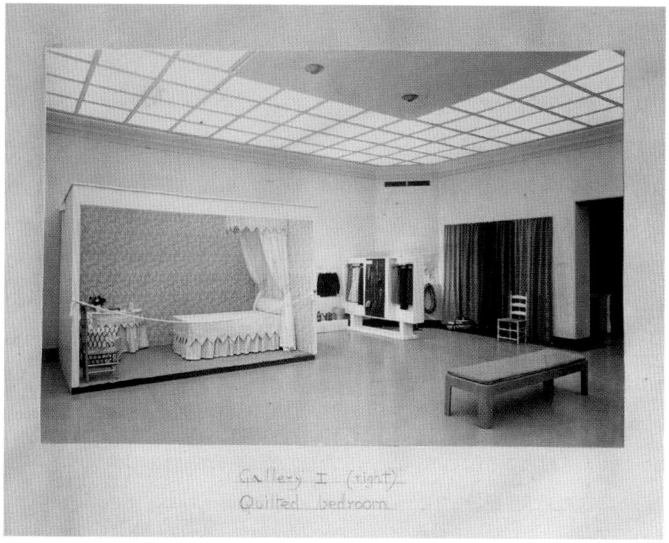

ABOVE AND OPPOSITE Two pages from Muriel Rose's scrapbook showing a 'room' installed in the Worcester Art Museum and exhibits in the exhibition

relayed to Rose in a letter.[8] As one New Yorker put it, 'It is a very great surprise that you should send us in these days such extraordinary evidence of British taste and skill and democratic culture.' The curator of the Museum of Fine Arts in Boston stated, 'This exhibition stands for the kind of life we are fighting to preserve. It speaks a universal language.' Meanwhile, the director of the Toledo Museum observed, 'the exchange of art brings our respective countries a better understanding of each other'. He continued, 'it is an excellent investment in the future happiness of the world'. These responses are heartfelt and human-centred, but they are political too; they recognize the strategic alliance-building purposes of the exhibition. What Winston Churchill would go on to describe as Britain and America's 'special relationship' was enacted as a family meal around a dining table. The cushion covers and teacups were comforting but enabled a performance of transatlantic engagement. As the director of the Worcester Art Museum in Massachusetts recognized, the exhibition's method was 'much more valuable than any direct form of propaganda'.

Trading handshakes

A secondary purpose of the exhibition was to encourage an export market for British goods. Trade bodies reflected on what Britain could do that the United States might not. The United States Advertising Corporation encapsulated it: 'There's a homely warmth to it which expresses the real English people in terms that appeal to the heart. Here, in a country accustomed to large spaces for swinging of arms and random talk, many people have failed to understand that the self-contained British manner, developing naturally in a more crowded land, represents consideration for others. They will know from this exhibit the human warmth that lies behind British reserve.'[9] While such national characteristics reinforce stereotypes, a key exhibition subtext was that Britain was a land of craft producers in opposition to America's industrial production. Charles Marriott's preface to the catalogue stated baldly, 'the machine still lags behind in England'. He confessed, 'we have not yet had anything comparable to the exhibition of "Machine Art" held at the Museum of Modern Art, New York, a few years ago, and to send examples of what we can do in that way to the United States would have been rather like "sending coals to Newcastle".'[10]

Rose was aware that 'the United States has a real respect amounting to almost reverence for English craftsmanship'. She saw it in the appreciation for tweeds, tailoring, and saddlery, and this was enhanced by the show: 'This confidence will perhaps be our strongest plank in competing for the United States export market.' Trade-building was part of the work that the exhibition was expected to do, including in direct sales, where possible. The inclusion of makers' addresses in the back of the catalogue was designed to create contacts 'when the tourist traffic begins to flow again'.[11] This element is notable now, when personal information is so carefully protected; it is hard to imagine contemporary artists' home addresses, for example, being published in an exhibition catalogue of their work, but this was not only a condition of the times. Meeting the maker was part of the exhibition's message about personal relationships over industrial production: the welcoming handshake of the handmade in contrast with the cold hard front of the machine.

History, modernity, nationality

The story of how Rose came to be involved with the British Council and its transatlantic project is worth recounting. The idea for an exhibition of British crafts had, in fact, been hers originally, imagined as 'a productive piece of War Propaganda epitomising our national heritage', but it would have taken a rather different shape had it gone ahead. Detailed plans drawn up in collaboration with the modernist architect Oliver Hill in 1939 imagined a much wider scope, taking in both rural and domestic objects from the fifteenth century to the present day, building on Hill's central contribution to a previous project, unconnected to the Council, the *Exhibition of British Industrial Design in Relation to the Home*, which had opened with dramatic backlit sculptural displays of scythes, hoes, and other agricultural implements, and proceeded through room sets designed in the most modernist of architectural styles.[12] Hill and Rose's original exhibition proposition included 'the hand-forged airscrew and crankshaft in Metal, the huge hand-blown broadcasting valves in Glass and the fine stoneware insulators used in electrical distribution in Pottery'. Arguing that these communicated 'a supreme intrinsic beauty', they were said to provide 'an appropriate climax to the finest work of the past'. While this wildly ambitious exhibition would not come to pass – and one marvels at the impossibility of transporting such enormous items by boat in any instance, not least across wartime waters – the aim of the original concept was the same as the one that would be realized at the Metropolitan Museum of Art: to provide a reminder to the public 'of the Britain for which they are fighting'. Similarly, the two projects aimed to 'give encouragement to the living craftsman, both studio artist and anonymous rural worker'.[13]

When Rose had been forced to close the Little Gallery on the outbreak of war in 1939, she felt a responsibility for 'abandoning the artists whose work we have been selling and at a most difficult time'. One of her key ambitions was to keep these artists in work. 'Without their stimulus', Rose noted in her original plans, 'we cannot hope to build up the Overseas market upon which our national life so vitally depends.' Rose cast about for sponsors of an exhibition, approaching Dorothy Elmhirst, the wealthy American benefactor of Dartington Estate in Totnes, Devon, an experimental site of rural revivalism, arts education, and progressive thought. The British Council was on the list of possible funders in part due to its 'handsome Treasury grant', but also because Rose was already connected with Kenneth Clark, a member of the Fine Arts Committee, so hoped to have some leverage. Government support – even at arm's length – was needed to circumvent the issues of import duty.

In the end, under the initial chairmanship of Sir Lionel Faudel-Phillips, the Fine Arts Committee took up a revised version of the plan. Rose was persistent in making herself useful, sending the British Council polite but firm letters, with the result that she was appointed in 1941 to assist with accessing the craftspeople from whom exhibited articles would be selected; some five hundred were contacted in the first call.[14] As planning developed, she became secretary to the Arts and Crafts Exhibition Committee. She was notably the only woman on the team, although many of the exhibitors and much of the exhibition's audience were female, and she received bottom billing on the exhibition line-up of lettered and titled luminaries with H. M. The King at the top, as the British Council's patron. Despite this status, many exhibitors were from Rose's

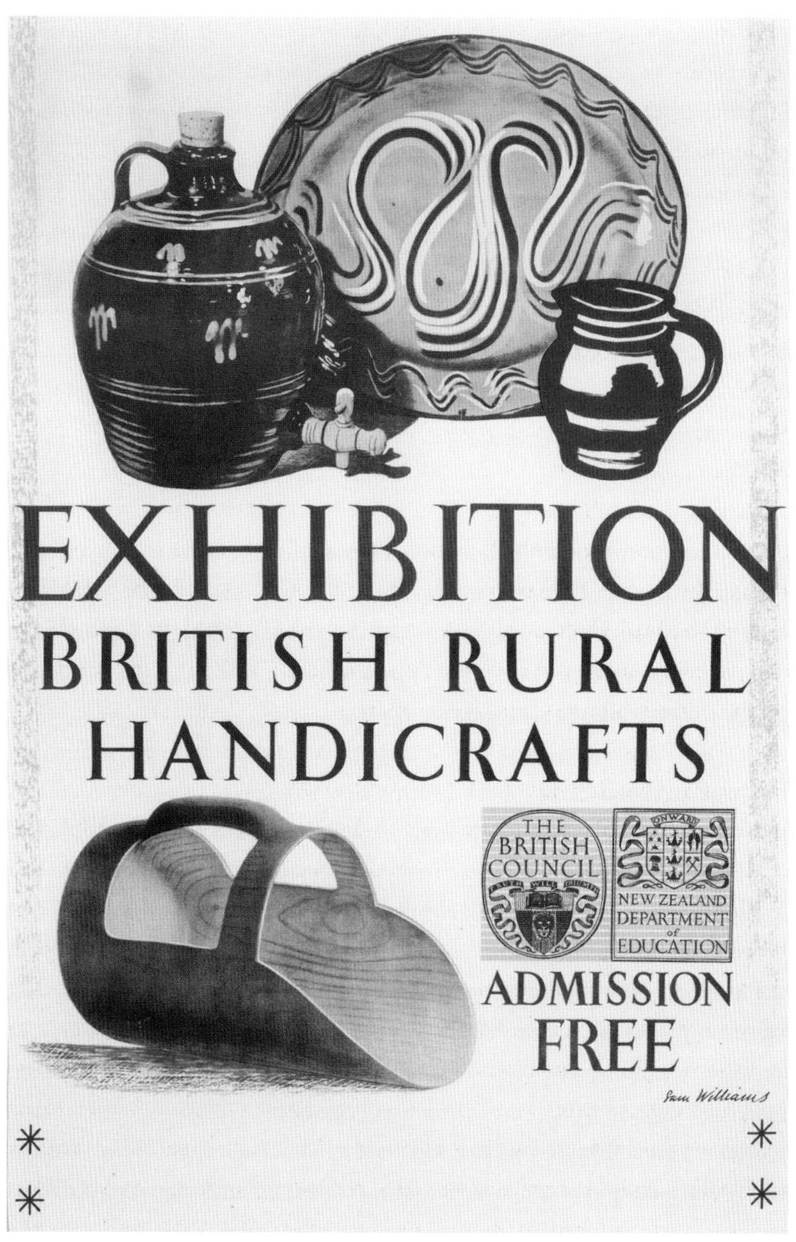

A promotional poster for the *British Rural Handicrafts* exhibition, 1945–6

capacious contacts book, and some were personal friends. She accompanied the exhibits around fifteen cities in the United States and Canada, building up important connections for future exchange with craftspeople and museum professionals, while promoting the moral and aesthetic values of craft through hundreds of gallery talks.

While Rose promoted British craft overseas, her understanding of British national identity was internationalist in outlook. This is corroborated by archival notes towards another wartime exhibition that she planned, to support the status of displaced persons by showing 'the contributions made in the past to our national culture by refugees'. Rose's focus was refugees' contribution to 'our applied arts and industries'. This included contributions by Flemings and Walloons to wool trades and clog making; the international origins of the Manchester cotton industry and the Sheffield cutlery trade; and European influences in architecture 'brought up to date by Prof Gropius ... and other living refugee architects'. The ethos was underpinned by a quote from the sixteenth century (credited by Rose to the reign of Henry VIII): 'good workmanship of all artificialitie is most comenly seen in strangers'.[15] Britishness in Rose's craft exhibitions was strategic but not xenophobic.

Turnip draggers, fag hooks, and hedge slashers

By the time that she coordinated a second British Council crafts exhibition, *Rural Handicrafts from Great Britain* (also known as *British Rural Handicrafts*), which would travel across New Zealand and Australia during 1945 and 1946, Rose had become the British Council's officer for crafts and industrial art. The purpose of *British Rural Handicrafts* was to celebrate country crafts in recognition of the 'knowledge and inspiration' that they offered to artist-craftsmen of the present day. Commonality was highlighted for the Commonwealth. Shared roots in 'pre-industrial ancestors' underscored shared investments in the war effort. Enormous geographical distances were bridged by an emphasis on unchanging essentials. Finally, in order to counteract any impression that Britain might be technologically stuck in the Middle Ages, photographs of 'recent developments in agricultural machinery' were also included.

Michael Cardew, *Giant Tea-Pot*, as shown in Muriel Rose's scrapbook

The contents of the exhibition were eclectic, from horseshoes and brasses to 'thrift crafts' prompted by war shortages, such as men's carpet slippers made with string soles. There were spoons and baskets for specialist uses and evocatively titled tools, including turnip draggers, fag hooks, and hedge slashers. There was evident pleasure taken in the archaic language associated with many items, as shown in the catalogue's glossary, which included 'cnocker' (a small wooden club used to stun salmon), 'kishie' (a Shetland peat-carrying basket), 'sneath' (scythe handle), and 'thwart' (the seat of a rowing boat). Given the huge global popularity of 'Waltzing Matilda', described as Australia's unofficial national anthem, it is tempting to think that the Brits were asserting a lexicon to rival the jumbuck, billabong, and swagman of that famous song.

H. J. Massingham, the British rural revivalist, praised the 'quality and durability' of rural items, but also their visual pleasures, whether they be 'comely' or 'sturdy'. In his catalogue essay, he admired the items in the show that expressed a singular function, in most cases rather alien to twentieth-century

A corn dolly from the *British Rural Handicrafts* exhibition, from Muriel Rose's scrapbook

urbanites: the rabbiting spade, reaping hooks, and potato hoppers. He was also enamoured of items of more recent production, such as Michael Cardew's 'giant tea-pot, from which Og, King of Bashan, might have poured his tea'. Of this object, described as a large slipware teapot on an iron base, used for country gatherings, he claimed: 'Cardew was thinking of what tea-pots are for and only as an afterthought of their appearance.' The braided corn dollies in the show were harder to argue for in relation to utility, but Massingham gave it a go. Their use, he argued, is 'valid and crucial' in that they are 'charms or amulets or good luck tokens, made from the last sheaf to be reaped in order to woo the blessing of the corn spirit'. In changed times, the dolly remains 'an integral part of harvest as the grain or the sickle that cut it'. Another important aspect of the exhibition, in Massingham's estimation, was the status it afforded its makers, who were in many cases unknown. This inclusive approach signalled that artistic ability was not 'freakish ... absurdly temperamental or superior' but in the hands of everyone, everywhere.[16]

Teapots and bedspreads

The inclusion of hand-thrown ceramics by Cardew in both of these two early exhibitions might indicate simple folk crafts practised, as Massingham would put it, by 'ordinary folk engaged in normal service to the needs of the community' rather than 'fancy men or, as we call them, artists'.[17] This rather belied the truth. Cardew was an Oxford-educated intellectual. As his biographer Tanya Harrod has written of him, he was of 'the Mandarin class', an elite; a theorist of his craft, as well as a practitioner trained under Leach. Cardew had a passion for primitivism as a result of learned engagement with the progressive ideas of the craft revivalists. Those were the craft supporters that Leach had dismissed in 1938 as 'collectors, purists, cranks or "arty" people', quite unlike

ABOVE Ceramics displayed in the *Exhibition of Modern British Crafts* in the Metropolitan Museum

OPPOSITE Michael Cardew, *Jug*, c. 1947/8, stoneware, with persimmon glaze and painted decoration, height 12 cm (C295)

'the normal man or woman'.[18] Cardew's bold, warm wares were studied acts of plainness, their rustic slipwares redolent of seventeenth-century styles, assembled with traditional methods of throwing and firing in bottle kilns and rooted in a self-conscious rejection of the machine. They were not the product of a person untainted by the modern world. Cardew's ideas about the dignity of labour and the rejection of urban sophistications were anti-modernist; as such, they were very much of their time.

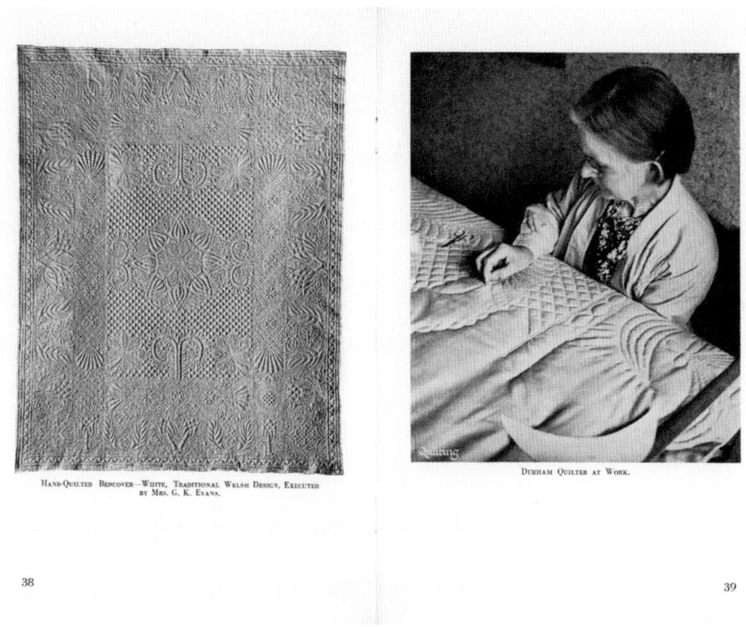
HAND-QUILTED BEDCOVER—WHITE, TRADITIONAL WELSH DESIGN, EXECUTED BY MRS. G. K. EVANS.

38

DURHAM QUILTER AT WORK.

39

Two pages from the catalogue produced for the *Exhibition of Modern British Crafts*

Both of the catalogues for the *Exhibition of Modern British Crafts* and the *Exhibition of Rural Handicrafts from Great Britain* showed exquisitely detailed quilts alongside photographs of quilters at work. Rose had a particular passion for these items as she had played a leading role in their creation as an advisor for the Rural Industries Bureau, which was formed in 1921 to regenerate rural handicrafts in areas of Britain suffering economic hardship. In this role, Rose sought ways to give work to the wives of unemployed miners. Along with quilter Mavis Fitzrandolph, she toured locations in south Wales and Durham on wash-days, looking for examples of handmade quilts pegged out to dry. They called at the doors of houses with promising examples fluttering in the breeze – always unannounced to ensure that the hard-up women would not spend their limited funds on preparing tea – and they appointed as paid needleworkers the women who were most skilled and most in need of support. Through this employment, the women became breadwinners, earning more than their husbands ever had. In their place, the former miners took on the housework. Rose's exhibition of quilts at her Little Gallery was the first of its kind and launched a fashionable interest in the form in the 1930s; Queen Mary ordered a quilted dressing gown, and the elite Claridge's Hotel bought quilts for the beds of the suites in its newest wing.[19] The examples that Rose toured in the United States, Canada, Australia, and New Zealand took the textiles further than their makers from the mining districts would ever travel.

Discordant textures: industrial ceramics

While Rose's predilection was always for the handcrafted, she was also in charge of 'industrial art'. An important aspect to the *Exhibition of Modern British Crafts* was its inclusion of machine-made wares, ranging from wallpapers and textiles 'produced under industrial conditions' to ceramic items produced by major suppliers.[20] This created an awkward mix. How could a solid brown stoneware pitcher with freestyle decoration speak the same design language as a fine china mug printed with hard, bright, hot pink graphics under a uniformly transparent glaze? Much of the input for this aspect of the exhibition came from the participation of Cecilia Dunbar Kilburn – known as Lady Sempill after her 1941 marriage to William, the 9th Lord Sempill – who was another rare woman in the early days of the Fine Arts department. A former sculpture student at the Royal College of Art, Dunbar Kilburn had run a London shop known as Dunbar Hay with Athole Hay, a tutor at the art school, between 1936 and 1940. Described as a 'marriage bureau' for young designers and manufacturers, the Albemarle Street venue provided a space for Dunbar Kilburn to commercialize the design and applied art of those in her close social circle of fellow graduates, including Eric Ravilious, Edward Bawden, and Enid Marx.[21]

Sempill was brought in to the *Exhibition of Modern British Crafts* 'to add colour'.[22] Major Alfred A. Longden, who had taken over as director of the Fine Arts department after the death of Faudel-Phillips in 1941, noted that while the craft objects assembled at Windsor Castle were undoubtedly of a high quality, the overall effect was 'a little sad in tone'. In part, this was due to the humble nature of the materials supplied; luxury items, such as those made from silk, had been refused by the Board of Trade and the Foreign Office because of the terms of the US Lease-Lend Act of that year, which reclassified raw materials as war supplies for defence purposes. Longden appeared concerned that the exhibition was going to appear dowdy. While he did not want the exhibition to look like 'a West End drawing room or a Fortnum and Mason department', he was also aware that some craftsmen, such as artist potters, 'have confined their efforts to schemes in white, grey and brown'. Sempill was sceptical of how handmade and mass-produced articles would work side by side in the display. She pointed out, 'the very textures of these factory-produced goods are bound to be somewhat discordant'.[23] The two were combined, and the result was a highly colourful parade. Bright patterned wallpapers and hand-blocked textiles offset the subfusc shades of natural materials, against gallery walls painted in a palette of 'cream, cocoa brown and sea-blue'.[24]

One of the results of Sempill's artistic-industrial partnerships, a set of nine Wedgwood ceramic carpet bowls, while strikingly beautiful in colour and print, was one of the more curious articles to appear in the *Exhibition of Modern British Crafts*. Here the rhetoric about craft's rustic utility comes undone in the

Josiah Wedgwood & Sons, *Set of Carpet Bowls*, *c.* 1938, eight bowls and a jack, with presentation box, produced for Dunbar Hay Ltd., London. Potteries Museum & Art Gallery, Stoke-on-Trent

Eric Ravilious, *Garden Implements Jug*, 1939, earthenware with printed design and lustre, height 19.6 cm (C189)

Eric Ravilious, *Rainbow and Camouflaged Ship*, 1942, watercolour and pencil on paper, 49.5 × 53.5 cm (P158)

face of a genteel parlour pastime played with fragile items on a soft surface. Coincidentally, Ravilious, a Wedgwood collaborator as well as the designer of a Dunbar Hay-commissioned Regency-style table and chairs at the centre of the exhibition, was playing bowls when war broke out in 1939 and playtime was declared over.[25] Along with many other artists, including several in the *Modern British Crafts* show, he was given paid work by the War Artists' Advisory Committee as a visual chronicler of the sites and sights of conflict. In paintings now in the British Council Collection, Ravilious produced soft and strange pastoral views that depict the fringes of war. Tragically, while on this duty, in the same year that his Wedgwood mugs and jugs were embodying the future of design for industry in the United States, the plane on which Ravilious was travelling was declared lost over Iceland. War was barely depicted in the *Exhibition of Modern British Crafts*, but its presence was never far away.

Craft turns and returns

Muriel Rose's exhibition successes preceded a new responsibility in 1948 to develop and purchase craft objects for the British Council's developing permanent collection. Most of the items in the two major exhibitions had been temporary loans. Some came direct from the makers or, in the case of the sycamore table made by Edward Barnsley, which Rose kept and cut the legs down to suit her diminutive stature, from collectors.[26] The purchases represented the first government-sponsored effort to create a national collection of crafts, and the acquisitions took their place alongside the Wakefield Collection of graphic art, discussed in the previous chapter, and the first purchases of original paintings, discussed in the next. By the early 1960s, after Rose's departure and with a changed ethos in the Fine Arts department, the crafts collection was reviewed, and many items were deaccessioned. Those deemed 'rustic' – agricultural implements and corn dollies, for example – were donated to the Museum of English Rural Life. Some textiles and sets of china were passed to the Victoria and Albert Museum, and some furniture went to the Holburne Museum in Bath; others had become infested with pests and were destroyed.[27] Further ceramic gifts and transfers took place in the 2000s, but the British Council Collection

A British Council exhibition of English artists' pottery, Singapore, 1966

has retained a nationally important range of studio pottery and industrial production ware.[28]

The crafts have held a particular place in British Council exhibitions over the last eight decades, with some curious turns and returns.[29] By way of example, the British Council assisted the Crafts Council in the organization of *La Poterie Anglaise Contemporaine*, which toured domestic ceramics by Janice Tchalenko, David Leach (Bernard's son), and Geoffrey Whiting, among others, around three French cites in 1979. This had a mixed reception. In Caen, it was perceived as disappointing, with the wares said to look too much like those that could be bought in the local market. The British Council's French representative reported that 'only half the exhibition was grudgingly shown, hidden away and unpublished'. In Orleans, however, leeks and cabbages were added to the display alongside 'tea-cosies, aprons, and a variety of scones and pork-pies etc bought especially at Marks and Spencer's in Paris'. Visitors were again encouraged to handle the exhibits. Archival notes also record that 'over 100 posters were removed within 24 hours by poster collectors – they were too attractive'.[30]

A revived interest in craft and design in the 1980s, under the custodianship of exhibitions officer Muriel Wilson, led to new British Council Collection purchases to underpin, for example, *Cloth, Clay, Wood*, a touring exhibition that travelled from Belgium to Brunei, via Malaysia and South Korea, to take in five countries in South America over six years. Pots and pitchers poured oil on troubled waters in the *British Studio Pottery* show in Mikhail Gorbachev's Soviet Union in 1986 as the country opened up to the West.

Front cover of the catalogue for *La Poterie Anglaise Contemporaine*, 1979

ABOVE Jill Crowley, *Teapot Hand*, 1996, oxidized stoneware, height 22 cm (P6618)

OPPOSITE Ara Cardew, *Very Large Teapot*, 1996, stoneware with tenmoku glaze, height 61 cm (P6639)

In the 1990s, the exhibition *Time for Tea* gathered together eighty teapots, including some fresh acquisitions and second-hand purchases, for a twenty-six-stop tour of Central and South America, Eastern Europe, and the Far East. Among its features was a specially commissioned 'Very Large Teapot' by Ara Cardew, grandson of Michael Cardew, as a replica of the six-and-a-half-gallon mounted pot from which copious tea was drunk at the original *Exhibition of Modern British Crafts*.

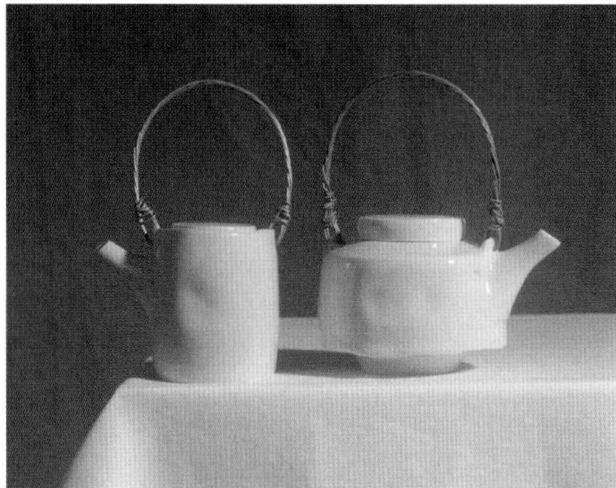

Edmund de Waal,
(left) *Small Upright Teapot*, 1996,
Limoges porcelain,
celadon glaze, and wire,
height 20.5 cm (P6754)

(right) *Blue White Teapot*, 1996,
Limoges porcelain,
celadon glaze, and wire,
height 21 cm (P6561)

Carol McNicholl,
Coffee Set, 1991, earthenware,
painted with coloured slips,
10 × 29 × 140 cm (P6033/A-H)

Richard Slee, *Pink Plate*, 1997,
earthenware, underglaze,
monoprint, and screenprint,
diameter, 42.3 cm (P6894).
This and the works above
all appeared in the 1997
exhibition *Time for Tea*.

Front cover of the catalogue for the exhibition *Everything But ...*

There were further widely travelled showcases of contemporary British kitchenware around the millennium. With a nod to Muriel Rose, these were arranged in table settings for *Dish of the Day* or placed into imagined rooms in *Everything But ....* Rather than pictured in ideal homes, however, the items were photographed, warts and all, among the kitchen sinks and the draining boards, mops, and buckets of real-life London abodes.

Perhaps the one British Council acquisition that sums up changing attitudes to historic crafts, and ceramics in particular, is Alan Kane's *Home for Orphaned Dishes*, purchased in 2011. Made up of mostly amateur ceramics hand thrown in the 1960s and 1970s in the studio tradition, such vessels had been pushed to the back of kitchen cupboards or abandoned to charity shops as their bulky bodies fell out of favour against the more fine-boned varieties.

Alan Kane's *Home for Orphaned Dishes*, installed at the Whitechapel Gallery, London, 2011, 300 ceramics from the 1960s / 70s, including 150 objects donated at the exhibition (P8367)

Kane cherishes vernacular creativity but also revels perversely in material that breaks boundaries between beauty and ugliness, the valued and the despised. A key part of his relational art work is that exhibition visitors add unwanted ceramic items of their own each time that the show is displayed. From mass-produced mugs to novelty toilet-brush holders, these additions expand the British Council's craft collection in new ways and add further layers to its meaning. When the work was shown in Tokyo in 2015, the donations were accompanied by emotional stories, rich with grief, embarrassment, and shame, about unwanted gifts, the possessions of dead relatives, and craft projects gone wrong.[31] The 'barrier of strangeness' that Muriel Rose noted could be overcome by displays of domestic goods was again at play. All over the world, in different places and at different times, in circumstances of conflict and of peace, exhibitions of household wares and human-scaled crafts have demonstrated the ability to break down cultural barriers and create powerful feelings of home.

Two of the ceramics from Alan Kane's *Home for Orphaned Dishes*

CHAPTER 2

Avant-garde ambassadors

In the aftermath of the Second World War, the Fine Arts department of the British Council continued to expand and develop its artistic and cultural relations activities. In 1946, the first oil paintings entered its collection, followed in 1948 by the first sculptures; by the end of the 1950s, more than three hundred art works had been purchased. The Council's attentions during and immediately after the war had been focused on the United States, Canada, and the dominions, as well as South America as a key site for trade. By the late 1940s and early 1950s, it was focusing on rebuilding relations across Europe. Key appointees to the Fine Arts Committee, among them Clive Bell, Herbert Read, and Lilian Somerville, made strategic purchasing and exhibition-building decisions that were to establish its core practices, including British representation at the Venice and São Paulo biennials, circulating exhibitions from the Collection, and the development of British artists' reputations through high-profile international solo shows in important cultural locations.

In a Cold War context, travelling exhibitions of 'advanced' art carried messages that were often opaque, but the very ambiguities inherent in art also enabled the projection of a broad range of sometimes contradictory values and emotions, encompassing freedom of expression, atomic anxiety, universal humanism, and national particularities. These were messages that the department was able to capitalize upon for the development of cultural relations in the mid-century. At the same time, its ambitions were constrained by contracting

Graham Sutherland, *Thorn Trees*, 1945, oil on canvas, 127 × 101.5 cm (P74) (detail)

ABOVE LEFT Graham Sutherland, *Tin Mine: Miner Approaching, Turning Towards Voice From Below*, 1942, gouache, chalk, wax crayon, and ink on paper, mounted on hardboard, 117.5 × 74.5 cm (P163)

ABOVE RIGHT Graham Sutherland, *Limestone Quarry, Loosening Stone*, 1942, gouache, wax crayon, and pencil on cardboard squared up for enlargement, 66 × 58.7 cm (P165)

budgets. As its activity grew, it also drew much press attention at home and abroad, not all of it admiring. Controversies in this postwar period demonstrate the challenges of communicating via modern art. They also reveal the fault lines that could appear between the British Council's aspirations and the perception of its audiences, and also between the agendas of Council officials and those of art historians. These examples illuminate various expectations of the role and purpose of sending art overseas in public service. Nonetheless, the practices of the Fine Arts department at this time set a template that would endure.

Building the Collection

After the end of the war, the building of a permanent collection developed in earnest. Following the purchases acquired with Wakefield funds, the next major set of acquisitions came in 1946 with works dispersed at the close of the War Artists' Advisory Committee (WAAC). Established by the Ministry of Information at the outbreak of the conflict in 1939, and overseen by Kenneth Clark alongside his Fine Arts Committee duties, this project had given commissions to some four hundred contemporary artists as a means of producing an official artistic document of the war, providing employment and protecting artists from front-line military service. More than 5,500 works were created, and these were used to populate regional and national public exhibitions across Britain, as well as to communicate British wartime experience to the United States and Canada under the auspices of the ministry. In 1946, the WAAC collection was broken up and distributed across sixty national institutions. Clark's role on the Fine Arts Committee meant the British Council was a natural recipient. Forty items were offered and twenty-five were accepted, including multiple works by Edward Bawden, Graham Sutherland, Henry Moore, the late Eric Ravilious, and Albert Richards, who had been killed by a landmine in Belgium on army duties the previous year.[1]

Albert Richards, *Take Off and Landing Field*, 1943, oil on cardboard, 62.2 × 75.5 cm (P161)

WAAC subjects in the British Council Collection include naval ships, bomber landing strips, ruined towns, military base camps, and air-raid shelters, but their treatments are never literal. These are documentary views infused with painterly perspectives. Sutherland's studies of limestone quarries and tin mines, for example, are as much studies of landscape, texture, colour, and rhythm as they are documents of scant resources utilized for war purposes. Richards' runway, intended as a base for a second front, is rendered as a patchwork of intersecting lines, mingling mud and concrete, earth and sky in an elemental scene that is part pastoral and part apocalyptic. In the same artist's *Building a Hutted Camp in Essex*, coils of curving corrugated metal – construction material used to assemble Nissen hut roofs – float free in the foreground like sculptural forms in parkland. Moore's bodies in bomb shelters are a mass of bony bumps bundled together in the textured shadows of Tube stations. In *Row of Sleepers*, he repeats the theme, with haunted and contorted figures increasing in definition and detail as they come closer into view, culminating in the form

ABOVE Henry Moore, *Brown Tube Shelter*, 1940, wash and crayon and Indian ink on paper, 37.5 × 54.5 cm (P152)

RIGHT Henry Moore, *Row of Sleepers*, 1941, watercolour and ink on paper, 54.5 × 32 cm (P15)

OPPOSITE Albert Richards, *Building a Hutted Camp in Essex*, 1941, oil on cardboard, 60.3 × 76.2 cm (P160)

of a child at the front of the frame, whose tiny piercing eyes ask searching questions to which there are no satisfactory answers.

The WAAC gift included works on paper and board in wax crayon, chalk, gouache, and ink, as well as the first oil paintings to enter British Council ownership. The next acquisition of oils was a more strategic selection resulting from a grant specifically for the purchase of art. In 1946, £1000 was provided from the Council budget 'for the purchase of contemporary British paintings and small pieces of sculpture', while a further £500 was designated for 1947 to result in 'the purchase of works of art suitable for more or less permanent loan to British Council Institutes in the more important capitals'.[2] From these humble beginnings, a nationally significant collection was born. The split between works bought for exhibition and those intended for insti-

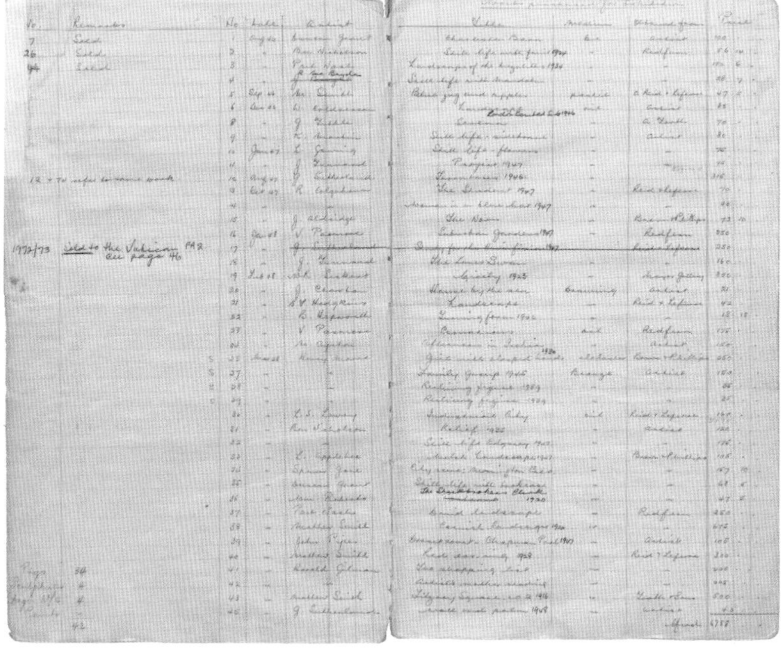

The British Council Collection's earliest acquisitions ledger, showing the entry for Duncan Grant's *Charleston Barn* as 'P1', the first painting acquired, in August 1946

ABOVE LEFT Clive Bell, photographed by Bassano Ltd, 1921

ABOVE RIGHT Herbert Read, photographed by Howard Coster, 1934

tutional decoration continued, with separate purchasing budgets, for several years, alongside the third strand of money from Lord Wakefield. Together with further gifts and commissions, these three strands would eventually intertwine to constitute a single unified collection.

During the war, two important figures joined the Fine Arts Committee. Clive Bell, the influential critic and champion of non-representational art, came on board in 1941. From his early promotion of Post-Impressionism in the 1910s to his central role in the Bloomsbury set – as husband of painter Vanessa Bell and brother-in-law to Virginia Woolf – Bell was a senior authority at the heart of modernist and formalist circles. In the same year, Herbert Read was recruited. As one of the most energetic promoters and prolific writers on avant-garde art – not to mention a poet, educationalist, and literary critic – his cultural credentials enhanced the credibility of the committee in its early decades. Together and separately, Bell and Read selected works for many temporary and touring exhibitions, nominated the practitioners who would represent Britain at international art events, and advised on the purchases that would shape the character of the British Council's collection of paintings and sculpture.

Duncan Grant, *Charleston Barn*, 1942, oil on canvas, 60.3 × 73.7 cm (P1)

In May 1946, the committee unanimously elected Bell and Read to make the first painting purchases, on the proviso that 'no individual work exceeding £200 should be purchased without the approval of the committee'; the allocation had been made on the assumption of 'an average price of £50 a picture'.[3] By the autumn, the first six paintings had been bought, comprising five oils and one work in pastel, split between four still lifes and two landscapes. The first item entered in the accession ledger represents the directorial hand of its selector writ large. *Charleston Barn* is a scene from the farm in rural Sussex that was Bell's sometime home, painted by Duncan Grant, who was at this point his wife's lover and the father of the child that Clive was then calling his own. The barn was a regular subject for both Grant and Vanessa Bell; Charleston farmhouse was their decorative canvas with walls, floors, and furniture all marked with their distinctive soft and dusty colour palettes of corn yellows, dusky pinks, and powder blues in abstract patterns and naive motifs. *Charleston Barn* had been purchased directly from the artist in a transaction that must have been more familial than formal. Although the subject showed a painted country scene adaptable for a range of communicative purposes and revealed nothing of the domestic dramas and Bohemian lives contained therein, Bell's Bloomsbury choice made a highly personal mark on the Collection.

The acquisition of the other non-still life in the first round of purchases, *Landscape of the Megaliths* by Paul Nash, appears to have been based more explicitly on decisions about quality rather than personal relationship, even though the artist, who died in 1946, had been well known to Read, who had been centrally involved in the Unit One group of British modernist artists and associates. Read had joined its founder Nash, Henry Moore, Barbara Hepworth, and others in Hampstead in 1933 to declare Unit One 'the expression of a truly contemporary spirit' in painting and architecture.[4] *Landscape of the Megaliths* appeared in the one and only Unit One exhibition, held the following year at the Mayor Gallery in London. A Nash work had previously been offered as part of the WAAC gift, but the Fine Arts Committee had turned it down; it was 'not considered to be of sufficient interest to represent that artist in the Council's collection'.[5] Instead, its members chose an example that represented Nash at his finest, and which

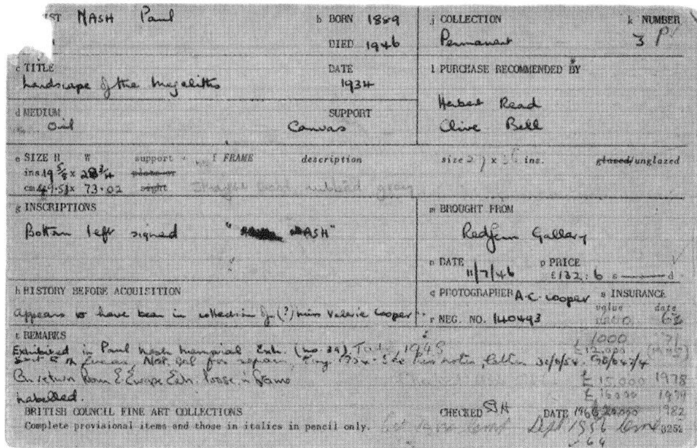

NASH Paul
b BORN 1889
DIED 1946
j COLLECTION Permanent
k NUMBER 3 P
c TITLE Landscape of the Megaliths
DATE 1934
l PURCHASE RECOMMENDED BY Herbert Read, Clive Bell
d MEDIUM Oil
SUPPORT Canvas
e SIZE H W support
ins 19 5/8 x 28 3/4
cm 49.5 x 73.02
f FRAME description
unglazed
g INSCRIPTIONS Bottom left signed "NASH"
m BROUGHT FROM Redfern Gallery
n DATE 11/7/46
o PRICE £132: 6 s — d
h HISTORY BEFORE ACQUISITION Appears to have been in collection of (?) Miss Valerie Cooper
q PHOTOGRAPHER A.C. Cooper
s INSURANCE value date
r NEG. NO. 140493
t REMARKS
BRITISH COUNCIL FINE ART COLLECTIONS
CHECKED
DATE
Complete provisional items and those in italics in pencil only.

Card record for the acquisition of Paul Nash's *Landscape of the Megaliths*

had already toured, as a loaned work, in British Council selections for the 1939 New York World's Fair and after. *Landscape of the Megaliths* combines the modern and the antiquarian, the representational – Avebury standing stones – and the dreamlike, with its wide-open spaces, squat pink skies, and looming shadow lands. Nash's peculiar view used a similar palette to *Charleston Barn*, but its bold, radical gestures makes Grant's paintbrush look uptight in comparison. Both are depictions of historic landscapes in southern England, but Nash's suggestive smudges and primitivist markings represent the most ancient of sites in the newest and strangest of ways.

Academicians versus the avant-garde

The purchases made through the postwar years show a commitment to the most challenging of contemporary art. In the phrasing of the Fine Arts department, they 'stressed the less academic aspect of British painting'.[6] This was by no means a popular choice; the tendency towards abstraction challenged conventions of beauty and could be hard to read for straightforward meaning. It was criticized vociferously by those invested in art's more conservative institutions. A famous invective of 1949 by Sir Alfred Munnings, president of the Royal Academy of Arts, about 'so-called modern art' was broadcast live on the

Paul Nash, *Landscape of the Megaliths*, 1934, oil on canvas, 49.5 × 73.2 cm (P3)

BBC and typified rearguard views. Munnings railed against the artistic choices of 'all sorts of highbrows'. He styled these figures as 'experts who think they know more about Art than the men who paint the pictures'. Critics in institutions such as the British Council were giving state support to the 'damned nonsense' that he saw embodied in the work of Pablo Picasso and Henry Moore. Munnings complained, in defence of realism, 'If you paint a tree – for God's sake try and make it look like a tree, and if you paint a sky, try and make it look like a sky.'[7] Despite being state-funded, the Fine Arts Committee was far from conservative in its aesthetic decisions; as such, its selections came to clash with audiences about what made art 'good'. This can be seen in two early examples of reactions to exhibitions of modern painting from the Collection.

Throughout the Second World War and into the 1950s, the British Council sent exhibitions of craft, graphic arts, and painting to Sweden; there was a clear need to keep good relations with this politically neutral nation. Although Council communications publicly discussed cultural relations as exchanges between equals, private discussions reveal hierarchies with some nations – and some cities within those nations – perceived to be more culturally developed than others. It is certainly true that in the early days, the British Council sometimes saw its paternalist purpose as bringing 'advanced' British culture to those apparently in need of it. However, in the case of mid-century Sweden, the aim was not to educate but to keep up. The Council's Swedish representative claimed, 'the Swedes are probably, in proportion to their population, the most highly cultured and educated nation in Europe'.[8] Scandinavia held a high watermark of artistic excellence, particularly in design, and Britain's reputation was not so distinguished. In this context, alongside awareness that the Rockefeller Foundation and other American associations were arranging 'funds for the interchange of museum collections throughout the democracies', the British Council competed for Swedish affections in the 1940s and 1950s.[9]

The artist and critic Michael Middleton, who worked in the Fine Arts department after the war, noted in 1948 that exhibitions in Sweden must be 'absolutely first-class' and lectures must be of 'star' quality; 'second-class productions are a waste of money' in that country.[10] The department's first attempt – graphic art – had been found by the Swedish press to be 'banal', 'academic and conventional', 'artificial and affected'.[11] Middleton further noted, 'A very small number of critics and museum authorities in Sweden are aware of current trends and developments in British painting.' He opined, 'ignorance of our work is complete and widespread'.[12] *Engelsk Nutidskonst*, the 1948 exhibition designed as an antidote, toured Stockholm, Malmö, Gothenburg, and Sundsvall, and included works by Moore, Sutherland, and Victor Pasmore. It did not have the desired effect.

Despite 'phenomenal goodwill towards Great Britain and a phenomenal general interest in painting', Middleton summarized, 'the general feeling was that British painting was tagging along behind Paris in a fairly unremarkable way'. Painters singled out for critique included Bell's nearest and dearest, Duncan Grant and Vanessa Bell. 'There was the strongest criticism of their work, some hanging committees refusing to show certain of their paintings, saying that to do so would make a laughing stock of the exhibition.' A Stockholm critic stated, 'in this exhibition every kind of "ism" was represented including nepotism'. Middleton weighed up 'whether to send to another country the paintings we know they will like, or the paintings we consider best at home'. He concluded: 'Either set out to please them, or set out to shock them: you can't do both simultaneously.'[13]

The Fine Arts department continued to assemble international contemporary art exhibitions; whether they pleased or shocked remained in the eye of the beholder. One example, *British Drawings and Watercolours of the 20th Century from the Collection of the British Council*, compiled in 1951 by poet and art critic Geoffrey Grigson, had an extraordinarily active global life. It included works by Wyndham Lewis, Eduardo Paolozzi, Barbara Hepworth, and Frances Hodgkins. Notwithstanding periodic replenishment and conservation, it toured for thirty years, taking in fifty-seven countries including Israel and Lebanon, Tunisia and Algeria, Gibraltar and Malta, Hong Kong and Korea, Greece and France, Argentina and Chile, Hungary and Romania, Finland and Austria, Spain and Portugal. In 1953, it travelled to eight locations in New Zealand, where its reception provided a striking contrast with the reaction to British contem-

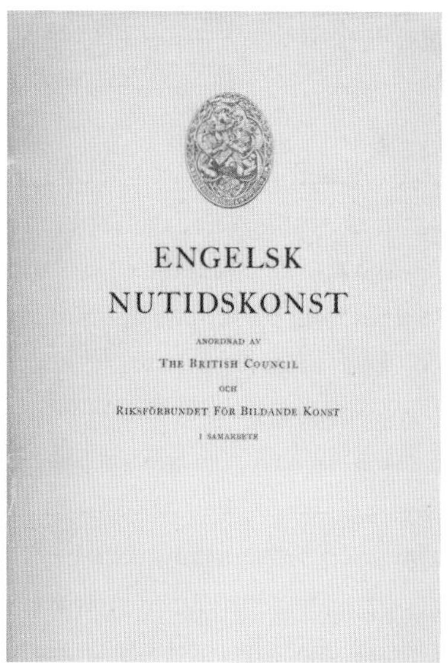

The Auckland Star
WITH WHICH IS INCORPORATED
The Evening News, Morning News, The Echo and The Sun
FRIDAY, JUNE 12, 1953

Henry Moore's "Row of sleepers" in wax chalk, pen and water colour.

Will British Art Jolt Auckland Too?

By TOM BOLSTER

The exhibition of modern British drawings and water colours that drew hot bolts of wrath from certain citizens in Palmerston North is now in the Wertheim Room at the Auckland Art Gallery, placidly awaiting the verdict of Aucklanders.

What is probable is that most Auckland gallery-goers will find the British show a provocative addition to the visual arts programme organized this year under the banner of the city's bustling Arts Festival.

Mentally, Aucklanders will no doubt compare the 60 or 70 British works with their counterparts in the local Society of Arts exhibition also on view at the gallery.

This comparison, on the whole, may not particularly favour our contemporary Auckland art; on the other hand, the British works, in certain instances, by no means have the ascendancy.

The British show is hung to its best possible advantage. Arranged chronologically, it moves from drawings by Sickert and Harold Gilman, done under the direct influence of the French Impressionists, into the post-impressionism that Gilman and several others from the Camden Town Group went on to explore.

What this show demonstrates very clearly is the impact that Wyndham Lewis' vorticist school made upon modern British painting.

Possibly, the Palmerston North gentlemen blanched as they peered into the Lewis abstraction in pen and wash done in 1912 (when Sickert was still absorbing 19th-century impressionism).

From here on the tide flowed strongly—Frances Hodgkins, Gwen John, Ben Nicholson and others in the present show carrying the experiments of the Parisian school into the main stream of British painting.

The English Channel may have halted Hitler, but it was no barrier whatever for the surging art which a handful of councillors now wish to bar from Palmerston North.

As single works, one of the Hodgkins fish studies, an exquisite little Gwen John and Barbara Hepworth's surgeons in oil and pencil imprint themselves on one's mind.

But it is the sweep of Henry Moore and Graham Sutherland that gives the present show its force and suggests a flowering of the modern trend in Britain.

Was it the Sutherland study for his important work at the Festival of Britain that aroused the ire of Palmerston North's art-lovers? Or, perhaps, his capriciously - titled, gloriously-coloured, "Landscape with estuary?"

If children in Palmerston North primer departments (as a headmaster has alleged) can match a Sutherland landscape in form and colour, they can do what few creative artists in New Zealand or Britain have achieved.

Keith Vaughan, John Minton, Eduardo Paolozzi, Robert Colquhoun and several of the younger figures in British art today offer examples of their recent work.

Vaughan's is introspective and interesting. Paolozzi is hardly up to his contributions to the lithograph show we saw here last season. There is nothing—for me—that reaches the level of Moore and Sutherland.

But, taken all in all, the present exhibition offers a microcosmic excursion through modern British art that is lively, enlightening and invigorating.

One may wonder (while admiring his stage decor) how Edward Burra's "The Band" slipped into the show. We can question the exclusion of a John Piper.

In terms of personal taste, we can like or dislike a number of things in this show. But in these drawings and watercolours we get a clearer picture of what seems to be happening in the British Isles than was obtainable from either the Massey Collection or the British Council's oils that toured here about the same time.

For this we can thank British critic, Geoffrey Grigson, for choosing the present works, and the British Council for sending them here.

ABOVE LEFT Front cover of the catalogue for the exhibition *Engelsk Nutidskonst*, which toured Sweden in 1948

ABOVE RIGHT Cutting from the *Auckland Star*, 12 June 1953, with a preview of the exhibition *British Drawings and Watercolours of the 20th Century from the Collection of the British Council*

porary art in Sweden. Where one exhibition was seen as rearguard, the other broke boundaries of aesthetic acceptability.

When the exhibition eventually arrived at Palmerston North, a city on New Zealand's North Island with a population of thirty thousand, D. C. Pryor, headmaster of the Central School, claimed, 'I could get similar in the primary departments of any school in this town.' He added, 'It is harmful that young people are being taken to these displays and told they are art when they are not.'[14] The art was likened by reporters to the 'untaught steps' of an eight-year-old child. One asked, with sarcastic rhetoric, 'If the British Council thinks that these things should be presented to the world to see where England has got to ... then who are they in Palmerston North to say nay?'[15]

Moore's *Row of Sleepers* was used as an illustration of works received with 'wrath' and described as 'trash'.[16] Complainants felt that the public was being held in contempt; the art was impossible to understand. British Council members were told to 'grow up or if grown up to act their age'. Modern art was nothing but 'a colossal leg-pull'. As a corrective, selectors were directed to the realist Munnings – 'who can draw and paint with a high degree of ability' – and were warned against Picasso, who, it was complained, dressed like a tramp, smoked in his own exhibitions and 'refused to say' of his painting 'what it was intended to be'.[17]

Not all held such antagonistic opinions. Some papers capitalized on the controversy to create headlines, but nonetheless pointed out, 'If children in Palmerston North primer departments ... can match a Sutherland landscape in form and colour, they can do what few creative artists in New Zealand and Britain have achieved.'[18] To counteract an angry resolution passed by city councillors, 'That the Council advise the British Council that it was very disappointed in the display of modern British water-colours', the Palmerston North Art Group wrote to the New Zealand representative to reassure him that 'the opinions expressed are certainly not shared by a large majority of people of this town'.[19] The group expressed their wish to be connected to a wider world, and their warm appreciation for British Council efforts in assembling 'the finest exhibitions it must be possible to arrange for a country so isolated as ours'.[20]

The sculpture of Henry Moore

Modern British painting, then, in different settings, could be variously perceived as imitative or boundary-breaking. Modern British sculpture had its own fortunes in the same period, and the Fine Arts department's promotion of three-dimensional art was to have a transformative and enduring effect on the perception of British modern art overseas. Its first purchase of a sculptural work began in December 1947, when approval was given for a bronze copy to be made from a Henry Moore reclining figure in lead owned by the Victoria and Albert Museum.[21] This commission was significant; the British Council Collection today has a particularly fine and extensive collection of contemporary sculptures, including many Moores. The early purchases, alongside gifts from the artist, underpin more than eight decades of touring his work globally. The close connection between the Fine Arts department and the sculptor have led to his being described as 'the British Council's greatest friend'.[22]

The British Council's first sculpture by Moore has many of the recognizable features that characterize the artist's work, from his experiments in organic form and his repeated explorations of the reclining female nude to his technical achievements combining voids and solids in a range of materials. Here these elements combine in a flowing form of a faceless figure in tawny bronze. A woman's neck, breasts, and shoulders emerge from smooth masses and negative spaces; together these suggest a raised knee, a torso lounging on a supportive elbow and a hollow for a single nipple. Modest in scale compared with Moore's later monumental works, the bronze is a mere foot long. The version it was modelled on was cast by the artist under humble conditions in the late 1930s. The undulating shapes had been constructed by hand from softened beeswax from Boots the Chemists, around which a plaster mould was built. The wax was melted out in a kiln improvised in Moore's back garden, and the space was filled with lead from a pipe melted by the artist in a domestic saucepan over a Primus paraffin stove.[23] The bronze British Council commission would have been cast professionally by a foundry from the lead version – the material is more resilient than lead and comes with greater sculptural prestige – and the final figure was mounted on an oval oak base.[24]

Henry Moore, *Reclining Figure*, 1939, bronze on oak base, 31.5 × 11.5 × 17 cm (P28)

Henry Moore, *Girl with Clasped Hands*, 1930, Cumberland alabaster, 42.5 × 30 × 23.5 cm (P25)

Reclining Figure took its place in the Collection at the same time as other key Moore purchases, including *Girl with Clasped Hands* from 1930. Sculpted in richly toned Cumberland alabaster, this striking half-figure was more typical of Moore's direct carving production methods and his favoured materials. Nine-tenths of his sculptures are in stone, and of the forty-one different stones used in his works, he favoured English quarry sources.[25] *Girl with Clasped Hands* stands forty-two centimetres high from flattened head to waist-cum-plinth. Its primitivist style shows a key inspiration: ancient non-European sculptures outside the classical Western academic tradition, in this case Mesopotamian votive figures. *Girl* borrows the reverent folded hands of the five-thousand-year-old Sumerian worshippers, along with their painted eyes, but her furrowed brow, squared shoulders, and sideways glance suggests anxious preoccupation rather than religious attentiveness. Moore often spoke of the importance of vitality to sculpture; here the squat young woman almost bristles with unarticulated tension. Both of these works began busy touring lives in British Council exhibitions from the first year of their purchase, most notably at the 1948 Venice Biennale.

Moore in Venice

An early responsibility of the Fine Arts department of the British Council, which continues to this day, was the selection of artists to represent the nation in the British Pavilion at the Venice Biennale. The process showcases British talent in an international forum and often forms the basis from which European tours are generated and from which collection purchases are made. Although there has been a biennial international art exhibition at Venice since 1895, it was only in 1909 that the United Kingdom established a pavilion in the city's Giardini della Biennale; and British representation became a state-organized affair only in 1930. Eight years later, the Fine Arts department took over the selection of British artists from the Department for Overseas Trade; at this point, the practice was to display multiple artists, with historic works shown alongside contemporary practitioners.[26]

The war led to a ten-year gap in official British representation at Venice. While the Biennale took place in 1940 and 1942, Britain did not take part. An exhibition had been organized for the 1940 edition, but it was withdrawn at the last minute, with the British Council showing the works at Hertford House in London (the home of the Wallace Collection) instead. The selected artists were Frank Dobson, Alfred Munnings, the late Glyn Philpot, Edward Wadsworth, Frances Hodgkins, and Duncan Grant. A group of wood engravings were also shown. The Biennale was suspended in 1944 and 1946. During this time, the British Pavilion was taken over by the Italian army, and it was temporarily renamed the Padiglione del Regio Esercito (Royal Army Pavilion).

With the festival's resumption in 1948, the pavilion became the site for a major Moore retrospective, comprising fifty-three works on paper and thirty-six sculptures, including *Reclining Figure* and *Girl with Clasped Hands*. Shown alongside paintings by J. M. W. Turner, the exhibition was to prove a triumphant choice; Moore was awarded the prestigious International Sculpture Prize.

TOP The British Pavilion at the Venice Biennale of 1948

ABOVE John Rothenstein, director of the Tate Gallery (centre, background), escorts Luigi Einaudi, president of Italy (centre foreground), around the opening of the Henry Moore exhibition in the British Pavilion

Henry Moore holding *Stringed Figure*, 1937, in his exhibition in the British Pavilion at the 1948 Venice Biennale

A European tour of the show followed, taking in Belgium, France, Netherlands, Germany, Switzerland, and Greece in its first three years, with further British Council exhibitions taking Moores across the globe throughout the 1950s and, indeed, far beyond. This energetic mid-century activity established Moore's prestige internationally as 'Britain's greatest living sculptor', while it also consolidated the humanist message of his works in the service of cultural relations.[27] Together these factors underpin Moore's inclusion in more than 160 British Council exhibitions to date.

Herbert Read's essay in the 1948 catalogue framed Moore in relation to reference points that would direct his reception for years to come. These included his background as the son of a miner, his attachment to the English landscape, his inspirations in so-called primitive sculpture, and his sculptural lineage in Renaissance tradition and European modernism.[28] Read's championing of Moore was by this point well established; he had been writing essays on the artist for more than fifteen years, and the two Yorkshiremen were close

Front cover of the catalogue for Henry Moore's exhibition at the 1948 Venice Biennale

friends. The qualities he attributed to Moore's work echoed the sculptor's own claims – including 'truth to materials', as an attempt to bring out the essential qualities of his sculptural sources, rather than trying to make, for example, stone look like flesh – but to these Read added several of his own. Moore was 'a humble and devoted exponent' of the 'element of art that transcends all periods and schools'. He tapped into eternal archetypes that captured the essence of what it meant to be human; indeed, his work, Read later said, communicated nothing less than the life-force itself.[29]

Moore in Mexico

The seemingly contradictory qualities that allowed Moore to communicate, simultaneously, the personal and the universal, the traditional and the modern, the national and the cosmopolitan, enabled the broadest reception for Moore's work as it travelled. By 1950, the Fine Arts department could claim: 'We have been asked by practically every capital in the world for a Henry Moore exhibition.'[30] The same year, a Moore drawing exhibition travelled to Mexico City and Guadalajara. As a means of building an alliance between the two nations, it was important for the British Council to make a connection between the artist and

Mexico. The exhibition leaflet included a copy of a handwritten letter from him in which he stated that the country was the place he would most like to visit, and that, 'Pre-Columbian sculpture has been the most important single influence in my own sculpture.'[31] The catalogue essay by Grigson styled the exhibition as a return gesture by the artist to the country from which he had taken so much: 'Mexican art has moved Henry Moore so considerably throughout his conscious life as a sculptor that an exhibition of his drawings here in Mexico City must gratify him as a quid pro quo.'[32]

Grigson positioned Moore's interest in pre-Columbian sculpture as a turn away from the academic art education that he had received in London in the 1920s. He quoted Moore: 'Mexican sculpture, as soon as I found it, seemed to me true and right. ... Its "stoniness", by which I mean its truth to material, its tremendous power without loss of sensitiveness, its astonishing variety and fertility of form-invention and its approach to a full three-dimensional conception of form, make it unsurpassed.'[33] Grigson linked all Moore's reclining

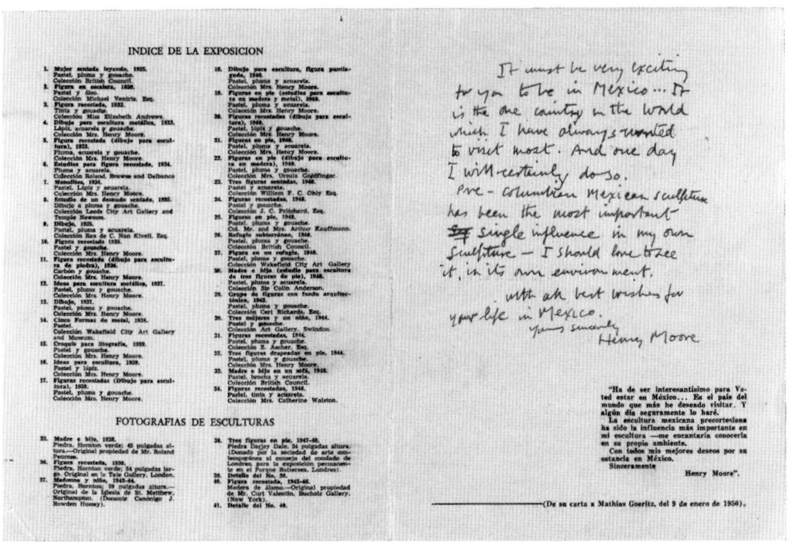

INDICE DE LA EXPOSICION

1. **Mujer sentada leyendo, 1925.** Pastel, pluma y gouache. Colección British Council.
2. **Figura en escalera, 1926.** Pastel y óleo. Colección Michael Ventris, Esq.
3. **Figura recostada, 1932.** Tinta y gouache. Colección Miss Elizabeth Andrews.
4. **Dibujo para escultura metálica, 1933.** Lápiz, acuarela y gouache. Colección Mrs. Henry Moore.
5. **Figura recostada (dibujo para escultura), 1933.** Pluma, acuarela y gouache. Colección Mrs. Henry Moore.
6. **Estudios para figura recostada, 1934.** Pluma y acuarela. Colección Roland, Browse and Delbanco
7. **Monolitos, 1934.** Pastel, Lápiz y acuarela. Colección Mrs. Henry Moore.
8. **Estudio de un desnudo sentado, 1935.** Dibujo a pluma y gouache. Colección Leeds City Art Gallery and Temple Newsam.
9. **Dibujo, 1935.** Pastel, pluma y acuarela. Colección Rex de C. Nan Kivell, Esq.
10. **Figura recostada 1935.** Pastel y gouache. Colección Mrs. Henry Moore.
11. **Figura recostada (dibujo para escultura de piedra), 1936.** Carbón y gouache. Colección Mrs. Henry Moore.
12. **Ideas para escultura metálica, 1937.** Pastel, pluma y gouache. Colección Mrs. Henry Moore.
13. **Dibujo, 1937.** Pastel, pluma y gouache. Colección Mrs. Henry Moore.
14. **Cinco Formas de metal, 1938.** Pastel. Colección Wakefield City Art Gallery and Museum.
15. **Croquis para litografía, 1939.** Pastel y gouache. Colección Mrs. Henry Moore.
16. **Ideas para escultura, 1939.** Pastel y lápiz. Colección Mrs. Henry Moore.
17. **Figuras recostadas (Dibujo para escultura), 1939.** Pastel, pluma y gouache. Colección Mrs. Henry Moore.
18. **Dibujo para escultura, figura puntiaguda, 1940.** Pastel, pluma y acuarela. Colección Mrs. Henry Moore.
19. **Figuras en pie (estudios para escultura en madera y metal), 1940.** Pastel, pluma y acuarela. Colección Mrs. Henry Moore.
20. **Figuras recostadas (dibujo para escultura), 1940.** Pastel, lápiz y gouache. Colección Mrs. Henry Moore.
21. **Figuras en pie, 1940.** Pastel, pluma y acuarela. Colección Mrs. Henry Moore.
22. **Figuras en pie (dibujo para escultura en madera), 1940.** Pastel, pluma y gouache. Colección Mrs. Ursula Goldfinger.
23. **Tres figuras sentadas, 1940.** Pastel y acuarela. Colección William F. C. Ohly Esq.
24. **Figuras recostadas, 1940.** Pastel y gouache. Colección J. C. Pritchard, Esq.
25. **Figuras en pie, 1940.** Pastel, pluma y gouache. Col. Mr. and Mrs. Arthur Kauffmann.
26. **Refugio subterráneo, 1940.** Pastel, pluma y gouache. Colección British Council.
27. **Figura en un refugio, 1940.** Pastel, pluma y gouache. Colección Wakefield City Art Gallery
28. **Madre e hijo (estudio para escultura de tres figuras de pie), 1940.** Pastel, pluma y acuarela. Colección Sir Colin Anderson.
29. **Grupo de figuras con fondo arquitectónico, 1943.** Pastel, pluma y gouache. Colección Ceri Richards, Esq.
30. **Tres mujeres y un niño, 1944.** Pastel y gouache. Colección Art Gallery, Swindon.
31. **Figuras recostadas, 1944.** Pastel, pluma y gouache. Colección Z. Ascher, Esq.
32. **Tres figuras drapeadas en pie, 1944.** Pastel, pluma y gouache. Colección Mrs. Henry Moore.
33. **Madre e hijo en un sofá, 1946.** Pastel, brocha y acuarela. Colección British Council.
34. **Figuras recostadas, 1946.** Pastel, tinta y acuarela. Colección Mrs. Catherine Walston.

FOTOGRAFIAS DE ESCULTURAS

35. **Madre e hijo, 1936.** Piedra, Hornton verde; 45 pulgadas altura.—Original propiedad de Mr. Roland Penrose.
36. **Figura recostada, 1938.** Piedra, Hornton verde; 54 pulgadas largo. Original en la Tate Gallery, London.
37. **Madonna y niño, 1943-44.** Piedra, Hornton; 59 pulgadas altura.—Original de la Iglesia de St. Matthew, Northampton. (Donante Canónigo J. Rowden Hussey).
38. **Tres figuras en pie, 1947-48.** Piedra Darley Dale. 54 pulgadas altura. (Donado por la sociedad de arte contemporánea al consejo del condado de Londres, para la exposición permanente en el Parque Battersea, Londres).
39. **Detalle del No. 38.**
40. **Figura recostada, 1945-46.** Madera de álamo.—Original propiedad de Mr. Curt Valentin, Bucholz Gallery, (New York).
41. **Detalle del No. 40.**

It must be very exciting for you to be in Mexico... It is the one country in the world which I have always wanted to visit most. And one day I will certainly do so.
Pre-Columbian Mexican sculpture has been the most important single influence in my own sculpture – I should love to see it, in its own environment.
With all best wishes for your life in Mexico.
Yours sincerely
Henry Moore

"Ha de ser interesantísimo para Vsted estar en México... Es el país del mundo que más he deseado visitar. Y algún día seguramente lo haré.
La escultura mexicana precortesiana ha sido la influencia más importante en mi escultura —me encantaría conocerla en su propio ambiente.
Con todos mis mejores deseos por su estancia en México.
Sinceramente
Henry Moore".

(De su carta a Mathias Goeritz, del 9 de enero de 1950).

The exhibition leaflet for Henry Moore's touring exhibition in Mexico, 1950, with a handwritten note from the artist

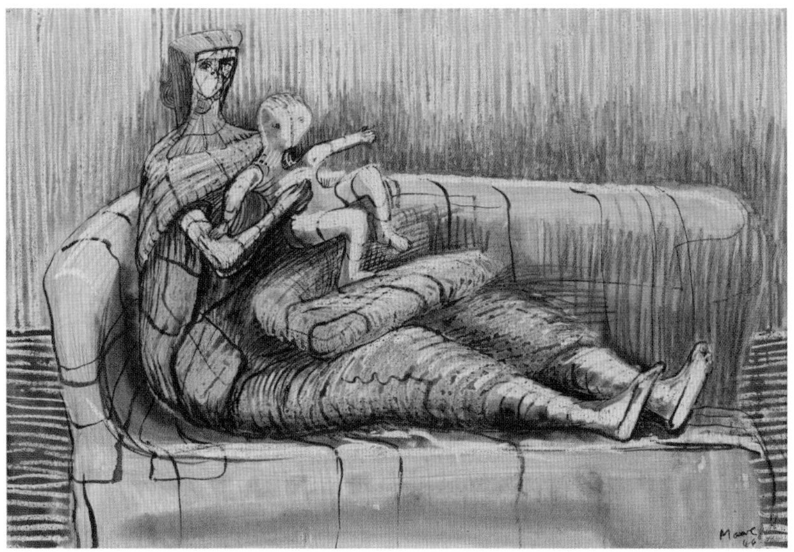

Henry Moore, *Mother and Child on a Sofa*, 1946, crayon, watercolour, and ink on paper, 37.5 × 55.5 cm (P121)

figures to 'an Aztec theme', and even his shelter drawings, which might seem more closely located to London under fire.[34] This narrative influenced how the exhibition was received. As one report put it, 'A man who has never been in Mexico and who knows and feels the pre-Cortesian art of Mexico only from the famous collections that are found in Europe, becomes one of the best and most authentic representations of a spirit intrinsically ours, the spirit of our ancestors, which animates us to-day.'[35]

British Council cultural exchanges, then and now, enable international communication between parallel communities – for example, between gallerists and artists, and art teachers and students. In Mexico, getting opposite numbers together was more important than pleasing diplomats or British visitors. This was just as well; these audiences were not impressed. The Council's representative in the country observed that the governor of the State of Jalisco 'expressed surprise and interest' in Moore's work, but he also noted that 'exclamations of horrified incomprehension' emerged 'from members of the British colony', who were heard to make dismissive comments about 'degenerate art'.[36] The British consul, an amateur flower painter, was also furious about Moore's positive reception; he was said to be 'running round telling everybody that his pictures were much better'.[37] Moore works frequently created controversy as embodiments of a new vision in modern art. In Mexico, this was offset by creating contexts that domesticated its strangeness. As the Mexican artist Mathias Georitz wrote to his friend Moore, 'New people look at your work with other eyes and are very touched to find in your work something "Mexican".'[38]

Moore in Greece

The following year, Moore sculptures were sent to Greece. Again, a strategic relationship was formulated around cultural correspondences; once more, the exhibition was a focus for energetic attention in a country with an eminent sculptural tradition. As the *Sunday Times* summarized, 'Few of our contemporary artists have done more for the reputation of their country abroad than that great sculptor, Henry Moore. As an ambassador for the arts of England in foreign lands he has something of the propaganda force of the Sadler's Wells Ballet centred on one person. It is, therefore, of interest that he is now in Greece. Never before has there been an English sculptor of international reputation. The phenomenon has been as rare as that of an English matador.'[39]

Moore's capacity to generate headlines added to his powers. Of his Greek reception, it was noted, 'Of course there has been controversy. ... One paper wrote that it is impertinent for the barbarians from a foggy island to send these objects to the home of the greatest sculptors ever born.'[40] The sculptures were described as 'an affront to the Acropolis'.[41] While this negative attention could be perceived as a failing, the press outcry had a positive effect on audiences: 'many must have come to see what all the fuss was about'.[42] One of the 34,000 visitors in the show's nineteen-day run at the Zappeion Gallery in Athens, 'came out flourishing a stick and saying, "The damnable thing is there must be something really good, it makes me so angry."'[43] Indeed, it was observed, 'Perhaps the greatest benefits will be among those most overtly hostile. ... People may say they dislike his work, but they will not forget it.'[44]

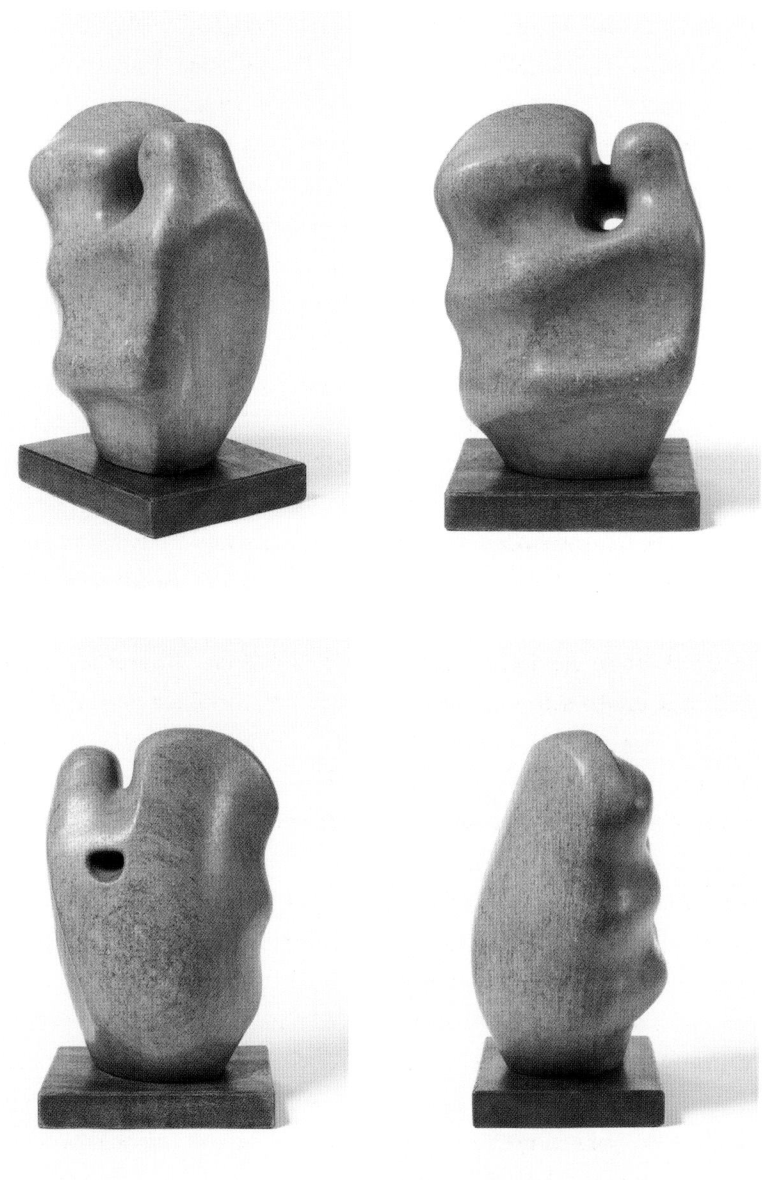

Henry Moore, *Mother and Child*, 1936, Ancaster stone, 50 × 31 × 28 cm (P48)

And in not forgetting the exhibition, they would also not forget the institution that organized it: 'The general public – at *all* levels – has been aware of the fact that an exhibition of modern English sculpture was organised by the British Council in Athens; the merits or otherwise of the sculptor were in a sense common café talk for the space of a few weeks, and the British Council was linked with the sculptor's name in all this talk.'[45]

Michael Tombros, director of the Athens School of Fine Arts, explained the hostile local reactions: 'We have only one art museum which is closed, contains very few things, ignores whole representative periods and is an example of the lack of interest shown to art by the government and society. When the public which has thus been deprived is confronted by the sort of works he has never seen, he asks himself: "What is this?"'[46] Positive reception of Moore's sculpture in Greece was enhanced when the artist and his wife, Irina, visited the country. Over seventeen days of duties, he attended museums and heritage sites, art schools and studios, lectures, performances, cocktail parties, picnics, and dinners with ambassadors, academics, artists, critics, curators, and collectors.[47] As he had done in Mexico, he built persuasive links with Greece as a pivot point in his sculptural practice, creating an alliance that rewarded all involved.

Moore the man was as much an ambassador as his works. His warm and generous personality softened his art, and moderated that which was perceived to be aesthetically outlandish. He was frequently characterized as a down-to-earth Yorkshireman; a family man of simple tastes who preferred to live in a country cottage than the art world of the metropolis. Appraisals read Moore's physical appearance as a measure of his approachability, to style him apart from the peculiarities associated with avant-garde artists. Greek newspapers noted with satisfaction that he was neither formal nor fanciful: 'Mr. Moore was wearing a beige suit, green coloured stockings, a shirt with a grey tie. His face was rosy, typically Anglo-Saxon, his small eyes bright blue and his hair brown.'[48] Moore's story as a miner's son wedded to the ancient English landscape combined with his Greek sculptural inspirations; as such, by the close of the exhibition, it could be claimed, 'Henry Moore has become a friend of Greece, and that the Greeks have become Henry Moore's friends.'[49]

A view of the exhibition *Henry Moore*, Moderna Galerija, Ljubljana, then Yugoslavia, now the capital of Slovenia, 1955

Sculptor as Cold Warrior

Moore's works continued to be in demand internationally throughout the 1950s, and exhibitions of his work travelled across Europe, the Commonwealth, the Middle and Far East to the fringes of the Iron Curtain. For all their mostly apolitical and ambiguous messages of universal humanism, his sculptures could function as symbols of artistic freedom, freedom of thought, and thus wider social freedoms, especially when seen in relation to autocratic modes of governance and their forms of aesthetic communication, which were considered didactic, state-prescribed, and aggressively realist in comparison. Non-representational works of art hold a double-coded position in cultural relations; as the historian Larraine Nicholas has put it, they are 'both innocent of politics and heavily implicated in it'.[50] British sculpture in these domains, art historian Pauline Rose has argued, 'represented honesty, quality and democratic values'.[51] It was the very antithesis of totalitarian monuments.

Moore's art inhabited a uniquely productive space, where it was well known enough to be in regular demand, but also challenging enough to garner regular press attention. Aesthetically, it sat between the figurative and the abstract, the experimental and the conservative. These particular conditions, along with Moore's warm ambassadorial talents, made him an ideal cold warrior in the British Council's mid-century arsenal of soft power. This was recognized by his contemporaries at the time. Artist Julian Trevelyan remembered Kenneth Clark saying, 'If it proved necessary to send an ambassador of the human race to Mars, Henry Moore should undoubtedly be chosen for the job.'[52] In addition, travelling exhibitions of Moores's work regularly led to international museum purchases and to public commissions, while the siting of his sculptures in urban redevelopments became potent symbols of the rebuilding of a divided Europe.[53]

Moore was not the only British sculptor to receive major promotion at Venice. Barbara Hepworth followed in 1950, in a display that included her biomorphic sculptures alongside her hospital drawings. Shown with contemporary paintings by Matthew Smith and the nineteenth-century romanticism of John Constable, the exhibition secured Hepworth's international reputation.

Barbara Hepworth's exhibition in the British Pavilion of the 1950 Venice Biennale

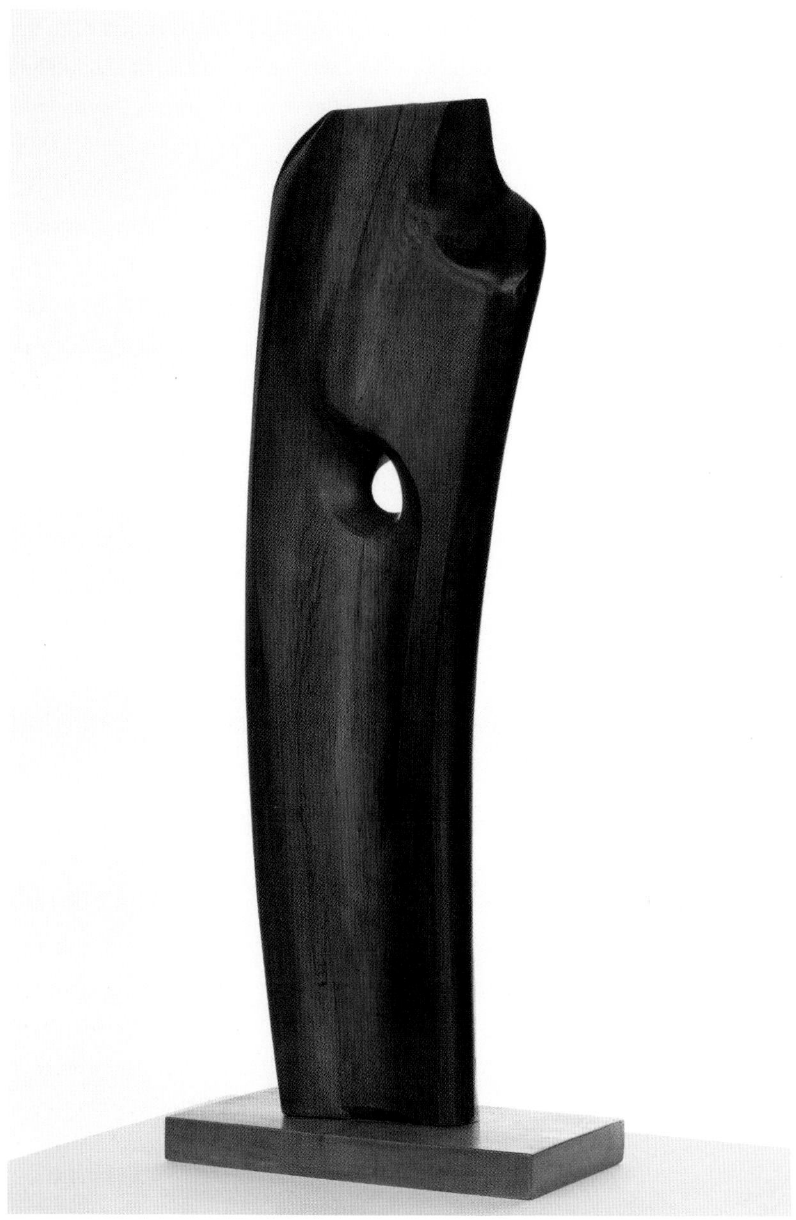

Barbara Hepworth, *Rhythmic Form*, 1949, rosewood on wooden base, 40.7 × 104.3 × 22.8 cm (P167)

Barbara Hepworth, *Two Standing Nudes*, 1947, pencil and oil on board, 30.5 × 37 cm (P2738)

Two views of Graham Sutherland's solo exhibition in the British Pavilion of the 1952 Venice Biennale

In 1952, Read was the commissioner for an exhibition within the British Pavilion at the Venice Biennale designed to build upon Moore's contribution, but also to move the debate on. He was part of a team that included the formidable painter-turned-arts administrator Lilian Somerville, who joined the Fine Arts department in 1941, and led it with fierce determination from 1947 for more than twenty years. Read wrote the catalogue essay that introduced the next generation of British sculptors to a European audience. Moore was positioned as the departure point for the exhibiting artists, all of whom were under forty years of age. His bronze *Double Standing Figure* stood, strategically, at the entrance of the pavilion, 'to give an orientation for the surprising developments that will be found within'.[54] Read's show, which was entitled *New Aspects of British Sculpture*, was part of a wider display called *Exhibition of Works by Sutherland, Wadsworth, Adams, Armitage, Butler, Chadwick, Clarke, Meadows, Moore, Paolozzi, Turnbull*. Sutherland and the late Edward Wadsworth had rooms of solo paintings, while the rest – with the exception of Moore, whose sculpture remained outside – clustered in a group show.

The prosaic exhibition title was enlivened by the poetic characterizations drawn by Read in his essay of this new generation, whose aesthetics were marked by 'an iconography of despair' or, more famously, 'a geometry of fear'.[55] Robert Adams, Kenneth Armitage, Reg Butler, Lynn Chadwick, Geoffrey Clarke, Bernard Meadows, Eduardo Paolozzi, and William Turnbull did not constitute a particular sculptural school of thought, but in Read's conception their work shared an ethos shaped by the gathering shadows of their historical moment. He perceived an existential mood of atomic anxiety; their generation was caught between world war and nuclear catastrophe. As such, they rejected Moore's soft shapes and massed grand monuments and turned instead to hard, brittle gestures, cold and sharp in tone, coarse and crude in finish, constructed from angular metal rather than smooth stone. In textures that Read argued communicated the mechanized and the traumatized, their skeletal, robotic forms embodied sculptural agitation rather than serenity.[56] Armitage, Butler, Chadwick, and Paolozzi in particular produced warped human–machine hybrid figures in the 1950s, standing uneasily on emaciated,

TOP Sculptures and works on paper by Bernard Meadows in *New Aspects of British Sculpture*, the group show in the British Pavilion of the 1952 Venice Biennale

OPPOSITE Eduardo Paolozzi, *The Philosopher*, 1957, bronze, height 188 cm (P323)

spindly limbs, encumbered with blocky, burdensome bodies. In blackened bronze, the staggering figures seemed to emerge as if from a fire, dazed and devastated, limbless and eyeless, monstrous yet vulnerable. The rupture they communicated was an overturning of sculptural tradition and a response to the convulsions of the political present.

The exhibition was received with high praise. Read noted, with embarrassment, 'As *commissario* I was overwhelmed with congratulations. Again and again I was told that the British Pavilion was the most vital, the most brilliant, and the most promising in the whole Biennale.' He explained, 'Whereas in 1948 the great success of the Henry Moore exhibition was a tribute to the artist, this time it was the British contribution as a whole which was felt to be so exciting and so vital.'[57] Salutes came from Alfred H. Barr of New York's Museum of Modern Art, who proclaimed it, 'the most distinguished national showing in the whole Biennale'. In his summary, 'the exhibition was astutely planned, boldly selected, and installed with exceptional taste and intelligence'.

Kenneth Armitage, *Figure Lying on its Side*, 1957, bronze, 23 × 80.1 × 39 cm (P291)

It was particularly important that it had not been orchestrated by 'some public official or administrator'; instead, 'the Council sent as British Commissioner one of the most distinguished philosophers of art now writing in English'.[58] The exhibition's success was compounded by subsequent purchases of the work of exhibiting artists by museums and private collectors internationally.[59] It also had a significant effect on reputations. Sutherland, the principal painter in the pavilion, stated that his high status in Europe was closely connected to British Council efforts.[60] Armitage credited the exhibition with beginning his professional life: 'I was totally unknown before that, and from those few weeks I was a known figure throughout the world.'[61]

Lynn Chadwick, *Encounter VI*, 1957, bronze, height 153.5 cm (P287)

Graham Sutherland, *Thorn Trees*, 1945, oil on canvas, 127 × 101.5 cm (P74)

Thorns and bombs

The sculptors that Read organized under the geometry of fear concept were communicating a particular Cold War anxiety; this was his political viewpoint, but it also captured a broader state of mind. The fear of nuclear annihilation was not just a stylistic metaphor; it was close to the surface in discussions of the mid-1950s and was addressed head-on by Sir Philip Hendy, chair of the Fine Arts Committee between 1956 and 1959, in a letter to the press calling for more funds for cultural relations. In his calculation, a further £55,000 a year would represent merely 'half the price of a tail of a misguided missile, a negligible amount in the cost of the cold war'.[62] Art, here, was opposed to armaments; it was a peacekeeper and nuclear deterrent. While an earlier foreign secretary had felt that exhibitions of modern paintings were less likely to 'produce quick returns in the political field' than other British Council activities, they were political projects nonetheless.[63]

Perhaps the clearest Cold War context in which works in the Council's collection circulated can be seen with Sutherland's *Thorn Trees*. Painted in 1945 and bought in 1947 as one of the Council's first dozen purchases of oils, Sutherland's picture has been classified as neo-romantic. Despite its ostensible representation of plant life against a hard green ground and a dark-blue sky, the contorted shapes do not constitute a comforting pastoral landscape but signal instead a cruel space of intense suffering. The snarling spikes are angry meditations on Christ's crucifixion as much as they are scenes from nature; rather than picturing the bucolic, they show the barbed wire that contains it. The angry result bristles with rage, clawing at the viewer's eyes.

The British Council owns more than forty Sutherlands, and *Thorn Trees*, like many other works in its collection, has led an amazingly active exhibition life, touring the globe in the service of a diverse range of thematic narratives and in conversation with a wide variety of cultures. As part of its travels, it went to Toyko in 1957 as the British submission to the fourth International Art Exhibition of Japan, where it won the Foreign Minister's Prize. To celebrate this achievement, it appeared on page three of the *Mainichi*, the English-language Japanese newspaper sponsor of the event. The front page, however, carried

The Mainichi

UK To Relax Trade Ban On North Korea Also

UK Tests 2nd H-Bomb In Christmas Is. Blast

US Resigned To Japan Eventually Easing Ban

NATO-Like Mid-East Mil. Body To Be Studied Soon

EDITORIAL

Int'l A-Test Control Urged By Matsudaira

Where to Shop, Where to Dine

International Art Exhibition Prize Winners

CHURCH SERVICES

Swimming Season Opens

let's tune in

ENTERTAINMENT GUIDE

SCREEN

YOKOHAMA

Announcements

STAGE

The front page and page 3 of the *Mainichi* newspaper, 2 June 1957

a rather different illustration as its haunting lead image: a mushroom cloud dominates the sky above Christmas Island, the result of British nuclear experiments. The cover also detailed clashes between police and Japanese protesters outside the British embassy in response.[64] The two pages, with their contrasting but corresponding images, testify to the chilling cheek-by-jowl proximity of British art and international politics in the period.

Indolent zanies?

In the mid-1950s, the British Council saw another shift in priorities. As budgets tightened, the focus turned away from Western Europe, with the exception of Austria, Italy, Spain, and West Germany, which were seen to remain politically unstable. With a new emphasis on the developing world, withdrawals took place in several countries, including New Zealand and Australia. The *Drogheda Report* of 1954 – written by the Independent Committee of Enquiry in the Overseas Information Services (better known as the Drogheda Committee) – which considered the ways government departments and other agencies, including the British Council and the BBC, administered overseas communications, praised the contribution of the arts in cultural relations and recommended its expansion, but money was no easier to come by.[65] By the middle of the decade, the proportion of Council budgets spent on the arts, including theatre and music, was just two per cent, with the vast majority of funds being spent on activities with more immediate returns, such as English-language teaching. A reflective essay in the mid-1950s by the Council's chairman David Kelly noted, 'Because of the publicity they attract, and the controversies inevitably associated with them, the Arts are often thought to constitute one of the main fields for British Council activity.'[66] Among the first surprises that Kelly experienced upon coming into post in 1955 was to find that Fine Arts department's budget was only £16,000 of the entire organization's annual £3 million. As he observed, 'these minute sums' covered the packing and dispatch of exhibitions, as well as staffing, and he compared the cost with 'the £2,000 a minute which some commercial firms have paid for television space'.[67] He regretted that, 'the Council lacks the resources to cope with the opportunities offered it'.[68]

Kelly also tackled widespread myths about the Council held at home, where the organization was little understood. A sustained campaign by the *Daily Express* over twenty years portrayed employees as Bohemian intellectuals; 'men with long hair and purple corduroys', as Stanley Unwin summarized it.[69] In 1954, frustrated Council staff self-funded a twelve-page pamphlet refuting press inaccuracies one by one. The aim of the slurs, Harold Nicolson noted, was to paint Council members as 'indolent zanies, wasting our slender resources'.[70]

While these characterizations are amusing, the claims that informed them were pernicious, and they had material consequences. In the second half of the 1950s, under the leadership of Paul Sinker, director-general of the British Council from 1954 to 1968, the Fine Arts Committee's decisions were called into question. Following instructions to withdraw from Europe, the department was seriously concerned about how it could maintain artistic legitimacy if it were unable to continue relations with Paris, the centre of the art world. The Committee wanted to keep its officer there, but Sinker was determined

Front cover of the catalogue for Lynn Chadwick's exhibition in the British Pavilion at the 1956 Venice Biennale

to curtail its activities to improve the Council's public appearance. He said the 'cranky' perception 'was made especially of some of the works of art the Council sent to the Venice Biennale'. He warned, 'The Council ought not to go too far ahead of opinion in showing art that was "avant-garde"'. Instead, it 'should concentrate mainly on what was accepted as good by those of authority'. Chadwick was used to illustrate the point; his sculpture had been in the 1952 Venice show and had been selected to represent Britain in 1956. Sinker wanted a more conservative choice, and he refused to continue the Paris appointment.

This decision caused controversy on two counts: the first was in relation to the authority of the Fine Arts Committee; the second related to Britain's artistic place in Europe. Speaking in a meeting of the committee in January 1955, Clive Bell, while declaring himself 'not in sympathy with Lynn Chadwick', said that unless the committee had the last word in aesthetic decisions, 'it had better resign'. Read, with immense restraint, asked after the artistic authorities to whom they should defer. Hendy, who had succeeded Clark as the

A view of Lynn Chadwick's exhibition in the British Pavilion at the 1956 Venice Biennale

Jack Smith, *Child Walking With Check Tablecloth*, 1953, oil on board, 153 × 122 cm (P286)

director of the National Gallery, was recorded as saying, 'If this Committee were not reasonably well-informed, he did not know who was.' Sinker said that ambassadors and British Council representatives abroad had advised him that artistically challenging exhibitions did not 'do much good'. He argued for more popular taste: 'It was time for the ordinary citizen to speak up.' Members of the Fine Arts Committee argued that British preferences should not be a basis for generalization: 'the ordinary citizen abroad was far more intelligently interested in the visual arts than he was here'. The British Council should not lower its standards, they maintained.[71]

The debate illuminated who the Fine Arts department saw as its main audience. Especially with limited funds, it was argued that the British Council should focus on those who influenced taste in other countries.[72] Interest in British art was growing in a way that was unprecedented; for example, 'dealers in Paris were beginning to stock the work of British artists'. The role of the British Council in this had been central. Britain needed to keep the dialogue going: 'The extinction of the Paris post would be regarded as a signal everywhere that this country had no longer any art of international consequence.'[73] Beneath these arguments sat competing ideas about cultural capital. Whitehall, committee members complained, saw English teaching as the British Council's primary activity, with visual art one of 'the frills'. This failed to acknowledge culture's enormous dividends. As a case in point, France 'had spent a great deal of money in persuading the world of the importance of her art and literature' and was thus 'regarded as a far more important power than her political or economic situation alone would warrant'.[74]

In the end, the Fine Arts Committee eventually located separate funding to support, on a temporary part-time basis, an officer in Paris, the well-connected artist, curator, and collector Roland Penrose. In order to concede some 'compromise on aesthetic matters', Kitchen Sink artists – including Jack Smith and John Bratby, with their images of washing lines and cornflake packets – were sent to Venice alongside Chadwick to appeal to a wider range of tastes.[75] Although the department was vindicated when Chadwick secured the 1956 International Sculpture Prize at the Biennale – beating major names such as Alberto Giacometti – the clash was the first of a number of fights over the value of its work and the authority of its decisions.

Conflict and consolidation

The challenges discussed in this chapter offer insights into the functioning of the Fine Arts department, set against the developing and consolidating years of the British Council. What should modern art look like, and what could it achieve when it travelled overseas? Should it please or shock? Should it compete or unite? Who gets to choose and who gets to say? Expectations differed between sender and receiver, individuals and institutions, politicians and press, British ambassadors and British Council employees, curators and artists. The tensions offer a measure of its productivity and the complexity of art in international intercultural conversations.

The debates reveal cultural values about aesthetic and political autonomy, freedom and direction. At mid-century, the British Council reflected on the paradox at its heart: it was more likely to produce political results by being non-political, and it was more likely to serve the national interest by being, as well as appearing, disinterested.[76] At this time, as Margaret Garlake has put it, art in the British Council was 'promoted as a metaphor, sometimes a substitute, for political action'.[77] In the service of cultural relations, especially in the context of world war and then Cold War, even non-didactic abstract art served political purposes, carried political messages, and was interpreted in political frameworks.

By the end of the 1950s, after fifteen years of postwar operation, the Fine Arts department had secured major international accolades. Its esteemed members and advisors were radical and adventurous in their choices. Despite its successes, it operated in a tense environment, with institutional clashes over purpose, priority, and vision. By the end of the decade, the painters and sculptors whose international reputations the British Council supported had matured, and a substantial and active collection was consolidated. In the following decade, a younger generation would shift the messages that the Council sent overseas in a period rich with new artistic forms and new political challenges.

John Bratby, *Three People at a Table*, 1955, oil on board, 120.7 × 120.7 cm (P281)

CHAPTER 3

Pop and protest

By the end of the 1950s, the British Council's Fine Arts department had an advisory committee boasting some of the biggest names in national arts institutions, a vigorous programme of international exhibitions, an impressive list of prizes for the artists it had exhibited, and a growing permanent collection of paintings, drawings, prints, and sculptures. It had proven its value, but funding remained painfully tight. Despite institutional reviews identifying the arts as a particular strength in British cultural relations, budgets remained too small to make regular and substantial purchases for the Collection and to meet the growing requests for exhibitions across the world.

In this context, the department sought external funding to buy more ambitiously and to expand its exhibition output. New external money would now shift both the quantity and the nature of acquisitions. Buying became focused on younger artists and reorientated the character of the British Council's art exhibitions in a decade when a burgeoning culture of youth was making itself firmly felt internationally. New media, including the Pop art print, shifted the material messages of art works sent overseas. As exhibitions expanded in number and form, they also grew in complexity. In the turbulent international politics of the period, the Council's practices aimed to create dialogue but became entangled in wider debates about democracy, decolonization, and decorum. The debates of the decade left a lasting mark on the Collection's scale, subject matter, style, and shape.

Peter Blake, *The Beach Boys*, 1964, screenprint, 30.5 × 52.9 cm (P813) (detail)

Public funding and private purchases

Tightening budgets throughout the 1950s meant that money dominated the Fine Arts Committee's discussions as the new decade approached. In 1957, an annual purchasing budget of £700 had been observed to be completely inadequate for building a nationally significant collection.[1] A year later, a review of arts funding in Britain, entitled *Help for the Arts*, concluded that the situation was dire. State patronage was weak, private patrons were few, and taxation was high. The report's conclusions were damning: 'The support and enthusiasm which the visual arts command in Britain is less than in other countries and public taste is much less developed in this than in other spheres.'[2] It lamented: 'Far too few people seem to recognise the place which the arts should play in the life of the nation – as a whole.' Equally, it said, they were ignorant of the part the arts could play in international promotion.[3]

The report was commissioned by the Calouste Gulbenkian Foundation, an international philanthropic enterprise established in 1956 at the bequest of the individual whose name it bears. Gulbenkian was an Armenian-born businessman with British nationality who was one of the world's wealthiest individuals by the time of his death, aged eighty-six, in 1955. His fortunes had been accumulated through dealing in oil and petroleum, and part of his money had been invested in art; he was an enthusiastic collector with a personal collection of some six thousand works. The cultural foundation that carries his name was established in Portugal – Gulbenkian's adopted country – and for almost seventy years, it has provided generous financial support for artistic, scientific, and educational endeavours, primarily in Britain, Portugal, and Armenia.

The committee sought to capitalize on the foundation's intervention. In May 1958, it appealed for a grant of £25,000 to purchase a 'special collection of painting and sculpture by living British artists which would be known as the Gulbenkian Collection of the British Council'.[4] Sir Philip Hendy, director of the National Gallery and chair of the committee, made the case. 'Under the conditions of today,' he argued, 'the artist is in much the same position as the manufacturer; he cannot exist entirely on the home market. For the first time in about a century Great Britain has a number of artists whose work can be considered as a valuable export.' To this he added: 'An important part of the work of the British Council's Fine Art Department consists of sending work by living British artists to international exhibitions; and we know from their extraordinary success in these that their work is very highly esteemed abroad. The effect of their appearance in those exhibitions, however, is ephemeral, and it would be an enormous advantage to them and to the prestige of this country if a permanent collection could be brought into being that could be maintained in circulation.'[5]

Hendy did not detail that a permanent collection of three hundred paintings and works of sculpture was a growing part of the Fine Arts department's assets, along with the four hundred Wakefield works of graphic art. Instead, he emphasized the other and then more dominant methods of operation. 'The paintings and sculptures which make up the British Council's exhibitions overseas', he stated, accurately, 'are almost all borrowed from public or private collections or from the artists themselves.' In order to clarify the role of public funding, he noted that this was 'for the purpose of increasing the prestige of Great Britain abroad through the arts. Any benefit the artist may receive is incidental, and not the purpose of the Council.' With the proposed Gulbenkian Collection, he strategically stated that it would be 'primarily and directly to assist the artists'; in this way, he was able to justify the organization's eligibility for private foundation money. Finally, he emphasized the British Council's distinctive function, and thus its value to Gulbenkian: 'The Council is in a unique position to enable such a collection to be seen throughout the world.'[6]

The Gulbenkian response to Hendy's appeal was to make a counteroffer of 'a sum of £10,000 immediately to enable the British Council to buy, on the Foundation's behalf, works of British artists, mostly perhaps young artists. These works would, we suggest, be the property of the Foundation; for the first few years, the Collection would be at the disposal of the British Council for exhibition and tours abroad, but eventually it would revert to the Foundation.'[7] While a loan was not what was wanted, it was still attractive since the Fine Arts department's purchasing budget at this point was only £1,200 a year.[8] Internally, it was hoped that amendments might be made to the restrictive conditions of the grant. Unless purchases were made available on a permanent basis, the committee 'will be faced with the embarrassment of having to decide whether an important work by a young artist should be bought for the Gulbenkian collection, and ultimately be lost to the Council, or whether it should be bought for the Council itself'.[9] With regret that the budget forced them into such a position, and that 'what was being bought for the Gulbenkian Foundation ought to be going into the Council's collection, and in a few years such works would be altogether beyond the Council's means', the money was accepted.[10]

Accordingly, in 1959, the Fine Arts department received £10,000 to acquire new art. The additional money did not seem to change the nature of the purchases made, but it did enable more purchases to take place. The Fine Arts department was able to buy thick and fast in a way it had never been able to do before, and the resulting acquisitions were immediately put to use, with each one going out on display or into exhibition. In 1963, Paul Sinker, the Council's director-general, wrote to the Gulbenkian Foundation to request further support. He stated: 'I need hardly tell you that the grant has been of the greatest value in enabling us to buy the work of younger artists, as well as to increase the representation in exhibitions overseas of certain important older ones, to a far greater extent than our own grant would have allowed.'[11]

A further £10,000 followed, and the acquisitions continued apace. A 1966 listing of Gulbenkian works and locations show that the oils, drawings, constructions, and sculptures purchased were visible in exhibitions and British Council properties in Brazil, Canada, Chile, Finland, France, Germany, Ireland, Japan, Netherlands, New Zealand, Peru, Portugal, and the United States.[12] The energetic activity of art in the Council's care is striking, and the Gulbenkian works were no exception. They were often bought and sent on their ambitious travels in the same year that they were made. With their paint barely dry, many took top prizes in international competitions. The fresh works offered an obvious enrichment to the Fine Arts department's capacity and prestige, as well as establishing and developing the reputations of a new generation of artists. Although only temporary loans, the Gulbenkian purchases significantly expanded and updated the Collection's holdings. By the mid-1960s, the department's activity included thirty-four travelling exhibitions in forty-five countries.

David Hockney, *Pigs Escaping from a Hot Dog Machine*, 1961, Indian ink on paper, 45.5 × 60.5 cm. Centro de Arte Moderna Gulbenkian, Lisbon

The purchasing emphasis on youth enabled the Council to buy works by new artists, who in some cases were still in art school. David Hockney produced the faux naïf *Pigs Escaping from a Hot Dog Machine*, one of the cheapest Gulbenkian acquisitions at a mere £19, while still at the Royal College of Art in 1961. Sketched in Indian ink, crude outlines of creatures, recognizable only as pigs by their curly tails, bound out of the paper to the left, while a comic pump-action device issuing mustard and hot dogs is scratched out on the right. Hockney said, 'I could quite well draw figures in an academic style, but that was not what I wanted to do.' Instead, he adopted what he called 'an opposite style', one close to children's art and to the outline patterns of Egyptian art.[13] This characterized his first exhibited works and marked the beginnings of his stellar career. In buying artists such as Hockney so early, the Fine Arts department could purchase cheaply but also anticipate trends and establish reputations.

At the other end of the purchasing scale, Peter Blake's *Love Wall* assemblage from the same year, bought with Gulbenkian money, cost £400, which would have consumed a third of the department's previous annual budget.

Peter Blake, *Love Wall*, 1961, wood, collage, and construction, 237 × 125 × 23 cm. Centro de Arte Moderna Gulbenkian, Lisbon

12345
LOVE

Gloss-painted wooden frames and a front-door section in oxblood and royal blue form the ground for a collage of mass-media fragments, from contemporary pin-ups and advertising images to the sentimental illustrations of early twentieth-century postcards. Embracing couples are shown again and again, and the repeated number two underscores the partnership theme. Through Blake's signature graphics in diagonal monochrome stripes to the punchy colours of his eye-popping LOVE screenprint, the assemblage is a shop window into Blake's Pop preoccupations and style that has flourished over the subsequent seven decades.

Both Hockney and Blake had been showcased in the influential *Young Contemporaries* exhibition in London in 1961, alongside Derek Boshier, Allen Jones, Patrick Caulfield, Peter Phillips, and others. All were current or former Royal College of Art students, and the speedy purchases of these young artists' works for Gulbenkian helped the Fine Arts department consecrate their productions into an emerging Pop pantheon. Fine Arts was also able to buy young works for its own collection, but this did not happen with the same speed, at the same scale, or in the same media. Hockney and Blake, for example, are first represented in the British Council Collection in the form of prints bought in 1963 and 1964 respectively. This was in part due to limited money, but also because the department continued to acquire more established modernists such as Henry Moore and Graham Sutherland, whose international reputations it had established and whose works were still much in demand. As the British Council reported in 1961, 'The demand for exhibitions of the work of Henry Moore is inexhaustible.'[14]

The purpose of the British Council Collection by this time was not to gather a fully representative body of work that covered all bases of art production and style; this was simply not possible with a few hundred pounds per year. Instead, the Collection was pragmatically constructed to serve the cultural relations needs of the Council. To this end, in the early 1960s it was strategically populated to build critical mass around particular artists. Among the desired outcomes of the organization's cultural relations was the international promotion of individual British artists' reputations, the stimulation of an inter-

David Hockney, *Cleanliness is Next to Godliness*, 1964, screenprint, 92.7 × 58.4 cm (P814)

Peter Blake, *The Beach Boys*, 1964, screenprint, 30.5 × 52.9 cm (P813)

national art market for British works, and a change in perception of Britain's arts scene and cultural status. With the coming of a new generation, there was a risk that the Fine Arts department could fall behind the curve. An example of such a perception is found in novelist J. G. Ballard's autobiography. He recalls the freshness that he felt on first encountering Pop art at the *This is Tomorrow* exhibition at London's Whitechapel Gallery in 1956. He contrasted this with the activities of the British Council of the time, characterized as 'a supporter of Henry Moore, Barbara Hepworth, John Piper and Graham Sutherland, who together formed a closed fine art world largely preoccupied with formalist experimentation'.[15] The winds of change were blowing, and the Council would be swept along with it. Indeed, by the next decade, the Fine Arts department was adding to the new force of feeling and helping to shape its direction.

Emerging artists, receding works

Art historian Alexander Massouras has analysed the ages of artists collected by the British Council in the 1960s, revealing 'a very pronounced revision of the Council's collecting practice'; artists under thirty-five years of age made up between sixty-nine to eighty-three per cent of all purchases between 1961 and 1965. As Massouras argues, the Gulbenkian Foundation's 'express preference for young artists acclimatized the Council to a new and more speculative pattern of collecting'.[16] Undoubtedly, this focus was shaped by the Foundation's directive, but that was only one influence. Early career artists were more affordable and represented prudent purchases for a cash-strapped British Council, but there was also a growing hunger for new work in requests received from overseas. This shift in preference from 'the established' to 'the emerging' was part of a wider interest manifest in international art events such as the Biennial des Jeunes, established in Paris in 1959 to promote artists under the age of thirty-five. Youth was also a desirable exhibition theme, with regular requests in the period for shows of 'Young Painters' or 'Young Sculptors'. As purchases were made to populate such exhibitions, these demands shaped the Collection.

The final Gulbenkian purchases, overseen by the ever-energetic Lilian Somerville and Dennis Farr of the Tate Gallery, resulted in one hundred works by forty-nine artists. Although the Fine Arts department hoped to persuade the Foundation to gift the works, that did not happen, despite pleading letters pointing out the tremendous value that the works had for British Council purposes, the unique ability that the Council had to make the artists known worldwide, and the fact that the acquisitions made best sense alongside the British Council's own collection. The department was understandably concerned about the irreparable hole their loss would leave in its programme, not least because these were by artists who could no longer be bought so easily; even if their works were still available, their prices had skyrocketed. The combined Gulbenkian grants of £20,000 marked a substantial increase in Fine Art's coffers, but it represented a tiny expenditure to the Foundation. In just one year, 1968, for example, it made some £6,000,000 of grants to British arts, science, and education, with more than £350,000 going to British art.[17]

The Gulbenkian Foundation had its own plans. It opened a permanent home for its broader art collection, in the form of the purpose-built museum in Lisbon, in 1968. As a concession to the Fine Arts department's requests, it allowed around half of the purchased works to be used for British Council purposes until 1982, when all were returned to the Foundation. Since then, there have been several significant collaborations between the Gulbenkian and British Council, such as *Metamorphosis: British Art of the Sixties*, a jointly curated exhibition for Greece in 2005, and *Post-Pop: Beyond the Commonplace* in 2018, which brought together British and Portuguese Pop artists in Lisbon.[18] The British Council Collection has been both positively and negatively shaped by this moment in its acquisition history. Gulbenkian funds enabled the Fine Arts department to create many more exhibitions abroad and to include more original works than it would otherwise have been able to do, while the expanded budget gave it a bittersweet taste of what it could achieve if enabled.

Twentieth-century British art in Portugal

Having received the Gulbenkian money, the Fine Arts department made plans for an exhibition of modern and contemporary British art in Portugal. This would eventually be realized in 1962 as *British Art of the Twentieth Century*.

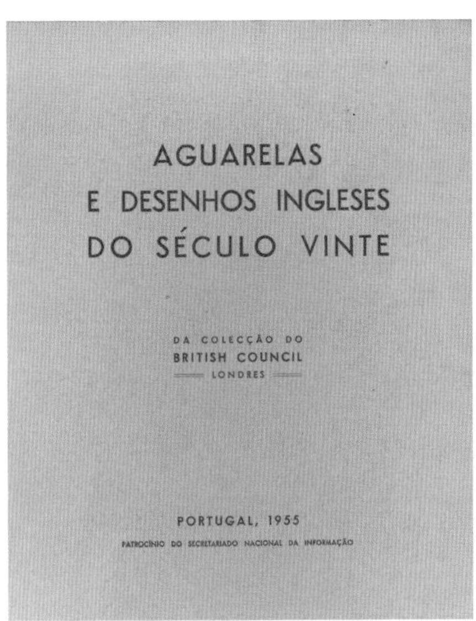

Front cover of the catalogue for the exhibition *British Drawings and Watercolours of the 20th Century from the Collection of the British Council*, which toured Portugal in 1955

It proved to be a highly contentious undertaking, implicated in political violence, a totalitarian regime, and artistic boycotts. Portugal had been under a dictatorship since 1926 and ruled by the nationalist government of Antonio de Oliveira Salazar since 1932. This political context, and in particular the colonial violence enacted at its hands in India and Angola in the early 1960s, had serious implications for the exhibition.

Prior to this show, Portugal had been the recipient of *British Drawings and Watercolours of the 20th Century from the Collection of the British Council*, the same exhibition that had caused such consternation in New Zealand in 1953. In his introduction to that show, its curator Geoffrey Grigson had noted art's capacity to unite through its universal language and its opportunities for international exchange. 'If there are aggressive forces of another, a fanatical, ideological kind', he optimistically proposed, 'the era of aggressive nationalism is coming to an end.'[19] It was striking, then, that the 1955 iteration appeared at the headquarters of Portugal's National Secretariat of Information, the body responsible for the Salazar regime's propaganda; it could not have supported such a view.[20]

Seven years later, the Calouste Gulbenkian Foundation was to provide the Portuguese finance (covering the mounting, publicity, and catalogue) for the touring exhibition of twentieth-century British painting and sculpture, while the Fine Arts department would pay for the packaging and shipping.[21] The foundation was separate from the government and ostensibly non-political, but in the context of the anti-Portuguese colonial uprisings that surrounded the show, its relation to politics came under intense scrutiny. As art historian Leonor de Oliveira has outlined, the history of Anglo-Portuguese relations helps explain why such an exhibition was wanted. In the Second World War, Portugal remained neutral but offered tacit support to the Allies, not least through the long-standing Anglo-Portuguese Alliance, the oldest international treaty still in force, which since 1386 had formalized a policy of mutual support in conflict. At the same time, however, Portugal also shared some ideological sympathies with the Axis nations.

Because of this position, the country became an important site for propaganda. From 1940, the British Council expanded its budget in Portugal and opened new cultural centres; activities continued in earnest after 1945. Despite the repressions of Salazar's regime, the leader tended to be treated sympathetically in Britain as a 'benevolent dictator'.[22] This perception was to change, however, as the Portuguese government attempted to preserve its colonies in the early 1960s, just as the Fine Arts department planned its show. The autonomy of colonial territories had been officially recognized by the United Nations after the Second World War, and the move of colonized people to independence gathered pace globally. Portugal, however, was not prepared to relinquish its colonies without a fight, and bloody confrontations took place in Angola and in the Indian territories of Goa, Daman, and Diu.

Dissident sculptors

A series of major incidents in Angola, including the violent military repression of striking workers and independence protests, left hundreds dead and injured and led to an international outcry against the Portuguese regime and United Nations sanctions. In this context, as Somerville sent out requests for artists to participate in the exhibition, she received principled rejections from several sculptors in particular. Hubert Dalwood, for example, explained:

> There are without doubt more villainous governments with more repressive colonial administration than Portugal but somehow the misdemeanours of Portugal (and of Spain) are disregarded in this country. For the sake of the debatable advantages of 'The Western Alliance', the government grant a complete indulgence to Spain and Portugal. It seems to me that any official exhibition will help to perpetuate the emotional fiction surrounding the phrase 'our oldest ally', and discourage those people in Portugal who wish for reform, and who look to this country for moral support. I would be obliged if you will bring my views to the notice of the Committee and thank them for considering me.[23]

Bernard Meadows expressed similar sentiments:

> For some time now, in fact ever since the idea of sending an exhibition to Portugal in the Autumn was first mentioned, I have not been happy at the idea of lending works in view of the recent happenings in Angola. I feel it is necessary to make some gesture of protest against the barbarous and inhuman reprisals perpetrated by the Portuguese. ... One has no right to interfere with the internal politics of Portugal, but also one need not condone Portuguese action. I feel lending one's works would do just this.[24]

Perhaps the greatest blow came from Barbara Hepworth, who had initially responded warmly but then withdrew support:

> I have been approached by the Council for Freedom in Portugal and Colonies and after giving the matter some very serious thought I have allowed my name to go forward as a sponsor and must ask you,

LEFT Lilian Somerville, photographed by Jorge Lewinski, 1965

OPPOSITE Walter Sickert, *Cicely Hey*, 1922/3, oil on canvas, 64 × 77 cm (P19)

> therefore, to allow me to retract my participation in the exhibition in Portugal. Please do make it absolutely clear to your Committee that my decision does not contain any criticism whatsoever of either The British Council or The Gulbenkian Foundation. I have the greatest possible admiration for (and appreciation of) the magnificent work done by all of you.[25]

Somerville wrote to those who turned down the invitation to reinforce the Council's independence as 'a non–political body' that 'does not differentiate between countries or political systems'. She explained, 'exhibitions are chosen to show in other countries the best paintings and sculpture produced in this country', and noted that the Portuguese government was not involved.[26] The British press picked up the story and declared the sculptors to be 'dissident' and 'courageous'.[27] The action was described as 'no idle inexpensive gesture ... the artists were risking giving offence to an important source of patronage'.[28]

Exhibition planning continued, even when further political actions – violent battles for independence in Portuguese-owned Indian territories – had major implications for Britain. Faced with a large-scale, Indian army-backed uprising in Goa in 1961, Portugal called on Britain for military support. Britain argued instead for a peaceful resolution. When the Portuguese conceded defeat – overpowered by the scale of Indian forces – the blame was directed at Britain. Across Portugal, the Union Jack was burned in the streets, the British embassy was bombarded with white feathers as symbols of cowardice, and the British Council's headquarters in Lisbon was stoned.

What has all this to do with an exhibition of modern art? The exhibition comprised works by Graham Sutherland and Victor Pasmore, Ben Nicholson and Ivon Hitchens, among others. What do its exhibited artefacts – Harold Gilman's and Walter Sickert's claustrophobic paintings of Camden Town domestic scenes of the 1920s, for example, boxed in with bedsteads and busy wallpaper, or Matthew Smith's brightly coloured Fitzroy Street nudes – have to

Harold Gilman, *Interior*, 1917, oil on canvas, 59.7 × 44.5 cm (P138)

Matthew Smith, *Young Girl*, 1925, oil on canvas, 73 × 61 cm (P96)

do with dictatorships and conflicts in sub-Saharan Africa and western India? The answer is everything. All stages of the planning, realization, and results of the exhibit were affected by politics, even as the British Council repeatedly stated its distance. Throughout the show, plain-clothes policemen patrolled the galleries as works were at risk of intentional damage. As a survey of twentieth-century painting, from realism to abstraction, the art did not carry explicit political messages, but the show was a diplomatic occasion of the highest tension.

In the event, the exhibition was received enthusiastically in Portugal, where it was celebrated as 'the artistic event of the year'.[29] Concluding notes in the documentation also display other results: 'We can take pleasure in the fact that the exhibition enabled the Embassy to re-establish relations with the Portuguese.'[30] Yet it is arguably the works that did not appear in *British Art of the Twentieth Century* that left the most significant mark. Their makers recognized

A view of the *British Art of the Twentieth Century* exhibition at the Museu Nacional Soares dos Reis in Oporto, Portugal, 1962, showing works by Francis Bacon (left), Graham Sutherland (centre foreground), and Roger Hilton (background)

Another view of the *British Art of the Twentieth Century* exhibition in Oporto, showing sculptures by Reg Butler and Lynn Chadwick in the foreground

that art can be an endorsement and perform allegiances. As will be seen, the British Council has variously sent and withdrawn exhibitions to and from international regimes in the service of specific diplomatic needs, but in Portugal the decision was to remain neutral and carry on. The official Council position in the 1960s was independence from government; as a cultural organization, it would not be 'swayed by transitory political exigencies'.[31] In this respect, the 1962 exhibition attempted to make manifest that which Grigson promised in 1955: that modern art speaks across national borders and it can antagonize nationalist ideologies.

The sculptors who refused to participate suffered no penalty; their snub was directed at Portuguese policy. Bronzes by Dalwood and Meadows were bought for the British Council Collection in the early 1960s, and Dalwood was selected to represent Britain at the 1962 Venice Biennale as the *British Art of the Twentieth Century* exhibition travelled to Portugal. Of the seventeen works by Hepworth owned by the British Council, eleven were purchased in

Barbara Hepworth's sculptures in the fifth Bienal de São Paulo, 1959, with works by Francis Bacon in the background

the years when the exhibition was being planned. As the tone of her letter conveyed, Hepworth had a positive and long-standing relationship with the British Council. She had been a close associate of Herbert Read's since the 1930s. Having represented Britain at Venice in 1950, she triumphantly took the Grand Prix at the Bienal de São Paulo in 1959. By the early 1960s, she was one of the biggest names in international sculpture, with several solo exhibitions supported by the British Council. Her works in the Collection appeared in fourteen shows before *British Art of the Twentieth Century*. *Rhythmic Form* of 1949 (see page 96), with its arabesque asymmetry and characteristic eyelet, was bought in 1950, exhibited in the British Pavilion at Venice that the same year, and is one of the Collection's greatest assets. It has appeared in twenty-five British Council exhibitions to date, but it was strategically absent from Portugal in 1962. As a masterpiece of Hepworth's celebrated powers in direct carving, the elegant posture of the rosewood sculpture also contains a silent gesture of resistance.

Barbara Hepworth, *Sea Form (Porthmeor)*, 1958, bronze, 117 cm long (P338)

Hubert Dalwood, *Divided Column*, 1962, bronze, height 53.5 cm (P403)

Bernard Meadows, *Large Flat Bird*, 1957, bronze, 111 × 69.5 × 36 cm (P397)

The medium is the message

Just as the acquisition committee supported a new generation, so too new forms came to the fore in their collecting. As I previously noted, prints had long held a dominant place in the Fine Arts department's thinking and activities: of the twenty-six British Council exhibitions going around the world in 1967, for example, nine were made up of prints in one form or another. These permanently circulating exhibitions – which travelled widely on tours that lasted many decades – could be broad in coverage, and might include displays of children's paintings and English handwriting alongside facsimiles of works by William Blake and J. M. W. Turner. Some of the exhibitions of the 1940s and 1950s, particularly those sent unaccompanied to developing locations without gallery infrastructures, were made up of photomechanical reproductions of sometimes mixed quality. By the 1960s, the department endeavoured to send original works wherever possible. Copy prints were not appreciated by host countries; the fact that they were low risk was rather too visible. The material values of art conveyed moral messages, and the effort required to send high-value and large-scale works overseas signalled trust, care, and prestige, not least to the recipient.

In the immediate postwar period, many Fine Arts exhibitions had been relatively modest. For example, correspondence with the Caribbean in the late 1940s noted, 'transport of framed, glazed, pictures, is not easy – particularly from island to island in the Eastern Caribbean. Air freight is expensive, and shipping sporadic.' Instead, a 'handy' exhibition was proposed, based on postcard-sized reproductions to be mounted on an easel or a display board.[32] Logistics take up a lot of space in the documentation of the Fine Arts department, especially when customs paperwork and transportation were not globally standardized and could be capricious. Works might travel by plane, ship, train, car, caravan, or handcart, and exhibition negotiations, country by country, could be idiosyncratic. Notable examples of the challenges of sending art far and wide include sculptures stuck off shore in violent storms in the Gulf of Mexico and prints ensnared in bureaucracy for more than a year at the Chile–Peru border.[33] When works arrived in countries without galleries or museums, they could be exhibited in reading rooms, educational institutes,

One of the British Council Collection acquisition ledgers, showing the fate of a number of works in the Collection that were lost or destroyed on their exhibition travels

or municipal halls, and they were often displayed with readily available materials for maximum flexibility. Art was variously presented behind glass or in the open air, pinned to peg boards, or mounted on impromptu plinths, as suited the hosts and the site. The Fine Arts department of the British Council led the field in expertise on international art handling, but its advice was not always followed. It is remarkable that works so infrequently went astray. Notes scribbled in early acquisitions registers reveal occasional tragedies, with works listed as, for example, 'lost in Uganda', 'stolen in Argentina', 'destroyed by fire in Lahore', or 'destroyed in civil riots in Cyprus'.

Richard Smith, *PM Zoom*, 1963, screenprint, 88.9 × 58.4 cm (P2268)

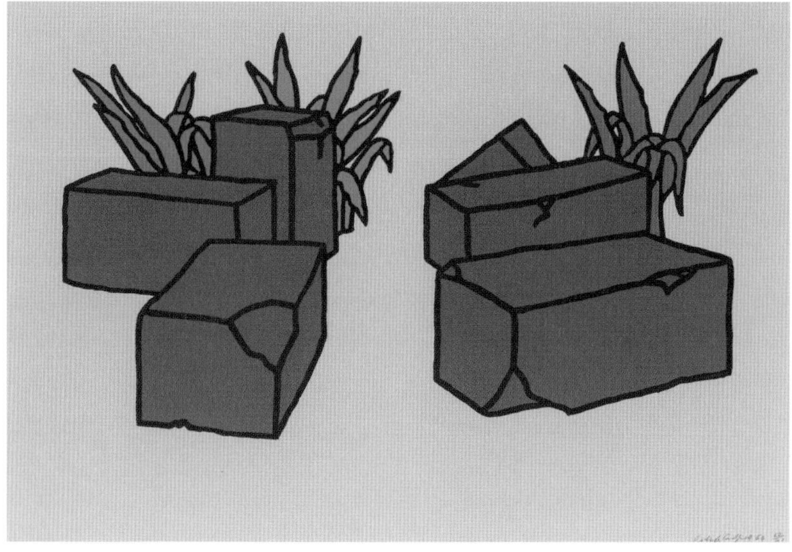

Patrick Caulfield, *Ruin*, 1964, screenprint, 91.5 × 58 cm (P817)

Richard Hamilton, *The Critic Laughs*, 1968, photo-offset lithograph, laminated, screenprinted, and retouched with enamel paint on coated stick, 59.8 × 48.9 cm (P1272)

Trust-building was a core part of the British Council's purpose, and this was embodied in exhibitions. International newspaper reports in the 1950s and 1960s, for example, regularly emphasized the enormous labour that large-scale sculptures by Henry Moore required to install, including improvised roller mechanisms, fork-lift trucks, and the muscle power of many men. Effort, expense, and care was read as an indication of how much the Council valued the country in which the work was shown. The changing value and status of artists' prints in the 1960s at the hands of the Pop generation thus provided new opportunities. Exhibition descriptions of these new forms noted their particularity. Silkscreen prints, for example, were 'prepared personally by the artist in limited editions and are usually signed by him'. Originality was underlined. 'A print ... is an original work of art, even though it exists in fifty or a hundred versions, the point being that each one has been made by the artist himself.'[34] The commitment to prints met two agendas. First, they fitted within the Fine Arts department's small budget – most cost no more than £10 a time – and second, they represented the development of artistic production through innovative and creative new methods. In the context of Pop, where mass culture informed subject matter and form, artists' prints encapsulated new mass-communication systems and the democratization of art. They became 'the chosen medium for the new age'.[35]

'These filthy pictures'

As part of its commitment to artists' prints, the Fine Arts department sent a print exhibition, *New Tendencies*, as Britain's contribution to events accompanying the Mexico Olympics in 1968. A body of etchings by David Hockney, *Illustrations for Fourteen Poems from C. P. Cavafy* from 1966, attracted particular attention. Constantine Cavafy was an Alexandrian-born Greek poet whose plain-spoken and proud erotic poetry detailed his homosexual encounters in Alexandria in the early twentieth century; its translation into English in the 1960s had been an inspiration to Hockney. Some of the etchings explored the poet's sites and moods, while others were drawn from the young artist's observation of his circle in his Notting Hill flat. To Hockney, the images – with their tender portrayals of intimate friends, their references to his travels in Cairo, Luxor, and Alexandria, and their inspirations in literature and physique magazines – were 'propaganda', but not in the British Council's use of the term: they championed his queer way of life.[36] Their affectionate representation of bodies in loving lines is hardly challenging to liberal twenty-first-century eyes, but to the British ambassador in Mexico in 1968 they appeared highly inflammatory.

In a series of anxious letters sent at the time of the exhibition opening at the Mexican Museum of Modern Art, the ambassador, Peter Hope, noted that he had been alerted to 'a series of prints by John [sic] Hockney' depicting 'a homosexual attachment between two adult males which was treated in a fairly explicit fashion'. Although the outrage was all his, he claimed to be concerned about local reaction. Mexicans, in his estimation, were 'very much less outspoken in such matters'. On inspection, he found that seven of the one

David Hockney, 'Two Boys Aged 23 or 24' from *Illustrations for Fourteen Poems from C. P. Cavafy*, 1966, etching and aquatint, 39.5 × 57 cm (P1180)

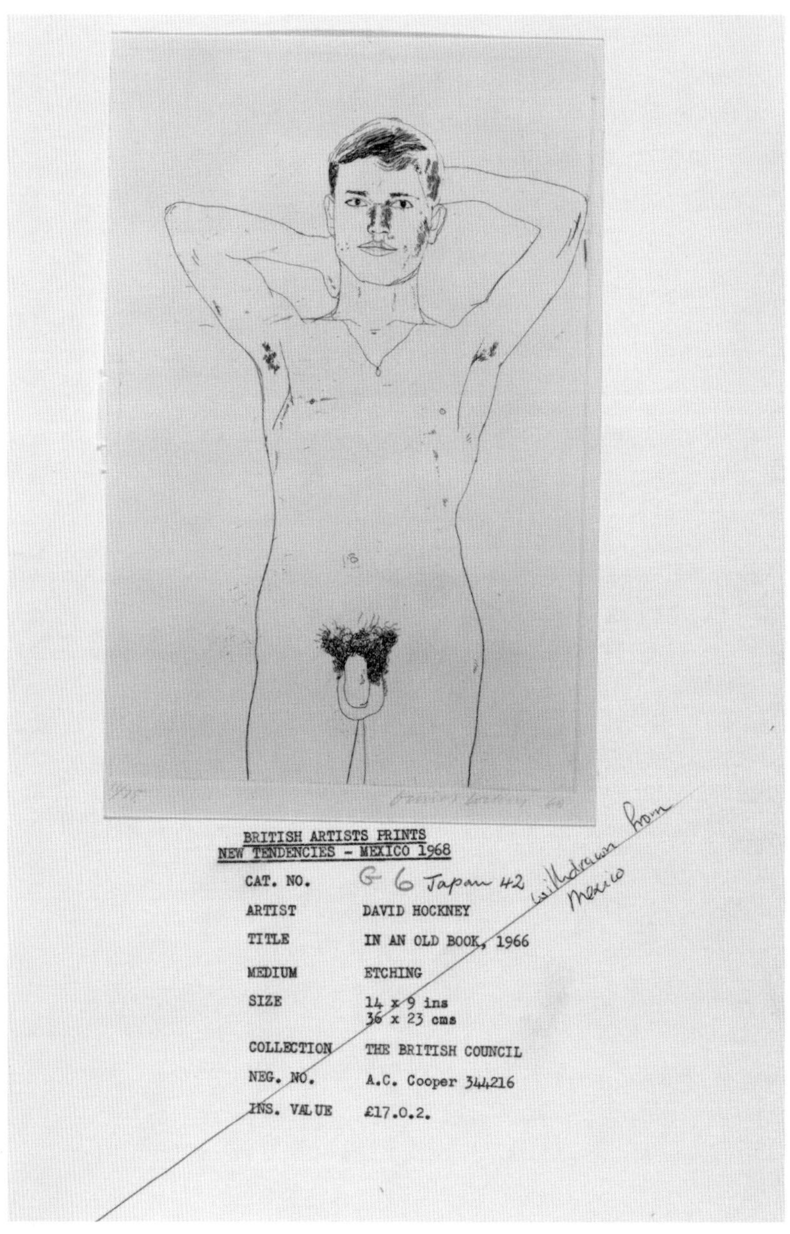
BRITISH ARTISTS PRINTS
NEW TENDENCIES - MEXICO 1968

CAT. NO. G 6 Japan 42
ARTIST DAVID HOCKNEY
TITLE IN AN OLD BOOK, 1966
MEDIUM ETCHING
SIZE 14 x 9 ins
36 x 23 cms
COLLECTION THE BRITISH COUNCIL
NEG. NO. A.C. Cooper 344216
INS. VALUE £17.0.2.

withdrawn from Mexico

A British Council record for *New Tendencies*, showing Hockney's print 'In an Old Book', which was withdrawn from the exhibition in Mexico and Cuba

hundred and twenty exhibits 'dealt with a pair of nude or semi-nude men in various compromising situations, mostly in bed'. He brought the prints to the attention of the museum director, Carmen Barreda, who, he claimed, 'had never seen anything like them in her life'. Hope was concerned that the prints could not be shown in provincial Mexico, where the exhibition was to travel, and he was also concerned about effects locally. He expected they would 'draw to the exhibition a crowd of young queens and beatniks who might create disorderly scenes'. Secondly, 'they might encourage homosexual artists' to think they could 'get away' with similar works.[37] This would cause damage to Britain's reputation, he concluded. He asked that the prints be withdrawn.

Much deliberation followed, with the Fine Arts department vouching for their 'highly regarded' quality, for their acceptability internationally – they had previously been shown at São Paulo, Rio de Janeiro, Montevideo, and Buenos Aires with no concern – and especially for their endorsement by the eminent figures on the Fine Arts Committee, from Hendy to Read, who had advised on their purchase for the permanent collection.[38] Homosexuality was, in any case, legal for men over the age of twenty-one in Britain, and the etchings – of a full-frontal naked man, of partially naked men in bed, and of men in underpants – were sexually implicit rather than explicit.

Members of the British Council acted as moderators between the Fine Arts department and the ambassador. D. Warren-Knott stated quite reasonably that there were no sexual acts on show, arguing 'were the figures female the drawings might well be taken as demonstrating simple affection in the classical nude'. In any case, if there were national views on the depiction of homosexuality, 'should we not leave the burden of censorship on the Mexicans rather than leap to adopt barriers to artistic expression we would not otherwise defend?'[39] After further discussion, it was decided to withdraw the seven contentious prints, even if this risked drawing negative attention. As one British Council official noted, 'It would be better to offend a few Mexican aesthetes than a lot of solid citizens.'[40] Artists and queers, it seems, were of minor value where public relations were concerned, even if there had been no opportunity for public opinion to be offended, and the offence was all in the eyes of the

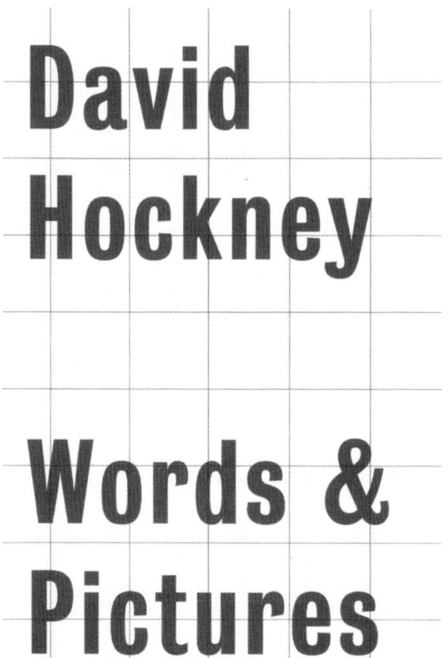

Front cover of the catalogue for the exhibition *David Hockney: Words & Pictures*, 2015

ambassador. Officials were also concerned about the reception of 'these filthy pictures' in Cuba. Hope was convinced that, 'Cubans are particularly puritanical at the moment.' The prints were thus withdrawn from the Cuban stage of their journey.[41]

Nevertheless, Hockney's *Cavafy* prints went on to appear in British Council-organized exhibitions in Australia, Austria, Belgium, Brazil, Chile, Colombia, Finland, France, Germany, Greece, Iceland, Israel, Italy, Korea, Lithuania, Malta, Mauritius, Netherlands, Nigeria, Portugal, and Spain. The story of their travels demonstrates not only how the Council's art exhibitions can be truly adventurous in their reach, but also that times and attitudes change – and are changed – as they circuit the globe. In 2010, the British Museum used one of the etchings to encapsulate a key moment in shifting attitudes to sexual relationships in their exhibition *History of the World in 100 Objects*.[42] Hockney had produced the prints at a time of intense debate about sexual freedoms in Britain. When the prints were withdrawn from Mexico in June 1968, homosexual acts in private had been decriminalized in England and Wales for less than a year; the ambassador had not moved apace. Ironically, they had been legal in Mexico since 1871. In 2015, a British Council Collection show of the artist's prints, entitled *David Hockney: Words & Pictures*, took the same works back to that country as part of the official UK/Mexico Year of Culture, coinciding with Mexico's legalization of same-sex marriage.[43]

Contractions and expansions

In 1970, the British Council reflected on the growing role of the arts in their activity. 'Now that London has achieved a leading position among the artistic centres of the world', its annual report that year noted, the organization could take credit for 'the contribution made by this Council over thirty-five years in nurturing this sensitive plant through a series of chilly financial climates'.[44] With money constantly tight throughout the 1960s, the Fine Arts department sought financial assistance elsewhere, leading to cultural allegiances that were not always warmly received. The net result, however, was a legitimate claim: British artists had become household names at home and abroad, and British Council efforts were paying off.

The expansion and export of British youth culture worldwide by the end of the decade positioned the department's activity within new 'youthquake' scenes, but the permissive pleasures of the Pop generation also met challenges when its attitudes were considered too progressive. As art travelled, it became entangled with moral values about form, content, and message. Its funders, makers, organizers, critics, and audiences all created rich and competing contexts for the work. As well as exploring additions to the British Council Collection and their display in the 1960s, I have investigated the ones that got away: the purchases not made, the exhibitions boycotted, and the works banned. In the midst of complex world conflicts, the travels and uses of the Collection in this decade show the continuing power of art to break down barriers, repair relationships, and challenge cultural conventions.

CHAPTER 4

Expanding the field

In the 1970s, the British Council focused once again on cultural relations with Europe, following organizational changes and broader political shifts that included the United Kingdom's 1973 entry into the European Economic Community. In a period of greater international exchange, what could or should British art communicate across the Continent and beyond? National frames, such as 'British' or 'English', provided the logic for many important Council exhibitions in this period, and the art was consequently read for national character. But whose Britain was being articulated, and whose was excluded? The emergence of new and expanded art forms in the decade challenged the supremacy of easel painting and plinth-based sculpture, but it also posed challenges to the modus operandi of the Council. These shape-shifting forms, especially in their most experimental manifestations, provided fresh directions and provocations that could challenge popular taste and government agendas. The radical ruptures of artistic practice, including its increasingly dematerialized nature and explicit politics, prompted heated debate about the possibilities and limits of avant-garde art in cultural relations.

International unities and rivalries

At the beginning of the 1970s, the Fine Arts department continued to have a mixed range of duties, including the facilitation of temporary exhibitions of loaned works from national museum collections, sometimes supplemented

Bridget Riley, *Cataract 3*, 1967, emulsion PVA on linen, 221.9 × 222.9 cm (P996) (detail)

with British Council Collection works; circulating shows made entirely of works from the Collection that toured more widely and for longer periods; and the selection and delivery of contributions to international art exhibitions and festivals. This latter category included biennials at São Paulo, Venice, and elsewhere. At each of these events, the department managed the British representation, though sometimes with frustration at the national structures with which they were organized.

The Council of Europe, for example, had been founded in 1949 as a political forum with cultural events attached to foster continental unity after the Second World War, but the focus of art exhibitions held under its aegis had long been noted by the Fine Arts Committee to exacerbate international rivalries.[1] In the mid-1960s, the Paris Biennale was criticized in similar terms by art critic Norbert Lynton. 'The idea of parcelling art into nationalistic packets and setting these on competitive display is in itself abhorrent', he complained. 'And, anyway, what is being judged: a country's current art production, many artists' individual performance, or the cunning of the national selection committees?'[2] The Venice Biennale of 1968 had been disrupted by student and artist protests – in the spirit of the revolutionary fervour rising across Europe – and these crystallized around its nationalist structures. Bridget Riley was the first British artist and the first woman to win the International Painting Prize. She did so against a backdrop of boycotts and arrests, amidst art works deliberately turned to the wall or strategically draped with anti-war and anti-fascist banners. The effect of these protests was a collectively agreed ambition that national prizes should be abolished in favour of non-competitive exhibitions with an international focus.[3]

The following year, the tenth Bienal de São Paulo was also caught up in its own political controversy, with an international boycott movement begun by expatriate Brazilians in protest at the dismissal by the military regime of liberal professors and government interference in the selection of Brazilian art for exhibition.[4] By the end of the decade, international exhibitions were showcases for artistic achievements, but also spaces where nationalist ideologies were performed.

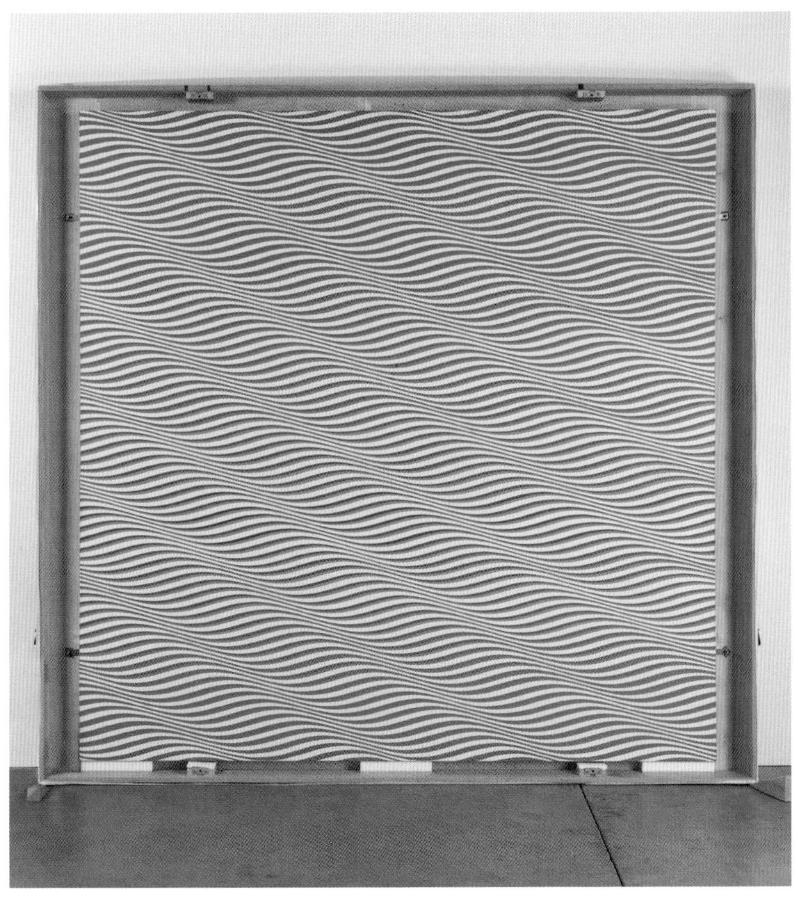

Bridget Riley, *Cataract 3*, 1967, emulsion PVA on linen, 221.9 × 222.9 cm (P996), in its British Council Collection transportation case

Bruce McLean, *Fallen Warrior*, 1970, photograph, 62.5 × 93 cm. National Galleries of Scotland

A New English Enquiry

The representation at the 1971 Bienal de São Paulo, entitled *A New English Enquiry*, marked an innovative departure in stylistic form for the Fine Arts department but, notably, not a move away from a national interpretive frame. Featuring graphic, photographic, and typographic works by a dozen artists aged between twenty-six and forty-one, including Keith Arnatt, Bruce McLean, and Richard Long, the exhibitors shared some characteristics in style but, in the words of their selector, John Hulton – now the director, following Lilian Somerville's retirement – they were 'concerned more with the underlying idea, the concept, than the means of expression'. In many cases, they produced performances that resulted in pictures, but the preceding activities were the art work. Hulton saw the group as displaying a 'lightness of touch and an element of wit' that belied their more fundamental mission: 'to destroy Art, at any rate, with a capital A'.[5] This endeavour was framed temporally and geographically as new and English.

Arnatt, McLean, and Long embody some of the experimental nature of the period, through works that reflect on the means of representation. They are as much *about* photography, performance, and sculpture as they are photographs, performances, and sculptures. McLean, for example, used his body in *Fallen Warrior* to model contorted sculptural forms on an improvised plinth in the landscape. The resulting photograph, taken at the Thames Embankment, records him denaturalizing figurative sculpture. The reference points include Henry Moore's *Falling Warrior* (see page 303), but also works such as Kenneth Armitage's *Figure Lying on its Side* (see page 102). The solidity and enormity of this postwar sculpture was perceived as an obstacle by the new generation. In his satirical critiques, McLean performed sculptural attitudes with his body. These were a kind of pantomime dialogue with the ponderousness that had built up around Moore's work.[6] The British Council had established the sculptor's international reputation, but they also engaged with its legacy in works that showed a debt to and a departure from his canonical forms.

The work in *A New English Enquiry* shared similarities with what American art historian Rosalind Krauss would later term 'sculpture in the expanded field'. Through these new manoeuvres, the form became, in Krauss's words, 'infinitely malleable'.[7] It no longer hung on narrow definitions that were bound by pedestals and galleries but was widened to encompass landscape, architecture, and bodies, as well as marks, movements, and gestures, however impermanent, however recorded, in any medium. Krauss's essay cited mostly American examples, but British works exhibited by the Fine Arts department expressed the same concerns. Whether there was something quintessentially *English* about this enquiry, then, is open to question. Indeed, as was claimed at the time, 'structurally the British situation is not exceptional'.[8] That geographical limits were irrelevant to art in this new experimental mode was taken as a given.[9]

The British Council in Europe

By the early 1970s, institutional agendas meant that British Council funds were directed towards Western Europe after a break of eighteen years.[10] The years 1971 and 1972 saw Britain's domestic politics dominated by the country's preparation for entry into the European Economic Community on 1 January 1973. Cultural relations in the wider world remained central to the Council's programme, but now operations closer to home resumed. It had been a long-standing point of Council frustration that its European activity had been limited, and statements communicated a sense of continental unity. 'Our own culture has grown out of a common European culture', it was observed; 'more than ever today we are expected to join in maintaining that common culture and its component parts'.[11]

Throughout the decade, there was a flowering of the European exhibitions programme, including loan shows that took place under the British Council's expertise, as well as exhibitions populated with works from its collection. Many had a national frame, such as *British Painting 1945–1970*, which assembled British Council Collection works for Norway and Poland in 1972; *La Peinture Anglaise Aujourd'hui*, held in Paris the following year; and *Two Centuries of English Painting: British Art and Europe from 1680 to 1880*, a show of almost four hundred paintings, drawings, and engravings that was organized by the Council in collaboration with the Haus der Kunst in Munich and held there in 1979. Privately, though, the Fine Arts department wondered whether surveys organized only around national output had 'outgrown their usefulness'.[12] Hulton said of the exhibition *British Painting and Sculpture 1960–70*, co-curated with the Tate Gallery and held at the National Gallery of Art in Washington, DC from November 1970 to January 1971: 'this kind of anthology exhibition was outdated'. What was wanted were 'smaller exhibitions of the work of younger artists and of an experimental nature'.[13]

From this impetus grew two striking exhibitions for European audiences: *Arte Inglese Oggi 1960–76*, held in Milan in 1976, and then *Un Certain Art Anglais ...*, which opened in Paris in 1979. Both exhibitions used the term 'English' to describe their aesthetic and rationale, but both posed major challenges to the visual culture traditionally associated with that nation. It should be pointed out that 'English' and 'British', and their extrapolations of 'Englishness' and 'Britishness' (in terms of both mentality and identity), were used interchangeably in the naming of British Council exhibitions during this period, and consequently in the language of their international reception. Their slippage as synonyms belied casual attention to national borders; Scotland, Wales, and Northern Ireland were sidelined. 'English' and 'British' were also flexible in meaning; they did not necessarily signal the location in which the work was produced, nor its subject matter, nor the citizenship of its creator.

The Englishness of British Council exhibitions

Art historian Nikolaus Pevsner – a member of the Fine Arts Committee from 1962 to 1970 – is best known for his treatise *The Englishness of English Art*, first delivered as a lecture in 1955, expanded into a book in 1956, and never since out of print. German-born Pevsner aimed to capture common cultural characteristics as a way of exploring whether art could be as distinct as language and as expressive of geography. He appraised mixed phenomena – including climate and queuing – to construct a theory of English artistic tendencies characterized by the timid, the taciturn, the modest, and the restrained. His premise – 'There is a spirit of the age, and there is a national character'[14] – contained a caveat. 'National character does not at all moments and in all situations appear equally distinct. The spirit of a moment may reinforce national character or repel it.'[15]

English art's hushed tones and small-scale efforts were challenged by the drama of new art; Pevsner was thinking of Moore 'and other younger sculptors' who disrupted certainties.[16]

Pevsner's claim that a national mood was readable through the visual was echoed in the reception of British Council exhibitions in the 1970s. A German reviewer, for example, asked in relation to the 1979 survey show at Munich's Haus der Kunst, 'Is there such a thing as a typically English painting? Just as there is English furniture, English weather, English fireplaces and English eccentricities?' He concluded that he was 'more interested in the Englishness of English painting' than in the paintings themselves. British Council exhibitions were seen to provide information about art, but also 'new, inexhaustible and happy insights into the English character'.[17] A print exhibition, *Artistas Gráficos Británicos de la Década del 60*, was reviewed similarly in Spain: 'The English have never had their island invaded, not even aesthetically. They have always been importers', the reviewer argued. 'They imported Gothic and Modernism, but they adapted them to their manner and rhythm, making them characteristically theirs. This is what they are doing to the latest "isms" that are tumultuously invading the countries of Europe.'[18]

Outside Europe, the Council's exhibitions also prompted reflection on nationhood. An exhibition of work by British printmakers that travelled to Ghana in 1971 was praised locally for bringing artists and art students into dialogue with international styles and international stimuli, countering the effects of working in national isolation.[19] Chon Syng-boc, writing in Seoul, reviewed a 1974 exhibition based on drawings and watercolours from the British Council Collection and considered it in relation to Paul Nash's 1934 questions: 'To what extent has contemporary art in England a national character? ... Can we find in our short history of painting and of sculpture, quantities so peculiar as to identify their subjects beyond doubt, and, if so, do these qualities persist today?'[20] A review of *Colour in British Painting*, held in various venues in Brazil from 1977 to 1979, put the relative merits of Brazilian and British art into competition, but the outcome was a sense of unity. The Brazilian reviewer noted that cultural production, 'showing an ever-increasing global scale, does not remove various expressions of socially-economically [sic] conditions, but asserts the reality of communication, transport and world interdependence'. He surmised: 'the lessons, for example of Constable and Turner, were of equal benefit to all and therefore are more than just a national cultural heritage'.[21]

As seen repeatedly, many found value in art's potential to interconnect; travelling exhibitions necessarily provoke debate about national identity and its limits. Art exhibitions that foreground national collections and tendencies as their central structure provide temporary spaces for reflecting on similarity and difference, geographical specificity, and aesthetic universality. These kinds of reflections were particularly prominent in the context of a newly federated Europe where terms such as 'we' and 'they' were under intensified scrutiny, but the debates also reflected an international consciousness in the arts more broadly, where an ever wider range of cultural exchanges between individuals and organizations was taking place.

Arte Inglese Oggi 1960–76

Following *Pittura Inglese 1660–1840*, a major British Council-sponsored show of 153 works produced in collaboration with Birmingham City Museum and Art Gallery in 1975 for Milan's Palazzo Reale, *Arte Inglese Oggi 1960–76* populated the same location the following year with fifty, mostly young, contemporary artists. This format attempted to resolve the problems of nationally themed survey shows by substituting a structure that showcased, instead, singular artistic points of view.

Reflections on the national dimension of the exhibition were provided in the bilingual catalogue.[22] In setting out the frame for the show, Guido Ballo, curator of contemporary Italian art, and fellow art historian Franco Russoli quoted Herbert Read from 1934: 'What will be carried out in England in future years will form an integral part of what will be done in Europe and America, and even if there should be local differences, these will take place within the sphere of a coherent, world-wide movement.' Read seemed, in this statement, to argue against national distinctions, but Ballo and Russoli were determined to locate 'the particular "British" aspect and meaning of the recent artistic

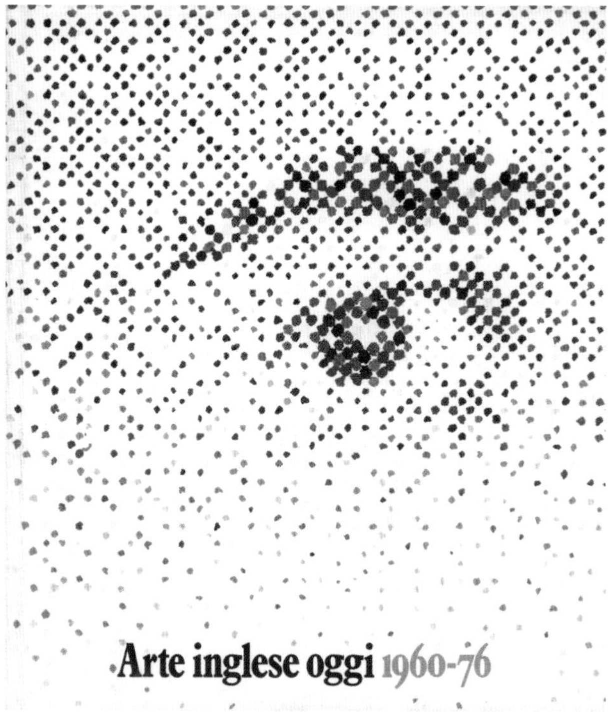

Front cover of the Italian edition of the catalogue for the exhibition *Arte Inglese Oggi 1960–76*

expressions'. New British art, in their appraisal, simultaneously incorporated polar opposites: 'physical and the metaphysical, pure form and the punctilious description of what is real, with both detached self-restraint and complete abandon'.[23] What was British was evidently hard to pin down.

Also in the catalogue, under the title of 'Alternative Developments', critic and member of the Fine Arts Committee Richard Cork provided an account of the expanded art practices that had also expanded geographical borders. Positioning English experimentation in relation to the interdisciplinary practices of the Italian Futurists, and thereby making reference to the home audience, Cork also saw English art as a reaction to American Abstract

Expressionism with its 'gargantuan' mural-sized canvases and price tags.[24] The importance of place was not a centrifugal force to Cork, however; there was no sense of art shaped by weather. If there was any myth of origin, it was more localized in the educational environment of St Martins School of Art, from which so many conceptual artists of the day had emerged.

If any kind of English characteristic can be detected in the artists of *Arte Inglese Oggi 1960–76*, it may be a particular type of deadpan wit and black humour. Gilbert & George, for example, were aligned by Cork with the popular comedians Morecambe and Wise, and with Flanagan and Allen, the music-hall double act that the artists mimicked for their famous singing sculpture. Their tone might be equally indebted to the contemporaneous *Monty Python* in its sense of national absurdity. In a spirit shared with McLean, artistic categories were undone by Gilbert & George, who posed as living sculptures

Gilbert & George, *Magazine Sculpture*, published in *Studio International*, Vol. 179, No. 922 (May 1970), pp. 220–1 (words blacked out by the magazine's editor), mixed media, 30.5 × 24.2 cm (P8208)

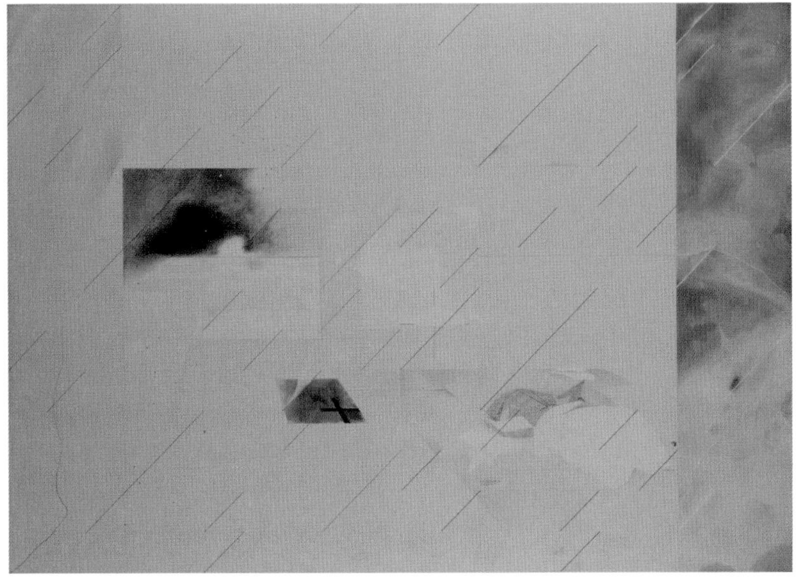

Rita Donagh, *Evening Papers Ulster, 1972–74*, 1974, oil, pencil, and collage on canvas, 140 × 200 cm (P2034)

while challenging all traditions of the medium. They produced – at least in name – sculptures from bodies, postcards, moving image, and, in the case of a later work in the Collection, printed matter (the *Magazine Sculpture* from 1969). These are smirkingly produced, complete with obscenities and expletives, behind a straight-faced facade of polite English gentlemen in Savile Row suits (although Gilbert is Italian by birth). Their arch mannerisms are all surface, hovering between impeccable respectability and outrageous offence.

Keith Arnatt's *Visitors* is a series of portrait photographs of day-trippers to Tintern Abbey, made at the historic site on the border between Wales and England in 1975.[25] The repetitive pairs of friends, lovers, and relatives are touchingly awkward in their monochrome depictions, showing best-dressed bodies in hats and handbags, shirts, and ties. The couples attempt to look presentable, but always end up appearing slightly off-key. Arnatt's series is less aggressively anti-authority than another of his submissions to *Arte Inglese Oggi 1960–76*, which consisted simply of a framed textual proposition: *Is it Possible for Me to Do Nothing as my Contribution to this Exhibition?* Yet in exhibiting prints that mimicked everyday camera culture and the aesthetically despised category of the snapshot, Arnatt reflected on cultural value and on art and artlessness. Like all his works, it was the irreverent result of a deconstructive strategy that challenged genres. The warm results are neither vernacular objects nor studious works of contemplation. They are English in their subject matter but also, perhaps, in their particular wit.

Not all the work included in *Arte Inglese Oggi* 1960–76 was playful; some dealt with deadly issues. A sequence of eleven paintings by Rita Donagh was discussed in the catalogue essay by Norbert Lynton in purely formal terms. The critic considered Donagh to be a post-Pop artist as she worked with graphic techniques and mass-produced materials found, he said, by chance encounter. In fact, the materials Donagh used in her work were politically motivated and carefully selected. Maps and newsprint signal locations across the island of Ireland that were the sites of sectarian violence. Donagh reflected on how such events were mediated through the text and image of English newspapers by incorporating these as collaged elements. Crime scenes were precisely plotted by dots and dashes onto sparsely painted canvases marked by topographical signifiers. In *Evening Papers Ulster*, 1972–74, X marks the spot where a car bomb victim fell, in a real-life case where the crumpled figure in the landscape was literally covered by newspapers before ambulances arrived.

Performing the avant-garde

Among the works in *Arte Inglese Oggi 1960–76* that dematerialized objects, critiqued categories, and produced ruminations on the powers of representation were some of the Fine Art department's first displays of performance art. According to Ted Little, director of the Institute of Contemporary Arts (ICA) and author of the exhibition catalogue essay on the subject, around 150 British artists were working under this category by 1976. Refusing to define the art form within a set of parameters, he nonetheless noted its shared characteristics: the rejection of art and life as separate spheres, and a repulsion for the art market. As performances often took place outside of theatrical venues – railway sidings and agricultural shows were listed as likely locations – the lack of box-office takings and their inability to produce tangible works for purchase meant that artists' salaries were topped up by public subsidy, including by the British Council.[26]

Alongside international exhibition organization and purchasing for the Collection, from 1973 the Fine Arts department administered the Grants for Artists scheme designed to support British artists to tour work internationally. One recipient, represented in Milan as part of *Arte Inglese Oggi 1960–76*, was the performance-art group COUM, mostly comprised of Genesis P-Orridge and Cosey Fanni Tutti, but with a cast of fluctuating guest members. Little described their practice as concerned with 'large, central, universal issues such as sexuality, death, life, decay, definitions of space and the nature of authority in society'.[27] By 1976, COUM had produced almost one hundred and fifty actions in six countries since 1968.[28] This included their British Council-supported production for the Paris Biennale in 1975, where they performed *Jusqu'à la Balle Crystale*, comprised of three evenings of cryptic performances in a white-walled gallery space, based around motifs of debasement, entrapment,

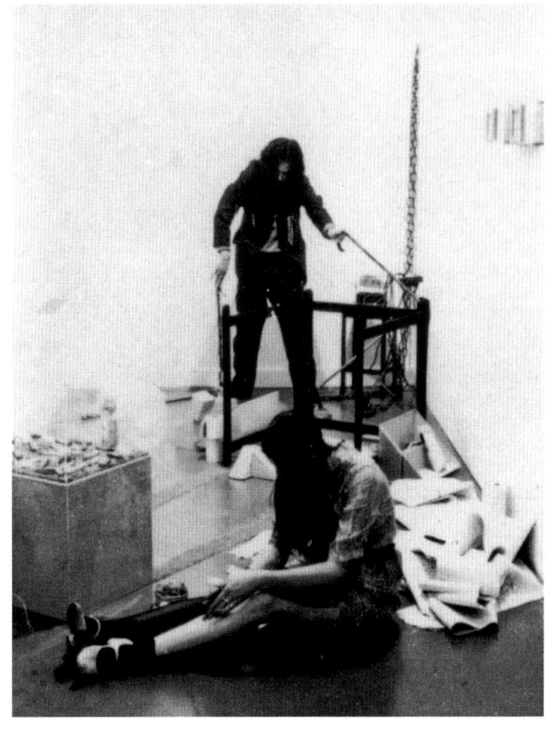

ABOVE AND RIGHT
COUM (Cosey Fanni Tutti and Genesis P-Orridge), *Jusqu'à la Balle Crystale*, performance, 9th Paris Biennale, Musée d'Art Moderne de la Ville de Paris, 18 September 1975

COUM (Cosey Fanni Tutti and Genesis P-Orridge), *Towards Thee Crystal Bowl*, performance, Galleria Vittorio Emanuele II, Milan, 24 and 25 February 1976

and liberation. Using knives and scissors, cling film and bandages, fruit and blood, caged mice and tampons, Tutti and P-Orridge acted out spontaneous scenes exploring pain, shame, and bodily taboos without linear narratives or supporting explanation.

In Milan, their deliberately misspelled performance piece – *Towards Thee Crystal Bowl* – took place in the Galleria Vittorio Emanuele II arcade in the busy shopping district of the city; it involved a scaffolding structure and a bath of white polystyrene pellets, enclosed in a fenced-off circle. Photos of the performance show a crowd of a few hundred, arranged five deep, watching carefully as Tutti and P-Orridge perform their hour-long work. Through suspended gestures, echoing each other's bodies, the lovers acted as light and shade, with P-Orridge dressed in dark colours and Tutti all in white. As P-Orridge ascended the scaffold, supported by heavy chains, Tutti slowly submerged herself in the white matter below. With no narrative and messages reduced to bodies and forms, the meaning was in the eye of the beholder, but the effect was well received by arts audiences. Cork, writing for the *Evening Standard*, described it as a 'restrained and remarkably balletic dialogue' delivered 'at the heart of Milan's public city life'.[29] Norman Reid, director of the Tate Gallery, called it 'effective and moving'.[30] In the department's appraisal of *Arte Inglese Oggi* 1960–76, 'It was quite the most important exhibition ever organised on contemporary British art.' The scale and ambition of the exhibition were vindicated by 120,000 visitors over eleven weeks.[31]

Wreckers of civilization?

The year 1976 was a challenging one for avant-garde art supported by public subsidy. The British press, informed by the pound's shrinking value, drew regular attention to artistic productions underwritten by state aid, especially when their materials were humble or their messages hard to fathom. The year began with public denigration of the Tate Gallery's acquisition of Carl Andre's minimalist sculpture *Equivalents VIII*, which the museum had bought four years earlier. When it was exhibited in 1974 and 1975, the work had drawn little reaction, but in February 1976, when it was not even on display, it was dismissed by some in the press as a nothing more than a pile of 120 bricks. The arrangement of industrial building materials directly on the gallery floor was seen to be a waste of taxpayers' money and a failure of artistic standards; the debate resulted in the vandalism of the work. Later the same year, Mary Kelly made headlines when she exhibited *Post-Partum Document*, a meticulous account of the mother–infant relationship, exploring her son's articulation of self through the acquisition of language. This took the form of psychoanalytic reflections and a sequence of visual documents, including her son's nappy liners. Press reaction characterized the work as excrement on the gallery wall. As the exhibition venue, the ICA, received Arts Council funding, there were further accusations of avant-garde art's waste of public resources. The ICA followed with a show by COUM called *Prostitution*. Intended as a critique of artists' commodification, it included materials related to Genesis P-Orridge and Cosey Fanni Tutti's body mortifications: blood, Vaseline, and meat cleavers. These combined with photographs that Tutti produced as performance pieces while working as a pornographic model. The content was designed to shock, and it achieved its result. Although the Arts Council came first in the line of fire, press furore also implicated the British Council.

Under a series of headlines, including 'State Aid for "Cosey" Travelling Sex Troup'[32] and 'British Council attacked for "porn subsidy"',[33] the Fine Arts department's support for COUM was closely scrutinized. *Arte Inglese Oggi 1960–76* as a whole was said to have cost Fine Arts £50,000 to produce; of this P-Orridge received £650.40. A total of £272.50 had covered fares, subsistence, and meals for Paris; following invitations to appear in eight galleries in America, £496 was added to that cost. Although the *Evening News* framed this as 'Sex Show Man's Amazing Free Tour',[34] other papers were more reasonable in their description of the work and the modest funds. The *Guardian* noted the academic authority behind the decisions: 'A number of critics here and abroad regard Mr P. Orridge as a leading young performance artist. All council supported tours are funded after recommendations by its fine art panel, headed by Professor Peter Lasko, of the Courtauld Institute.' Inflammatory comments came from the Conservative MP Nicholas Fairbairn, who stated, 'Now we are getting the lid off the maggot factory. Here, at the expense of the taxpayer, the British Council apparently sends these spurious and bogus destroyers around Europe to destroy the values of Western civilisation.'[35] Challenging art thus put debates about moral values and cultural relations under a particularly bright spotlight.

Rebel art on diplomatic display

These press reports prompted intense discussion among the Fine Arts department and the wider British Council. The Executive Board met to discuss the implications in late 1976; if their 'gross inaccuracy' was taken at face value, the results could be 'disastrous' for the organization. The British Council regretted not submitting a formal complaint to the press ombudsman and speaking up more loudly to clear its name.[36] The result was that the department was asked to establish new and clearer criteria for selecting artists. Connected to this, a Collection and Purchasing Committee was assembled in 1977, composed of a sub-committee of the Fine Arts Committee and the curator of the Collection, to provide six-monthly consultation about the disbursement of funds. Conversations about what should be supported applied to the purchase of art works as well as grants for artists.

The Fine Arts department was agreeable to this formalization; its staff understood the sensitivity. Bigger debates were raised about experimental art. Should it be supported? Norman Reid spoke in its defence, arguing that, 'the Council's responsibility for displaying experimental art was analogous to expenditure on research projects in other fields, where ultimate value could not be assessed in advance'; risks had to be taken. The Executive Board tried to distinguish between the differing remits of national organizations, arguing that the Arts Council existed to support all art, but the British Council should promote only 'the best'. The Fine Arts Committee, however, did not agree. Dennis Farr, director of Birmingham City Museum and Art Gallery, argued that, 'it was necessary to display works both of a recognised high standard and those which were experimental'. Members understood the British Council's cultural relations remit and reiterated the importance of considering 'the suitability of the receiving country when exhibitions were planned'.[37]

In the case of COUM at *Arte Inglese Oggi* 1960–76, modifications had, in fact, been made. The artists had wanted to perform naked, but instead wore monochrome clothing. Tutti was to be submerged in gallons of milk, but this was adjusted to polystyrene granules in part because of British Council anxieties about a contemporary political sensitivity, that is, milk quotas in the EEC.[38] Beyond this, while works in the Milan exhibition were experimental, it was not a location that had to be treated with particular caution; major European cities had lively contemporary-art scenes, and the show was designed to communicate with those who spoke a similar aesthetic language. The controversy, indeed, was the product of Britain rather than Italy. That senior Council executives did not speak the language of those conducting artistic experiments can be seen most clearly in photographs of the 1975 British Council board and the 1976 Milan delegation, illustrating the different worlds of the mature, besuited executives and the young, dishevelled artists arrayed around Trafalgar Square in flares and fur coats, carrying babies, smoking cigarettes, and flicking V-signs.

Regardless of these culture clashes at home, the debate about the art that publicly funded institutions should support offered a valuable moment of self-reflection. At the start of 1978, the Fine Arts Committee met to agree policies. They asked 'whether it is our function to present the newest thing or whether we should limit ourselves only to that which has been proved at home'. Some members stated 'something which is suitable for one country may not be so elsewhere, and diplomatic considerations must be taken into account'. Others pointed out the problems of making national assumptions about moral and artistic conservatism. It was noted that 'many countries' – Poland and Australia were cited – 'asked particularly to see the most recent experimental art and to learn what was happening now in Britain'.[39] It was the British Council's duty to give what was wanted; mutuality was a core premise. The matter remained unsettled, not least in relation to work that carried political messages. Michael Compton, a curator at the Tate Gallery, contended that, 'The objective of the British Council was to give a picture abroad of life in Britain. This meant that we should not be afraid of art forms which contained a polemical element if they were representative of the current climate.'

TOP The board of the British Council, 1974–5

ABOVE A promotional photograph of the artists in the *Arte Inglese Oggi 1960–76* exhibition in Trafalgar Square. Both of these photographs were reproduced in the *British Council Annual Report 1975*.

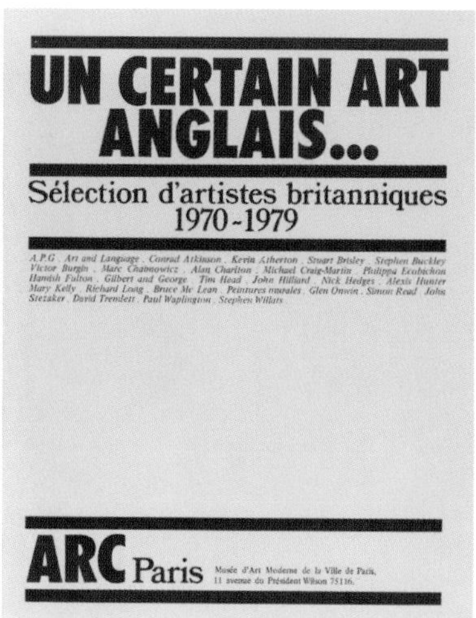

Front cover of the catalogue for the exhibition *Un Certain Art Anglais ...*, Paris, 1979

In particular, he asserted, 'In the case of work with a political or sociological content, the quality of the work could very often not be isolated from by its political potency.'[40] Precisely this point arose in relation to an exhibition held in Paris the following year.

Certainties and uncertainties

Un Certain Art Anglais ... Sélection d'Artistes Britanniques 1970–1979 was shown at the Musée d'Art Moderne de la Ville de Paris from January to March 1979, co-organized by the Fine Arts department and Suzanne Pagé, director of ARC, an independent French arts organization. As Gerald Forty, by then director of Fine Arts, asked in his introduction to the French-language catalogue, 'Can one speak of typical English characteristics in the art produced in Great Britain today?' His reply was that it was hard for an Englishman to judge, so he would leave it to French audiences to decide. 'Luckily,' he added, 'at least in the art world, we have left behind the era of overt jingoism.' That said, 'plants grow differently in different soils'; a study of comparative variations could prove instructive. As a second question, Forty asked whether one should speak of English art in the singular or the plural; on this, he was more definite. Variety characterized art of the 1970s due to the political diversity of contemporary society, but also because artists considered themselves as individuals and disliked being corralled into a homogenous group.[41]

To Pagé, there were three main characteristics in English contemporary art of the 1970s. The first was an extension of a national tradition of landscape studies, although its contemporary manifestation was tempered by a mode that was sober, careful, and even austere. The second aspect focused on relationships between art, reality, and illusion, including immersive installations and new ways with still life. Finally, and most significantly, Pagé observed energetic artistic political critique, through the analysis of ideology and direct engagement with social conditions of the time.[42]

The first category included the landscape work of Richard Long – although it should be noted that the artist has sought to distance himself from a national tradition. Indeed, by 1979, he had produced his art not only in England, but in Australia, Bolivia, Canada, Chile, France, Iceland, Ireland, Japan, Kenya, Malawi, Nepal, Netherlands, Norway, Peru, Poland, Switzerland, Tanzania, United States, and Zambia. Long's land art combines formal elements of minimalism with a meticulous engagement with the rural, marking and shaping sites

Richard Long's *Slate Circle*, 1979, installed in *Un Certain Art Anglais ...*, 214 pieces of slate, diameter 660 cm

ABOVE Richard Long, *Circle in Africa*, 1978, b/w photograph with text, 83.8 × 114.3 cm (P5641)

OPPOSITE Richard Long, *Stone Line*, 1979, Cornish slate, 239 × 130 cm (P3876)

through walking or other interventions, including the gathering and reordering of found materials, including driftwood and stone. The works are processes as well as products, sometimes involving intense physical labour, extended travel, and feats of endurance. The results include textual accounts, photographic documents, and three-dimensional structures, and have been described as ritualized practices, landscape poetry, and adventurous acts of discovery.

Long's slate circle at *Un Certain Art Anglais ...* comprised fragments from a Welsh quarry enclosed in a perfect circle more than six metres wide on the gallery floor; its evocation of ancient monuments and minimalist sculpture raised intriguing tensions about time and space, as traditional methods inhabited modernist settings. Another of Long's contemporaneous works, the 1978 photograph *Circle in Africa*, was subsequently purchased by the British Council.

Richard Long, *Spring Circle*, 1992, Delabole slate, 300 cm diameter (P6284)

Here Long recorded the temporary ring of burnt cactus – the material closest to hand – that he had assembled on Mulanje Mountain in Malawi. The collection also contains Long's *Stone Line* from 1979, where a simple linear sequence of Cornish slates brings the promise of a rural footpath into the gallery. His later three-metre-wide slate *Spring Circle* is a statement sculpture of the Collection. Quietly profound, the work's visual and material references are rooted in its West Country origins, but its adventurous travel around the world – to exhibitions in Cyprus, Czech Republic, France, Germany, Kuwait, Malta, Morocco, Oman, Pakistan, Portugal, Romania, Russia, Saudi Arabia, South Africa, Taiwan, and Zimbabwe – rivals the artist's own global walking endeavours.

Art / Illusion / Réalité

In Pagé's second category – the relation of objects to space, and reality to illusion – *Un Certain Art Anglais ...* showcased the first British Council purchases of installation art. The long-standing emphasis on practicality had emphasized the robust and the reproducible, the modestly scaled, and the easily transportable; by the 1970s, as art proliferated beyond the boundaries of frame and plinth, so too did the Council's collecting policy expand. Tim Head's *Still Life* and Michael Craig-Martin's *Picturing: Iron, Watch, Pliers, Safety Pin*, both from 1978, exemplify this parameter-busting.

Head's *Still Life* is a mix of image and objects, textures and dimensions, *nature morte* and *trompe l'oeil*. Playing with spatial dynamics and inverting orders of value, the artist mixed the material and immaterial, projecting bricks onto the wall via a slide projector, incorporating ladders and chairs as screened images, and three-dimensional props that the viewer must decode as representations or realities. Seated nudes and fire extinguishers brought the subject matter of fine-art painting and the pragmatic facts of exhibition management into juxtaposition; two- and three-dimensional layers of ropes and saws brought the garage to the gallery. Space and place are dislocated; 'here' is unclear.

Craig-Martin's *Picturing: Iron, Watch, Pliers, Safety Pin*, one of several taped wall pieces that the artist produced for the *Un Certain Art Anglais ...* exhibition, rendered everyday objects as shadowless and textureless as those from

Tim Head, *Still Life*, 1978, mixed media and slide projection installation, 240 x 300 cm (P3699)

a draughtsman's hand. In *Alice in Wonderland*-style, the safety pin loomed large as an iron or, seen from another perspective, the iron was reduced to size of a wristwatch. Together, their overlapping forms torqued into an intersecting tangle that the eye needed to retrace repeatedly to isolate its elements. *Picturing* made strange the materials of daily life and recast common tools as icons. As a work of art in the service of global communication, *Picturing* travels well, not only because its component parts are everyday essentials recognized and utilized everywhere. The work comprises a single 35mm slide whose projected object outlines are traced anew with black sticky tape in each exhibition setting. Infinitely repeatable, *Picturing* can be assembled by anyone and scaled up or down to suit the site, sliding between readymade and re-enactment. Since its first appearance in Paris in 1979, it has been taped to the walls of museums and castles, forts and gymkhanas, arts centres and galleries in Bangladesh, Canada,

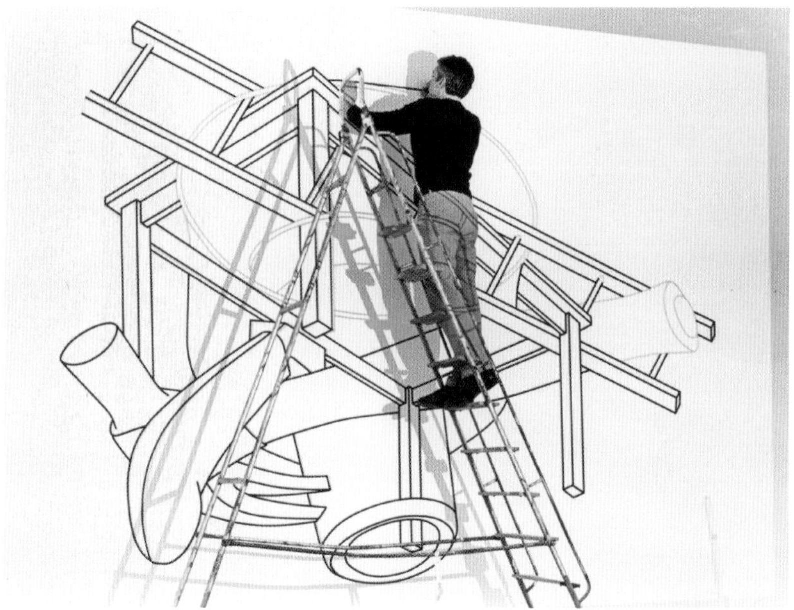

Michael Craig-Martin installing another of his taped wall pieces at *Un Certain Art Anglais* ...

Cyprus, Czech Republic, Germany, Hong Kong, India, Ireland, Kazakhstan, Malaysia, Malta, Morocco, Pakistan, Romania, Russia, South Africa, Spain, Taiwan, United States, and Zimbabwe. It is a still life that will not sit still.

Exposing conflict

Pagé's third category concerned politically engaged practice. In representing this substantial focus of British artists of the 1970s, the exhibition reignited debates about challenging art in cultural relations. On its opening night, Sir Nicholas Henderson, British ambassador to Paris, was met by artist Kevin Atherton in the middle of a naked performance piece. Much British press amusement was expressed on this meeting of worlds, under headlines such as 'British Art has Paris Exposure' (*Daily Telegraph*) and 'More Sex Please We're the British Council' (*Evening Standard*). The *Daily Telegraph* noted that Henderson

LEFT AND BELOW Kevin Atherton, *The Audience's New Clothes*, 1979, performance at *Un Certain Art Anglais ...*, Musée d'Art Moderne de la Ville de Paris, 1979

OPPOSITE Stuart Brisley, *Une Nouvelle Oeuvre pour la Consommation Institutionel*, three-day-and-night continuous performance, Musée d'Art Moderne de la Ville de Paris, 1979

was 'shocked' at 'the sight of a naked man walking up and down the main staircase'.[43] The *Evening Standard* gleefully noted, 'Paris is laughing. The British Council, who funded the effort, is blushing modestly.' The newspaper used the opportunity to kick its old enemy, contemporary art, noting that the ambassador and his wife had experienced, 'Stuart Brisley enjoying a 72-hour sojourn in a dog kennel and Bruce McLean playing with cardboard cups and a teapot while his assistants shouted nonsense at them'. In direct reference to previous press outrage, the article concluded: 'Such cavorting makes the Tate's bricks of yesteryear look very passé.'[44]

Atherton is and was a serious educator, sculptor, and performer; his 1970s work included site-specific and spontaneous performances that deconstructed conventions of art, entertainment, and audience. Nonetheless, he was keenly aware of the awkwardness of such operations, and the clashes that can occur when experimental art carries out diplomatic duties. In 2005, he explained how his performance at the Paris exhibition, which he called *The Audience's New Clothes*, involved his stripping on the gallery steps until he was naked and examining the clothes of the audience. Atherton recalled the moment that he met the official gaze of the ambassador and his wife: 'There was a naked man literally looking up his own arse. The timing was the best. The whole performance wasn't with my head between my legs. It was just at that moment that they came down the stairs.'[45]

From the perspective of the Fine Arts department, the art in *Un Certain Art Anglais ...* had been understood by those with whom it aimed to communicate. As a British Council spokesperson noted in the *Evening Standard*, 'The exhibition has been a success with the French, who really don't think it's very revolutionary.'[46] *Un Certain Art Anglais ...* generated positive Parisian press coverage and substantial attendance figures.[47] Yet for all the mockery of artistic eccentricity in the British press and the amusement that it generated among the artists, the show prompted serious issues. Henderson's anger overflowed as he apprehended Atherton, but his principal offence was with Conrad Atkinson, whose contributions were unflinching representations of the Troubles in Northern Ireland, accompanied by a narrative uncompromisingly opposed to British government policy.[48]

Through extended photographic documents that depicted political murals on Ulster streets and paintings of political paraphernalia, including green-white-and-gold-trimmed rosettes featuring a crucified Christ and the slogan 'Remember Our Glorious Dead', Atkinson caught the visual culture of the conflict. In the catalogue notes, he described the situation in Northern Ireland as a civil war of ten years' duration and stated that – with the exception of Rita Donagh (see page 162) – British artists were indifferent to it as a subject. Parliamentary debates seemed to do nothing about the violence carried out at their command. With explicit reference to the location of the exhibition, Atkinson argued that while Northern Ireland might be at the periphery of the EEC, it held a central metaphorical position in the heart of Europe. Citing the revolutionary slogans of Paris 1968, which aimed to take the museums to the streets, his aim was to bring the street to the art museum.[49] In mapping his work against international references, Atkinson strategically repositioned a war that risked being sidelined in the Englishness of *Art Anglais*.

Conrad Atkinson, *Colour photograph mounted on board of a rosette in the colours of the Irish flag depicting the crucifixion of Jesus Christ, surrounded by the slogan, 'Remember Our Glorious Dead'*, *c.* 1975, colour photograph, mounted on board, 12.7 × 6.7 cm. Tate

Ambassador Henderson argued that Atkinson gave a 'highly one-sided and critical interpretation of British action in Northern Ireland'. He took issue not only with the artist's political stance, but also with his aesthetics: 'These exhibits may qualify as interesting social and political statements. I do not see by what conceivable criterion they can be called art.'[50] Gerald Forty responded that political engagement was dominant in Britain, and that the Fine Arts department's role was to represent contemporary art. As with his earlier support for Hockney in Mexico, he argued against censorship, making the important point that, in a cultural relations context, Britain's liberal reputation depended on free artistic expression.[51] This was a principle expressed in respect to cultural relations more broadly by John Llewellyn, the British Council's then director-general, in the same year: 'One of the aims of British foreign policy is to uphold and extend the basic values and freedoms of our democracy. There is also a virtue in giving those living under repressive regimes some glimpse of what it feels like to live in a society where you do not have to watch your every word.'[52] The British Council's statement was a major assertion in support of free speech, even if such speech contravened the government's line.

In subsequent meetings, the Fine Arts Committee again considered the challenges of experimental art; the reputational risk of supporting 'activities which appeared absurd or irresponsible to the public at home' had already been rehearsed. Further reflection was required on art as political critique. The British Council's official assertion was that, 'while political comment was legitimate there were areas in which the Government and particularly our missions abroad could be seriously embarrassed by the use of public funds to support artists whose work ran directly contrary to what the Government was trying to achieve'. The suggested guidance was that selection committees should bear this in mind. Although there were some who felt that this was 'an insidious form of back-door censorship', most recognized the request as realistic. Political works would continue to be shown and bought by the Council, but there was collective agreement that it 'should be backed by the conviction of those concerned with the selection that it was of real value and that it could be legitimately and strongly defended on artistic grounds in the face of hostile criticism'. A final caution aimed to prevent further embarrassment: ambassadors and high commissioners were to be informed of controversial material, 'so that they could decide to what extent it would be appropriate for them to be involved', for example, in attending, or not, the opening ceremony.[53]

Expansions and exclusions

The Fine Arts department in the 1970s pushed boundaries of form and content in the expanded fields of contemporary art through commissions, exhibitions, and purchases, supporting new conceptual strategies alongside politically engaged practice. For some, this demonstrated bold, risk-taking ambitions; from another perspective, however, it upheld the status quo. This was raised with force in 'An Open Letter to the British Council' in 1979 by artists David Medalla and Rasheed Araeen. 'We are appalled', they began, 'that no black artist was considered suitable to take part in the exhibition *Un Certain Art Anglais* ..., in spite of the fact that this exhibition is supposed to be representing all the new important aspects of art in Britain in the '70s.' This omission, they said, was not the first time that black British artists had been excluded: 'A glance at the official art exhibitions at home and abroad will clearly show a consistency in the official attitude.'[54] In 1976, a report by the journalist and activist Naseem Khan, *The Arts Britain Ignores: The Arts of Ethnic Minorities in Britain*, including research into British Council practices, concluded that black British arts were institutionally neglected.[55] Medalla and Araeen rejected the notion of 'ethnic arts', but they similarly targeted the British Council. They contended that the Fine Arts department was 'adamant in persistently projecting the *white* image of Britain abroad, as if there are no black people in Britain or they are not part of British reality, and as if black artists have done nothing significant in the field of art'.[56]

Arte Inglese Oggi 1960–76 was also included in their critique. Medalla and Araeen described it as a major retrospective of recent developments including more than sixty artists, 'but all of them were white'. The exclusion was all the more galling because avant-garde art, political practice, feminist, and 'so-called social art' were 'rightly recognised and represented'. The artists drew the angry conclusion that there must be 'official censorship in art based on political, ideological and / or racial attitudes'. They called on the British Council to explain its position.[57] Later that year, *Art from the British Left*, an independent artist-organized exhibition in New York, featured an image by Araeen as its invitation card. Pointedly titled *Un Certain Art Anglais!*, it showed two white policemen assaulting a black man at an anti-racism protest to visualize the racist treatment that black and Asian artists felt they received from the art world.[58]

As will be discussed in the following chapters, the Fine Arts department's response to the call for better representation can be measured materially through the constitution of, and reflection on, its subsequent exhibitions and purchases. While it is true that more black and Asian artists were added to the Collection in subsequent decades, Medalla and Araeen's provocation continues to resonate as a standing challenge. Emma Dexter, director of what is now called the Visual Arts department, recently explained her desire to improve the representation of black British art in the Collection:

> It seems obvious that the British Council Collection should reflect the diversity of the UK, not just in terms of who or what is depicted, but also the artists whose works are contained within it. The collection should represent the country as a multiracial nation, so that the works enable a nuanced and sophisticated conversation about what Britishness means. It should therefore provide the tools with which to analyse the complex and sometimes troubling nature of British history, and how that informs our current notions of national identity. As a collection that, even since its earliest days, has been used to present national characteristics and ways of living to non-British audiences, it behoves the British Council Collection to embrace inclusiveness at every turn.[59]

Britain / Britishness, and sometimes England / Englishness, are necessarily one of the principal subjects of a national organization focused on international cultural relations. The British Council must always ask: whose culture is communicated? whose international relationships are supported or encouraged? The 1970s was a time of self-scrutiny for the Fine Arts department, intensified by the formalization of a single European community and the challenges to nationalist thinking in an increasingly internationalized art world. National identity was reflected upon repeatedly through art exhibitions organized within geographical frames. Where these aimed to encompass alternative practices, new forms, and expanded parameters, boundary-marking and boundary-pushing raised ongoing questions about aesthetics and politics, places and identities, openness and exclusion, censorship and free speech.

Rasheed Araeen, *Un Certain Art Anglais!*, 1979, offset-printed duotone, 10.7 × 15.1 cm. The reverse carried the statement 'This postcard piece originally protested the exclusion of Third World artists from a recent British Art show in Paris.'

CHAPTER 5

Use value

Following the introduction of a new government in 1979, the British Council was subject to a series of reviews and reorganizations, as well as dramatic budget cuts, that brought new challenges for the Fine Arts department. Discussions throughout the 1980s about the value of art in cultural relations, amid repeated crises in public funding and increased prices in the art market, would have significant implications for the British Council Collection, whose constitution underwent several changes in this period. As a result, the department saw a refocusing of its purpose, an expanding remit in the field of photography, and a change of name. At the same time, global political shifts led to new international restrictions as well as opportunities for relationship building, not least in the Soviet Union. These changed circumstances drew attention not only to the strengths and weaknesses of the Collection, but also to its capacities as a cultural ambassador, one that could establish and develop connections in difficult circumstances.

Painful cuts

Spending reviews brought in by the new Conservative government required all publicly funded bodies to share reductions in its income from the state. In the case of the British Council, the projected cuts amounted to one quarter of its budget at the start of the 1980s.[1] Plans to shoulder the blow included a radical reduction in its geographical reach and the total withdrawal of support for the

Peter Fraser, 'Easton Near Wells', from *Everyday Icons*, 1985–6, printed 2014, photograph, inkjet print on paper, 42.8 × 53.2 cm (P5403) (detail)

arts as a whole. The proposed changes prompted an outpouring of support from many high-profile cultural figures; *The Times* alone received sixty letters of protest from prominent individuals.[2] Henry Moore wrote directly to Margaret Thatcher to voice his views. Evaluating the institution's successes financially as well as culturally, Moore pointed out the large benefits to the Exchequer of the tax accrued on his international sales and commissions, and he noted that this was likely to carry on with subsequent generations of practitioners:

> The Council continues to support young artists in the way it has supported me in the last thirty years – many of our painters and sculptors will benefit from its encouragement and practical help, and will bring credit to the cultural life of our country (as well as income from abroad). I feel sure, Prime Minister, that money spent on the full support of the British Council is financially profitable to the nation.[3]

Eventually, the government agreed to continue funding the Council so that its cuts would be limited to eighteen per cent of its annual budget and its support for the arts could be retained. Even so, a series of reviews put the organization under continuing pressure. For example, the *Seebohm Report*, an independent review conducted by Frederic Seebohm, completed in 1980, investigated the Council's structure, financial control, and administration in order to find ways of expanding its income base. As part of this, the report surveyed the art collection and made recommendations that the British Council should 'renew' its holdings by selling works.[4] As a result, in 1982, it sold off nineteenth-century sporting prints, drawings, and watercolours that had originally been purchased as office decoration. These had been consolidated into the Collection in the 1970s, but remained somewhat incongruous with its central focus on modern and contemporary art.[5] The same year saw a major purchase of a newly produced Lucian Freud painting, *Naked Girl with Egg*, almost four decades after the Collection had acquired its first Freud.

Lucian Freud, *Naked Girl with Egg*, 1980/1, oil on canvas, 75 × 60.5 cm (P4184)

Lucian Freud, *Girl with Roses*, 1947/8, oil on canvas, 105.5 × 74.5 cm (P79)

Early and enduring purchases

The British Council had purchased Freud's *Girl with Roses* in 1948, when the artist was in his mid-twenties. He had completed the painting, and married its pregnant subject, Kitty Garman, that same year. With characteristic clinical detail, he depicted the individual hairs on his wife's head, the stitches in her knitwear, and the reflected scenes in her wide, startled eyes. After appearing in shows in Britain and the United States, the painting was selected by the Fine Arts department to be shown at the first Bienal de São Paulo in 1951, and then again at the Venice Biennale in 1954. In the seventy-five years since its acquisition, it has appeared in fifty exhibitions worldwide covering around thirty countries, demonstrating an excellent return on a modest investment of £157.

By 1982, when Fine Arts bought *Naked Girl with Egg*, Freud's work had matured. As an unflinching portrait of a supine nude, *Naked Girl with Egg* was no less probing and psychologically penetrating, but Freud had become even more forensic and even less forgiving in his fleshy depictions. In the same year, he once again appeared as a Council choice for Venice, appearing as one of four artists selected for the main international exhibition of the Biennale.

The long-standing relationship between Freud and the Fine Arts department offers a good example of the British Council's support for artists' careers and the returns that such connections bring. The goodwill that existed between them subsequently enabled the department to organize Freud's first exhibition tour of international museums. In 1987, both of the Collection's Freud paintings – along with eighty others – were shown at the Hirshhorn Museum in Washington, DC at a time when the artist was barely known outside his home country. Both the Metropolitan Museum of Art and the Museum of Modern Art in New York had turned the show down at proposal stage; Andrea Rose, then an exhibitions officer but soon to become the department's director, remembers that those institutions quickly changed their tune when the exhibition was crowned with accolades and Freud was transformed into an international star.[6] Rose, like her predecessors, argued strongly for the importance of exhibiting British art in the United States for the purpose of establishing artistic reputations, even though it was frequently low on the Council's agenda for cultural relations. She also highlighted the important interconnectedness of the Fine Arts department's varied activities. The expertise, insight, and trust developed through its mixed practices – its involvement in loan exhibitions and artist-grant schemes, for example – produced close relationships with institutions and practitioners, which in turn fed into purchases. As a result, as she put it, 'The Collection has grown as a branch grows out of a tree.'[7]

New materials and new investments: photography

With a narrowing budget and little in the way of funds to purchase major works by established names regularly, the Fine Arts department took advantage in the early 1980s of shifting attitudes towards photography as a means to devise

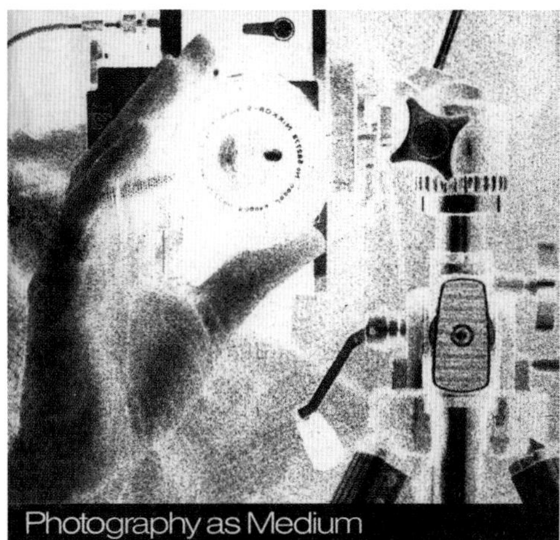

Front cover of the catalogue for the exhibition *Photography as Medium*, which toured from 1980 to 1986

new exhibitions and to develop the Collection. Within the British Council more broadly, photographic displays, separate from the activities of the Fine Arts department, had long been a staple institutional form. These were described by the Council as 'Visual Publicity' and provided didactic instruction about life in Britain for international circulation. For example, among the exhibitions of photographs produced in 1943–4 were *Women's Clothes in Wartime* and *Planning British Cities*, showing destroyed urban infrastructure alongside maps and architectural plans for reconstruction. Photographs had also been included as accompanying documentation in several postwar art exhibitions, where photographic prints, sometimes large in scale, had fleshed out occasionally modest circulating displays of three-dimensional material, for example work by Henry Moore. Before the 1970s, however, photography itself was not regarded as an art form in its own right within the British Council. In the decade that followed, this attitude began to change.

In 1970, what the Council classified as 'Photographic and Documentary' exhibitions included some forty-five displays for thirty-two countries.[8] While most of these displays did not encroach on Fine Arts' territory – such as those that depicted, for example, 'new approaches to science teaching' – some trav-

Fay Godwin, *Ruined Farm, Stanbury Moor*, 1979, silver bromide print, 17.6 × 17.6 cm (P3870)

elling exhibitions of work by documentary photographers, including Martin Parr and Ian Berry, blurred the boundaries between the organization's different departments. This blurring intensified as the Fine Arts department began to exhibit artists working with photography as part of their expanded repertoire. *Photography as Medium*, for example, was a circulating exhibition that showcased conceptual work from the likes of Tim Head alongside new practitioners of landscape photography such as Fay Godwin and the playful colour studies of Sharon Kivland.

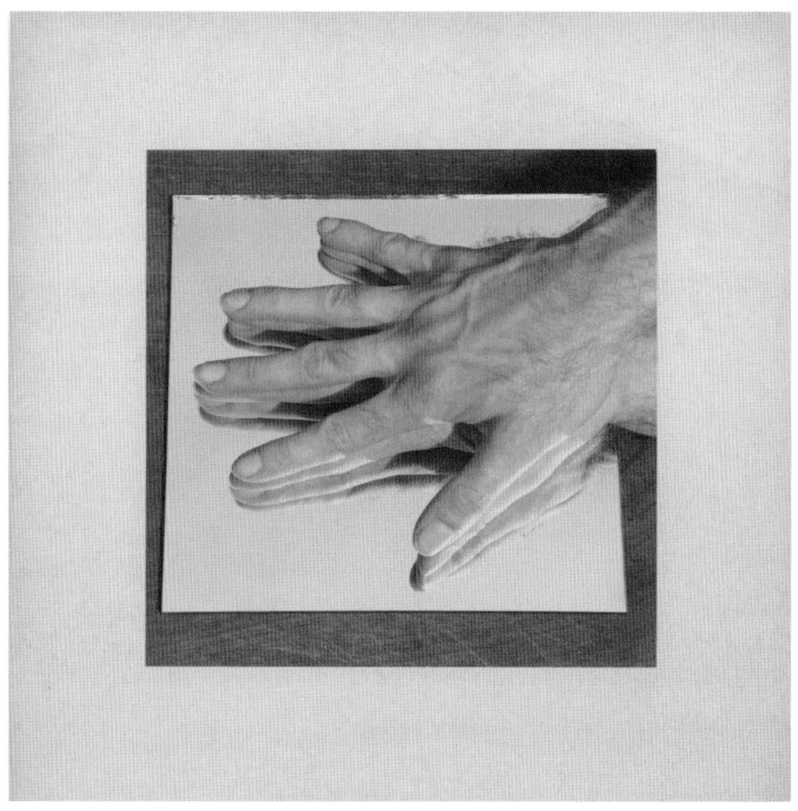

Tim Head, *Back to Front*, 1974, colour photographic print, 23 × 23 cm (P386)

Sharon Kivland, *Cocktails*, 1978, colour photographic print, 37.5 × 38.3 cm (P3718/B)

In the early 1980s, the institutional break-up of the General Exhibitions team, which had been responsible for the Council's photographically illustrated information displays, provided an opportunity for Fine Arts to explore the potential of photography at a time when the medium's status was undergoing revision more broadly. Two figures were at the heart of these debates: Alan Bowness, chairman of the Fine Arts Committee and director of the Tate Gallery, and Keith Arnatt, one of the first artists to be given a solo photographic show by the British Council. In 1982, Arnatt famously challenged Bowness on why the Tate collected only photographs made by artists and not photographs made by photographers. 'Making a distinction between, or opposing, artists and photographers is', Arnatt stated, 'like making a distinction between, or opposing, sausages and food.'[9] Photography, in his categorization, was a tool of artistic practice not a separate activity. Along with other national institutions in the period, the Fine Arts department reviewed its approaches to the medium, appointing Brett Rogers to develop a photographic strategy in that same year. Rogers had studied in London but had received several travelling exhibitions organized by the British Council while working as a gallery director in Sydney; she thus saw international operations from both sides of the desk.

Rogers' energetic activity included a series of judicious purchases for the Collection and the creation of around thirty international circulating exhibitions, which she organized until 2005, when she left to lead the Photographers' Gallery in London. As such, her contribution to photographic curating over the last four decades has been enormous. The adoption of photography by the Fine Arts department was partly practical; it was relatively cheap to buy and it travelled well, especially as copy prints that could be adaptable to display in a range of variable conditions worldwide, sometimes for many years at a time. From the outset, however, photography purchases and exhibitions were imaginative and significant, including major scholarly historical surveys of nineteenth-century British pioneers, from Julia Margaret Cameron to Henry Fox Talbot.

Particularly pertinent to the Council's work in cultural relations, and influenced by Rogers' own background – she described herself as very conscious in her Australian origins as 'a colonial' – were its exhibitions of

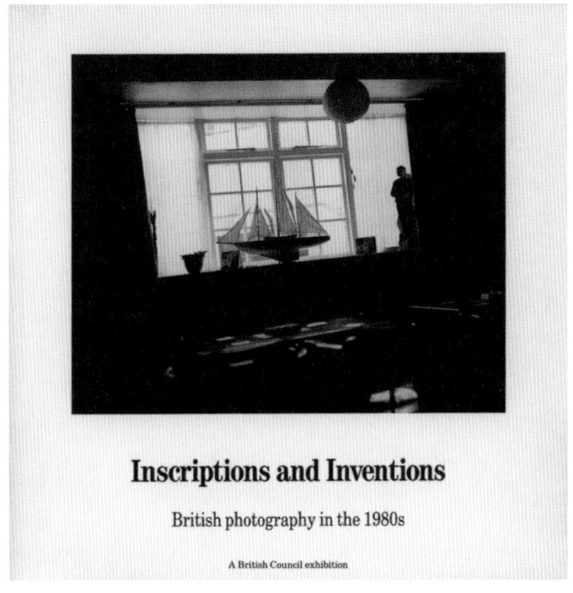

Front cover of the catalogue for the exhibition *Inscriptions and Inventions: British Photography in the 1980s*, which opened in 1987 and toured for three years

colonial-era photographs from British collections and archives.[10] Informed by postcolonial studies and thus aware of the skewed power relations that can be embedded and reproduced in some forms of visual culture, Rogers put imperialist practices under scrutiny, as photography exhibitions travelled to places where images had originally been taken but never previously seen. Photographs produced by the Scottish photographer John Thompson in Cyprus in 1878 were exhibited in that country in 1984; similar projects included James Robertson's views of Constantinople from the 1850s, William Ellis's contemporaneous photographs of Madagascar, and an exhibition of photographs of the subcontinent drawn from the British Library's Oriental and India Office Collection that travelled to sixteen Indian cities. As a result of these and other exhibitions, new transnational dialogues about historic world views took place in Barbados, Cuba, Cyprus, Haiti, Hawaii, India, Jamaica, Madagascar, Papua New Guinea, Sri Lanka, and Turkey. Reflective interpretations were co-produced with inter-

John Davies, *'Durham Ox' Public House, Sheffield*, 1981, silver bromide print, 50 × 60 cm (P6064)

national scholars, and in each case, copies of the photographic prints were presented to the exhibiting country as part of the process.

Rogers also developed a substantial new strand of purchases of contemporary British photography for the Collection, reflecting the principal preoccupations of current practice, from constructed photographs to new adaptations of the documentary form. The latter included the acquisition of challenging bodies of work that appraised the post-industrial political climate in Britain. The exhibitions *Inscriptions and Inventions: British Photography in the 1980s* in 1987 and *Documentary Dilemmas: Aspects of British Documentary Photography 1983–93* six years later presented images that examined the raw edges of British social inequalities. Examples included John Davies' lush, large-scale, silver-bromide landscapes. These romantic pictures in unromantic places, as Davies has described them, explored urban sites across the country where the old order was being dismantled – at times, painfully – to make way for regen-

Julian Germain, *Consett Bus Station Built with Italian Steel*, 1981, C-type colour print, 61 × 80 cm (P6167)

eration. The last pub standing in the long shadows as the ground is cleared for new development in *'Durham Ox' Public House, Sheffield*, for example, showed a poignant moment where communities were being reordered by new political priorities. Taking a similar perspective but a different visual style, Julian Germain's photographs of the shifting fortunes of Consett, County Durham, the location of a major steelworks shut down in 1980, followed the intimate realities of tough times. *Consett Bus Station Built with Italian Steel* offers a layered view of smashed glass, raindrops, and empty buses, framed by the mournful message that industry is elsewhere. To share the authorship of the project, Germain juxtaposed his own photographs with private perspectives from family albums and public moments of celebration from local press archives.

In other series, such as Richard Wentworth's *Making Do and Getting By*, Peter Fraser's *Everyday Icons*, and Verdi Yahooda's *The Mantelpiece and Its Thirty-Six Objects* (see pages 204–5), the textures of quotidian experience become the subject for contemplative still lifes. These photographic images, of domestic items usually thought to be of little consequence, borrow from the genres of oil painting while undermining that medium's associations of grandeur. The focus of these photographs is the marginalia of existence; their mode is 'muddling through', as the title of Wentworth's series suggests. 'A pink shirt and two red towels hanging on a clothes line will tell you next to nothing about British life in the 1980s', photography historian Ian Jeffrey asserted in his catalogue essay for *Inscriptions and Inventions*, with reference to a 1985 photograph by Fraser.[11] If one goes looking for the photographic equivalents of topical headlines, he implies, they will not be found in still lifes of laundry. Yet together these works show subject positions that eschew the spectacular in favour of the fine grain of lived experience, where the personal is definitely political. To borrow from the

Richard Wentworth, *New York*, 1978, from *Making Do and Getting By*, colour print made from transparency, 11 × 7 cm

Peter Fraser, 'Easton Near Wells', from *Everyday Icons*, 1985–6, printed 2014, photograph, inkjet print on paper, 42.8 × 53.2 cm (P5403)

ABOVE AND OPPOSITE Verdi Yahooda, *The Mantelpiece and Its Thirty-Six Objects*, 1985, colour photograph, 390 × 20 cm (P5426) (details above and work as installed opposite)

Martin Parr, *Untitled*, 1983/5, from *The Last Resort: Photographs of New Brighton*, Evercolor print, 50.8 × 61 cm (P5437)

title of a later photography exhibition organized by the Fine Arts department, they offer a 'reality check' to any aggrandized national self-image.[12]

Together, *Inscriptions and Inventions* and *Documentary Dilemmas* served as effective showcases for contemporary British photography as, between them, they travelled to fifteen countries across Western and Eastern Europe and Brazil. They also provide an indication of what the Fine Arts department saw as its role in promoting such work. A report on the reception for *Documentary Dilemmas* in São Paulo described the contents: 'A life-size cardboard cut-out of Margaret Thatcher spattered with red paint; a lone caravan parked on a deserted British beach in front of the rusting hulk of an abandoned trawler; a Union Jack caught in a solitary tree in a field in Northern Ireland; and a scrum of pink holiday-makers in a sleazy seaside hot-dog joint near Liverpool'. At the opening, an expatriate confronted the local Council representative. 'They're not exactly promotional, are they? Can't the British Council show something a bit more attractive?'[13] The visitor wanted to know why there were no scenic views of the Lake District, confusing the purposes of the Council with those of the British Tourist Authority. Rogers was clear that the job of the department was to represent photographic practice at the time, and national critique was undoubtedly an interest to photographers in the 1980s. Yet despite the reservations expressed by the nonplussed expat at the opening, local audiences loved *Documentary Dilemmas*. As reported by Mike Winter of the Council's São Paulo office, the three hundred Brazilian visitors who were surveyed appreciated the honesty. The exhibition told a truth that was valued.

Documentary Dilemmas was one of twenty-seven exhibitions from ten countries shown at the International Photo Meeting in São Paulo in 1993. Around 114,000 visitors attended the show in total, but it had slower-burning legacies too. The portfolio reviews that Julian Germain conducted in connection with the event introduced him to the Brazilian photographers Patricia Azevado and Murilo Godoy. From this meeting, the trio developed a long-standing collab-

A view of the exhibition *Documentary Dilemmas: Aspects of British Documentary Photography 1983–93*, held at the Museu de Arte de São Paulo in May 1993

oration that led to favela communities and street children in Belo Horizonte being provided with cameras to capture their own lives. The resulting books and international exhibitions, sustained over a twenty-year period, have developed new forums for marginalized groups and raised funds for a library and a community centre.[14] *Documentary Dilemmas* did not look nationally promotional, but it enabled intercultural interconnections that have endured.

Evaluating art in cultural relations: a new review

Amid increased scrutiny of public spending throughout the 1980s, the pressure for the British Council to prove its worth was a key feature of the decade. Few would dispute that publicly funded institutions need to be held to account to demonstrate their good value for money, but the regularity of reviews of the Council was notable. When eminent cultural studies scholar Richard Hoggart was commissioned to lead a review of the organization's arts activities in 1986, he and his co-authors remarked, 'It would be difficult to find a publicly funded body which has been so frequently and so publicly examined as the British Council.'[15] As an advocate for the social value of the arts, Hoggart was an interesting choice as auditor. His reflections provide poetic food for thought on the value of arts in cultural relations.

Hoggart argued for 'the profound long-term effect which the experience of a great work of art can have on its audiences' perception of themselves, of their own cultures and of the culture which produced that work of art'.[16] This was necessarily a long-term commitment; as such, its success could be fully judged only over time. The Council's 'magnificent exhibitions' were understood to 'work their special effects in the personalities of their audiences long after the events themselves have left town'.[17] Germain's slow-building, sustained collaborative activities based on deep knowledge, commitment, and trust provide an example of exactly this kind of after-effect. Other arguments made by Hoggart's report refer to specific Fine Arts activities, including an oblique reference to *Un Certain Art Anglais* ... of 1979 (see pages 172–82). 'An ambassador, or an ambassador's spouse, may be shocked by some manifestation of modern art', he hypothesized. 'It is a judgement an ambassador is entitled to make but it cannot be an order or an instruction.'[18] The arm's-length principle was fiercely defended.

Hoggart was passionately opposed to linking art to financial returns or to instrumentalism. It may be true that sales and commissions of British art could be directly linked to international exhibitions, and that the attractions of art galleries in Britain could be mapped against international tourist income. But rather than seeing a direct transposition of the British Council arts activities into the sales of cars, computers, or cream crackers, he argued that it was better to focus on building cultural affinities, sympathies, and allegiances.[19] Trade might result from a 'climate of respect and affection', but this was not the main purpose. 'The arts are not to be *used*. They are to be respected, admired, loved for and in themselves. The rest may follow, is perhaps likely to; but that must not be our direct business.' In a phrase widely quoted in the press, he declared: 'The arts are not to be seen as cultural polyfilla to a crumbling economy.'[20]

In relation to what kind of arts should be sent overseas, Hoggart was outspoken. 'The arts', he argued, 'are the supreme embodiments of and mirrors of a society, of a culture. They, not politics or wars, are the ways by which a society most perceptively and honestly explores and recreates its own nature, the way it sees the world and the orders of values it sees within the world.'[21] Art may resist as well as mirror social values, and this was to its credit. 'Some Council literature', Hoggart complained, 'speaks of art as though it were the cleanly scrubbed best face of British society, a face which exhibits all that is positive and instantaneously cheering in the nation's life. But the arts may be doing their best work for us, and for the understanding of us by others, when they are exploring our weaknesses.'[22] This self-critique applies well to British documentary photography of the 1980s, and Hoggart argued that it was just this kind of material that the British Council should support. 'Overseas audiences will be duly enlightened and will no doubt admire our capacity for honest self-criticism and perceptive insights into our own failings.'[23] The director-general at the time, John Burgh, felt similar: 'Cultural relations seek mutual understanding, they encourage activities which are fully representative of society and culture, not just those that are safe, undisturbing, traditional and self-flattering.'[24]

Shaping the Collection: particularities and preferences

While Hoggart's review characterized the British Council Collection as 'representative',[25] its shape is particular. It has been dictated by the limits of budgets, the tastes of the committee, the need to populate exhibitions, and the necessities of travel. In this sense, it is no different from any other collection; all are shaped by parameters, preferences, and pragmatics. It does not feature any work by Francis Bacon, for example. Why this should be is intriguing. Bacon had received an early champion in the form of Herbert Read, who boldly positioned a Crucifixion painting by the then little-known artist opposite a Picasso in his 1933 book *Art Now*. Bacon's paintings were first bought by New York's Museum of Modern Art in 1948 and by the Arts Council of Great Britain in 1952. He also represented Britain in exhibitions organized by the Fine Arts department for biennials in Venice in 1954 and São Paulo in 1959 (see page 136), and his works were included in many travelling shows, including Portugal's *British Art of the Twentieth Century* in 1962. According to Henry Meyric Hughes, director of the department from 1986 to 1992, institutional memory (fallible as it may be) recorded that Lilian Somerville did not like his work; she was an ardent supporter of abstraction and had little interest in most figurative painting.[26] Brett Rogers, on the other hand, thought the omission related to the personal preferences of Kenneth Clark.[27] However, Somerville was an early supporter of the figurative work of Lucian Freud, who, as I have shown, was also presented at the Venice Biennale of 1954 alongside Bacon in exhibitions that she organized; and Clark is known to have described Bacon as 'first rate' to Ben Nicholson and as having 'genius' to Graham Sutherland. The narrative of directorial exclusions on the grounds of personality is further complicated by the wide catholicity of other purchases made for the British Council Collection in its first two decades.

Everywhere described as formidable, Somerville, like earlier and later directors of the Fine Arts department, undoubtedly had her own particular tastes. At the point of her retirement in 1970, after some twenty-two years at the helm, the painter Patrick Heron reflected on what he described as 'her positively ferocious tenacity of purpose'. He noted: 'She is possessed by a burning *belief* in painting and sculpture and never hesitates for a moment to express her

ABOVE LEFT A view of *Masters of British Painting 1800–1950* at the Museum of Modern Art, New York, in 1956. Three paintings by Bacon can be seen: *Study for Crouching Nude*, 1952; *Fragment of a Crucifixion*, 1950; and *Painting*, 1946. The latter is in MoMA's collection.

ABOVE RIGHT Sir Roger Makins, British ambassador to the United States, with Lilian Somerville at the exhibition's opening. The British Council, under Somerville's directorship, assembled the loans from the United Kingdom and lent works of its own.

enthusiasm for (or condemnation!) of a particular work or a particular artist in a totally unambiguous manner. In a word, she has always stuck her neck out – right out: and made enemies as well as friends in the process.'[28] For all Somerville's forcefulness, one person, however persuasive, is only a single member of a decision-making body. As Meyric Hughes's successor Andrea Rose put it, 'The director cannot be an autocrat.'[29] Indeed, disputes about aesthetic and cultural value make some of the most interesting reading of the Fine Arts Committee's meeting minutes; tastes rarely align unanimously.

All collections are necessarily shaped by their collectors, and the other directors of the department each had moments where their personal likes and dislikes came to bear on what was bought or not. Gerald Forty, director during the 1970s, was remembered by Meyric Hughes as being even-handed in his preferences, supporting the work of performance artists, for example, despite not liking it himself. Forty was a keen painter whose tastes had been developed through an appreciation of British avant-garde art of the 1950s. He did not limit his purchasing to these forms, however, but nonetheless he drew the line at John Latham's *Skoob* works. These sculptural pieces, varied in shape and style, were based on destroyed literature, most famously in one work made of chewed-up and spat-out copies of modernist art criticism by Clement Greenberg. Forty's wartime employment in the Special Operations Executive, where, as the son of a native French speaker, he had trained British agents in Parisian slang for their work in occupied territories, continued to haunt him throughout his life; few agents returned from their postings. As Meyric Hughes interpreted it, the association of Latham's works with Nazi book burnings meant that Forty simply could not support their place in the Collection.[30]

In the case of Bacon, however, it seems that the central reason for his omission from the Collection is more prosaic than directorial prejudices. His absence was already observed in 1959. 'Judged in isolation, the Collection has as many gaps as strengths', Michael Middleton stated in the *Studio*. 'There is no Epstein, no non-figurative Pasmore, no Francis Bacon.' Middleton explained why gaps arose. 'It had originally been hoped, in the heyday after the war, to build up a full representation of British art in this country, brought continuously up to date', he explained. 'These ambitions were ended by the savage cuts of 1950/54.'[31] Purchasing in the 1960s emphasized younger artists and cheaper prints, while spending capacity in the 1970s was used to support new forms rather than filling gaps. Rapidly inflating art prices in the 1980s coincided with further slashes to funding to push Bacon very far out of reach; the annual purchasing fund would not have bought a corner of one of his canvases. Art critic Marina Vaizey reflected in 1988 that British success in the global art market had been produced, in part, as a result of international exhibitions, 'particularly the highly intelligent ones organised by the British Council, which also helps commercial galleries abroad'. The result was bittersweet: 'This welcome success for the artists is pricing their work beyond the grasp of our public collections', she wrote. At that point, Bacon held the record for the highest price paid for the work of a living British artist: $1,600,000 (£946,000) at Christie's.[32] The insurance value of a triptych in the 1988 Bacon exhibition in Moscow co-organized by the British Council was $4,500,000; it is no wonder that the show travelled across the Soviet Union under police protection.

Richard Hamilton, *Portrait of the artist by Francis Bacon*, 1970/1, screenprint over collotype, 82 × 69 cm (P1497)

Universal humanism to universal nihilism: from Moore to Bacon

If a collection is shaped as much by what is not in its possession as what is, understanding why there are no works by Bacon is just as important as understanding why there are hundreds by Moore. Moore's value to the Council was consolidated in the 1980s. A major sculpture, *Large Spindle Piece*, was sited at its London headquarters in 1982; and two years later, upon the organization's fiftieth birthday, Moore made a gift of more than two hundred prints. Staff members of the Fine Arts department held a formal silence to mark his death in 1986.[33] He is as central to the Collection as Bacon is peripheral. Yet, to say there are no Bacons in its holdings is to ignore images *of* and *about* Bacon, which include a print by Richard Hamilton based on a Polaroid taken by Bacon and photographs of the artist by Bill Brandt and Bruce Bernard.

Photographs of Bacon, and paintings by him, were used to communicate the artist's practice when the monographic exhibition and catalogue were prepared for Moscow in 1988. In the hands of the British Council, Bacon, just like Moore, functioned as a cultural ambassador. The message conveyed overseas was as much about the man as the work; yet Bacon's dress code was a

LEFT Bruce Bernard, *Francis Bacon*, 1984, cibachrome, 75.1 × 65 cm (P7301)

OPPOSITE Bruce Bernard, *Francis Bacon*, 1984, cibachrome, 75.1 × 65 cm (P7304)

leather jacket rather than Moore's comfy cardigan, and his lifestyle was less village family man than decadent metropolitan lush. The artist's image contributed to his reputation. As Grey Gowrie put it in the catalogue to the Moscow exhibition, 'Bacon himself looks very like a Francis Bacon.'[34] Bernard's photographs show Bacon at his most dissolute. Art books are piled high among rags and encrusted paint receptacles in his studio; walls and doors have been used as palettes; newspapers silt up around the artist's feet. As a working environment, it is wildly bohemian, dripping with colour and squalor. From these origins, the photographs seem to imply, Bacon makes meaning out of chaos. Now relocated to a Dublin museum, Bacon's studio is a rubbish tip-turned-still life, holding up a perished mirror to where Bacon's mess, mind, and mythology met. The photographs are testament to the deep friendship between the two men, which by the mid-1980s was four decades long. They and other images by Bernard of School of London artists, including Freud, are part of the Collection and contextualize its holdings as well as being art works in their own right. They capture works-in-progress and hero myths in the making.

Front cover of the catalogue for Francis Bacon's exhibition in Moscow, which opened in the Central House of Artists, in September 1988

The first textual page in the Moscow catalogue was a copy of a handwritten letter that Bacon wrote on the occasion of the show, now framed in the Collection stores in lieu of his paintings. It begins, 'It is a great honour to be invited to have an exhibition of paintings in Moscow. When I was young, I feel I was very much helped towards painting after I saw Eisenstein's films *Strike* and the *Battleship Potemkin* by their remarkable visual imagery.' In the same way that symbolic alignments were strategically constructed as diplomatic gestures between Moore and Greece, and Moore and Mexico, alignments between Bacon and Russia showed common cultures, travelling ideas, and the productive effects of cultural interchange.

Gowrie – poet, earl, former Conservative minister for the arts, and, by 1988, the chair of Sotheby's auction house – set the scene for the painter's subject matter by outlining the anxious conditions of the twentieth century as an age of extremes characterized by materialism, the horrors of war, the breakdown of religion, and existential threat. Bacon, he argued, is the man who gives this condition its imagery. His work ethic, his drinking, and his gambling was explored in the text with a Russian-inflected 'Dostoevskian intensity'. Like the

The original handwritten letter from Francis Bacon that was reproduced at the beginning of the catalogue

It is a great honor to be invited to have an exhibition of paintings in Moscow.
When I was young, I feel I was very much helped towards painting after I saw Eisenstein's films "Strike" and The Battleship Potemkin by their remarkable visual imagery. —
In one of Van Gogh's letters he makes this statement "How to achieve such anomalies such alterations and refashionings of reality that what comes out of it are lies if you like but ~~lies~~ lies ~~about~~ that are more true than literal truth"

Francis Bacon
London 4/6/88.

parallel words previously used to describe Moore, Bacon was characterized as 'the greatest living painter' on a worldwide stage. In Britain, Gowrie stated, 'It is still difficult to recognise how distinctive Bacon and the sculptor Henry Moore have made us in the visual arts.'[35] In contrast to Moore's romanticism and focus on landscape and the maternal, Bacon's vision was instead a primal scream, a nihilistic communication of purposelessness and despair; violent, theatrical, virile, and unflinchingly realist. Bacon's contorted bodies are painted with rags as well as hands; as such, he was portrayed as animalistic, wild, and untameable.

It was fitting that Bacon's introduction to a Russian audience should be made by a figure with such aristocratic authority as Gowrie; the brokering of Bacon in Moscow was a political act, albeit a rather unusual locus for building entente. Bacon was a slippery national representative, but his difficulty was part of his draw. When I asked Gill Hedley, exhibitions officer in 1988, why Bacon was so wanted, she said, 'He was not only the most famous artist in the world, but also a nihilist, glamorous, a queer Bohemian. He represented everything romantic about being an artist; he was the embodiment of the maverick.'[36] Meyric Hughes, however, remembered it differently. The Soviet ambassador to UNESCO told him that the exhibition nearly did not happen. The All-Soviet Union of Artists, the official hosts of the show, had decided Bacon was 'too hot to handle'. Meyric Hughes recalled:

> They had written a report which went up the ranks with comments to the effect that 'Bacon was a supreme example of Western decadence, and a homosexual to boot, and we cannot recommend this.' This got as far as Gorbachev's deputy, Yegor Ligachev, the Minister of Agriculture at the time, who was an arch conservative. He noted on the dossier, 'If this is as bad as people say, it will be excellent for the Russian people to see it as an example.'[37]

Whether it made him an object of fascination or of caution, the anomalies fit the occasion. Thatcher had described Bacon as 'that man who paints those *dreadful* pictures', and Bacon had previously refused a knighthood; his relationship with establishment interests was hardly straightforward.[38] David Sylvester, the principal interpreter of the artist's work, noted that his most important painting, a 'central panel of buggers', had been 'censored'. This apparently had disappointed Bacon but Sylvester explained that it was well understood. The British Council 'quite rightly toe the line', he stated; 'it's not like sending a cricket team to Russia is it?'[39]

Negotiations about securing loans for a politically volatile location had to be handled with care, and the Fine Arts department's experience and bargaining power was needed. James Birch, the young gallerist and drinking partner of Bacon, first developed the idea for the show and built the original connections, which were then formalized and delivered by the department alongside the All-Soviet Union of Artists and Bacon's dealer, Marlborough Gallery. The British Council Collection was used as leverage to persuade the Arts Council to provide its only Bacon; works of equivalent status were offered on loan in exchange. Everywhere the special nature of the event, as the first major exhibition of Western modern art in Russia and the only solo show by a living British artist, was emphasized. This secured the loan of the rarely travelled *Study for the Nurse in the Film 'Battleship Potemkin'* from the Stadel Museum in Frankfurt, which strategically underscored his Russian connection.

As well as being managed and selected by the Fine Arts department, the exhibition was opened by the Council's director-general, Sir Richard Francis. He described it as 'the fruit of an enthusiasm and of human conglomeration which transcend the normal bounds of cultural agreements and diplomatic associations'.[40] This may be hyperbole, but a sense of cultural significance prevailed. Russian critics described the exhibition as an opportunity for national reimagining under glasnost. As Mikhail Sokolov of the USSR Academy of Arts noted:

British Council exhibitions officer Gill Hedley unpacks works by Francis Bacon to install in the galleries of the Central House of Artists

> Our knowledge of world art is becoming broader and more comprehensive day by day, and we begin to understand our own cultural tradition more sensitively and thoughtfully. This is the substance of the international dialogue of the arts, which is becoming ever more active as the twentieth century draws to its close. The main purpose of Baconian art may be defined as 'truth at any price', and this naked truth – sometimes extremely cruel in its healing effect – is the thing most indispensable today both for our society and for our cultural life.[41]

The exhibition visitors' book included more than two hundred comments by professionals from culture, medicine, and industry. Strong reactions included bewilderment and disgust – Bacon was described as 'a cretin', a charlatan, misanthropic, and morally degraded – but there were also many statements of appreciation. It is striking that the exhibition provided visitors with an opportunity to take stock politically. As Hoggart claimed, art that is challenging has the potential for profound effects, and in this instance the exhibition operated as a productive site for reflection on self and other. 'Everyone who becomes familiar with this exhibition realises what a disaster totalitarianism is. It is a plague of the 20th century for all mankind', one visitor stated. 'The artist shows how the talent of any person can blossom in a democratic society based on the rule of law and how educated people perish in a bureaucratic command state such as ours.'[42] Another reflected: 'It is wonderful that now we have a chance to become familiar with modern movements in art, which exist apart from this notorious Socialist Realism. Only in such a way can one understand the controversial essence of man, the modern world and the relationship between them.'[43] Even those who disliked Bacon brought national reflections to their disdain: 'Bacon's exhibition depresses because of his pathologically distorted vision of man. Why do we, Russians, need acquaintance with alien culture such as this? Why do we need this foreign decay?'[44] At a time of seismic social change, a lack of comprehension was seen as a measure of cultural distances to be travelled: 'Unfortunately we (Soviet viewers) are not ready to understand abstractivism and surrealism', one visitor noted. 'During the whole period of Soviet power, we have been nourished by another type of art. We had ideas put into our heads which were convenient for somebody's plans. This deprived us of inner freedom, freedom of thought, of feelings. It will take some time for us to start understanding the paintings by Francis Bacon. Such exhibitions are vital if we really want to reconstruct our society.'[45]

Russian cultural relations: a longer view

The Fine Arts department handled the Bacon show without there being any Bacons in the British Council Collection because of its extensive experience in assembling international exhibitions, its connections with foreign cultural ministers, its access to government indemnity funding to cover large insurance costs, and the political significance of the occasion. Coordinating complex diplomatic teamwork was its specialism. Following the Bacon exhibition, during his visit to Britain in 1989, the Soviet minister of culture, Vasily Zakharov, claimed, 'Our present relations with Britain in the field of culture can be described as the best in the entire post-war period.'[46] The acknowledgment of peak harmony implicitly referenced a history of difficulties; indeed, the Fine Arts department had been putting together exhibitions for and with Russia for decades, with some triumphs and some setbacks.

The British Council did not operate in the Soviet Union in its pre-war years, and there was little activity immediately after; during the high tension of the Cold War, there was no cultural diplomacy with Russia at all. By the mid-1950s, however, some planning for exchange was permitted. As David Kelly, chairman of the Council put it in 1957, the organization continued to engage with the country in an official capacity via theatre, music, and exhibitions, of which, he said, the Council was 'the only body in this country with the necessary trained staff and experience'. A Soviet Relations Committee had been set up by the Council to coordinate cultural activities in 1955. In April 1956, the visit of Nikita Khrushchev, first secretary of the Communist Party and Nikolai Bulganin, chairman of the Council of Ministers, stepped up planning until, as Kelly put it, 'the effect of the Hungarian repressions in November on British opinion brought the whole programme into cold-storage.'[47]

During the Cold War, the British Council perceived cultural divisions between Britain and the Soviet Union; Soviet art was understood to be 'rigorously controlled by the Ministry of Culture, and organised as weapons of propaganda for the regime'.[48] British art, in the minds of its interlocutors, was characterized by independence from state control, freedom of expression, and stylistic liberalism. In mid-century, this contrast was embodied in the Soviet promotion of a didactic Socialist Realism and its strict rejection of abstraction and the avant-garde. This aesthetic-political distinction is visible in many of the Fine Arts department's papers, and informed British choices about the messages to be sent in exhibitions once cultural agreements were formalized at the end of the 1950s.

After *Russian Painting from the 13th to the 20th Century* at the Royal Academy in 1959, the department organized the return exhibition the following year. *British Painting 1720–1960* opened at the Pushkin Museum in Moscow and travelled to the Hermitage Museum in Leningrad. Containing 141 paintings lent by 66 museums and private owners, including Queen Elizabeth II, it was considered by the Council to be the 'first important exhibition of British painting ever to be shown in the Soviet Union'. It was seen by 370,000 people in total, averaging 7,000 visitors a day.[49] As art historian Verity Clarkson has observed, its contents balanced the communication of British aesthetic freedoms with a need to appeal to Soviet viewers. Catering to Russian tastes for realism led to anxieties; the inclusion of works by arch-traditionalists such as Alfred Munnings risked discrediting British artistic authority.[50] In the end, contributions to *British Painting 1720–1960* included a range of modern works. Freud's *Girl with Roses* (see page 192) was selected alongside Jack Smith's Kitchen Sink painting *Child Walking with Check Tablecloth* (see page 110). Graham Sutherland's *Thorn Trees* (see page 104) again performed diplomatic Cold War duties, while Victor Pasmore's *Abstract in Black, White and Ochre* was the most visually austere of Collection works on display. Its loose geometric gestures and floating forms of crescents, lozenges, dots, and dashes bore a provocative resemblance in their spatial dynamism and wintry palette to the Russian constructivist paintings deemed politically subversive by the Soviet authorities.

Victor Pasmore, *Abstract in Black, White and Ochre*, 1958, oil on board, 140.5 × 155.7 cm (P324)

Front cover of the catalogue for the exhibition *Great Britain / USSR*, held at the Victoria and Albert Museum, London, in 1967

In 1967, the Victoria and Albert Museum hosted *Great Britain / USSR: An Historical Exhibition* to illustrate cultural interconnections since the sixteenth century and to mark the visit of the Soviet premier, Alexei Kosygin, who opened the show with British prime minister Harold Wilson.[51] The main organizers were the Arts Council of Great Britain, which coordinated incoming international exhibitions, while the British Council organized those going the other way. The cultural agreement with the Soviet Union emphasized obligatory reciprocity, and thus it fell to the Fine Arts department to arrange the return effort for 1968. *USSR / Great Britain: An Historical Exhibition* was to feature 'objects illustrating significant connections between Britain and Russia'; this included art showing the influence of Russia on Britain.[52] The crated paintings were being loaded onto an RAF plane for transportation when the Foreign Office abruptly cancelled the exhibition. With the USSR's invasion of Czechoslovakia on 20 August 1968, all cultural exchanges were suspended.[53]

Art exhibitions for Russia have been handled with exceptional diplomatic care over sixty years of British Council cultural relations. Perhaps, in these transactions, culture's intersections with politics play out more explicitly than in other geographies. The Foreign Office has wielded the power to withdraw exhibitions just as it has initiated them. The same directions have taken place in reverse, with political disagreements leading to some Council endeavours being restricted in Russia. Nonetheless, cultural connections between the two countries continued to thrive in the twenty-first century, with the greatest successes taking place through the arts. For example, exhibitions in 2007 brought selections from the British Council Collection to regional museums in Irkutsk, Krasnoyarsk, Novosibirsk, Omsk, Tomsk, and Yekaterinburg, across the Urals and Siberia; the exchange also brought Russian art and curators to Britain in return. Since the Russian invasion of Ukraine in February 2022, all Council activities in Russia have been put on hold, but the British Council has stated its commitment to restart at the right time in the future.

Cultural exchanges operate on a sliding scale of distance from politics; the status of the British Council's government funding, but its separation from government policy, is of particular importance. As Rose observed, 'The Russians have never understood how the British Council can be independent of government. It is a concept that is foreign to them, and they always imputed spy motives to it.'[54] Ironically, the only spying incident associated with art went in the opposite direction, in perhaps the most famous, if not the only, intersection of secret agents with art history. Anthony Blunt, director of the Courtauld Institute of Art and Surveyor of the Queen's Pictures, was exposed in 1979 for having passed secrets to the Soviet Union from the 1930s to the early 1950s as one of the infamous Cambridge Five spy ring. Blunt had served on the Fine Arts Committee from 1949 to 1961 and was advisor to the *Great Britain / USSR* exhibition in 1967.

Useable art, critical art

The Council may operate independently of government, but on occasion political-cultural intersections are hand in glove with one another. In 1990, for example, when Thatcher was to meet Gorbachev in Kyiv (now Ukraine) as part of a four-day state visit, the department was called upon to contribute

Front cover of the catalogue for the exhibition *For a Wider World*, which toured from June 1990 until December 1991

to a cultural showcase under the banner 'British Days'. The exhibition *For a Wider World*, which went on to travel to a further three countries, was compiled entirely from Collection works. In the estimation of the committee – now operating under its new name, Visual Arts Advisory Committee – its scale, scope, and range showed 'a classic illustration of the importance of maintaining the integrity of the Collection, since it would have been impossible, at such short notice, for the Department to put together a loan exhibition of works of comparable quality from outside sources.'[55]

For a Wider World provided the backdrop for strengthening political relationships between Ukraine and the wider Soviet Union and Britain, although its contents barely touched the subject. The catalogue made only elliptical mention of building bridges in relation to intellectual exchange. Instead, the exhibition was a major survey of the Collection, starting with the oldest item – a view of Venice by Walter Sickert – and proceeding to new purchases, including emerging British talents such as Helen Chadwick. Together, the exhibits' materials ranged from oil on canvas to meat and light bulbs. They made statements of artistic innovation regardless of where the exhibition was shown.

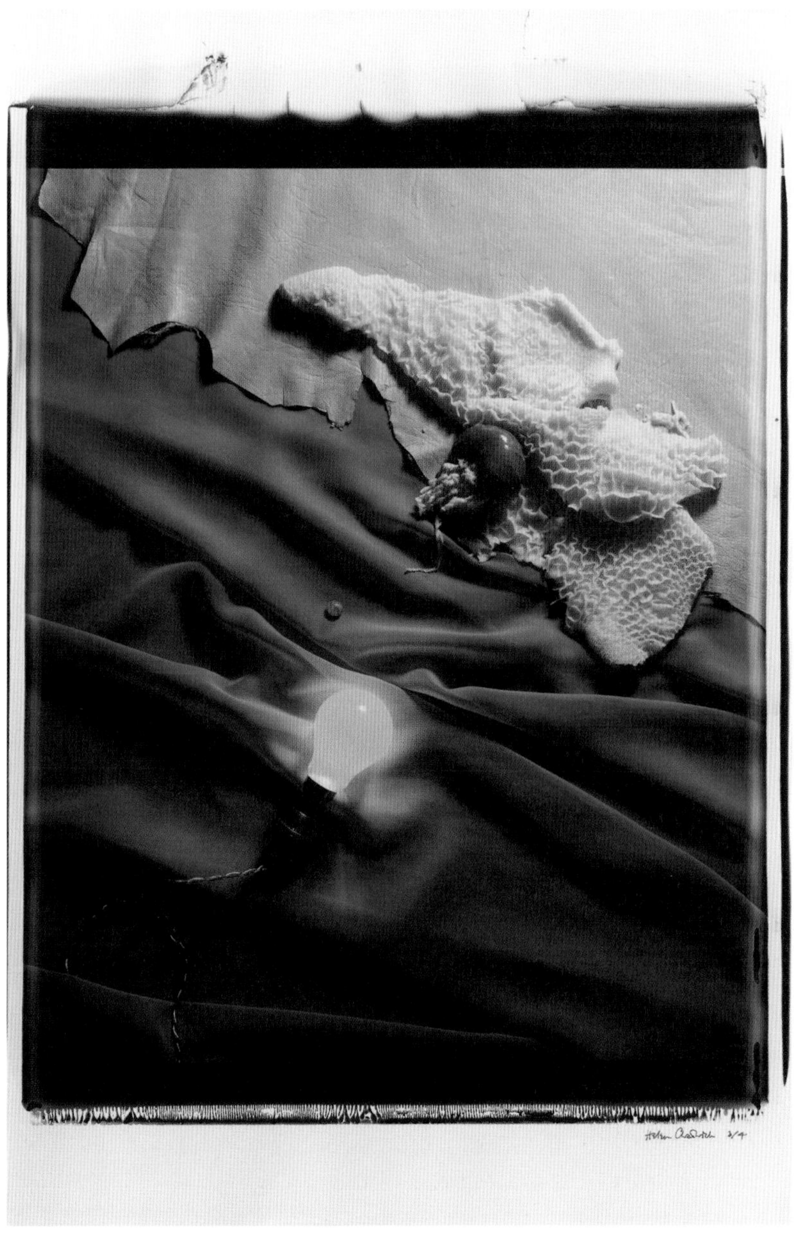

Helen Chadwick, *Meat Abstract #4*, 1989, colour polaroid print, 50.8 × 61 cm (P5761)

OPPOSITE AND ABOVE Bill Woodrow, *Point of Entry*, 1989, cardboard into bronze, 35.7 × 299.2 × 110.6 cm (P576)

As Rose recalled, 'The exhibition itself wasn't political, but the circumstances in which it was shown always were.'[56] Its destinations included Buenos Aires, where it marked the first time that the department had operated in Argentina since the British Council withdrew as a result of the war over the Malvinas, or Falkland Islands. Open ended enough to speak to a range of contexts without making explicit reference to any, art exhibitions may be perceived as an anodyne form of cultural relations, comprised of signs weak enough to be reinterpreted for a range of political ends. However, while the Council's exhibitions are designed to speak across borders, to last for long periods, and to adapt to the needs of specific sites, the works within them nonetheless often carry highly specific intentions and powerful messages.

A pertinent example is Bill Woodrow's *Point of Entry*. A fallen bronze form, suggestive of a person, spews out curling entrails as if from a bullet wound. The visceral message, in a cursive script, calls out 'Mum' and 'Dad' as a final haunting cry. Originally produced for a 1989 exhibition at the

Imperial War Museum, *Point of Entry* spoke eloquently of international conflict as it travelled worldwide as part of the British Council Collection, not least to Argentina. In Woodrow's explanation, 'There are at present wars or armed conflicts in the following countries: Afghanistan, Angola, Bangladesh, Burma, Cambodia, Chad, Colombia, East Timor, El Salvador, Ethiopia, Guatemala, India, Iran, Iraq, Israel, Lebanon, Morocco, Mozambique, Namibia, Nicaragua, Pakistan, Panama, Peru, Philippines, Somalia, South Africa, Soviet Union, Sri Lanka, Sudan, Turkey, United Kingdom.'[57] Many locations listed were exhibition sites. Such a work cannot be read apolitically; it is political in origin and in use. As it travels under a cultural relations remit, its message is enhanced rather than diluted.

A dual vision

During the 1980s, the British Council Collection was put under increased scrutiny. What did it cover and what was it missing? How could its effects be captured? Measures of its value, both monetary and otherwise, were examined ever more closely as public finances were limited and results were quantified. As a result, the decade saw a stronger articulation of what art was for in the British Council. Following a run of reviews, its art holdings were ultimately designated a nationally significant collection that would 'hold and maintain works for the nation' and would not be 'broken up for financial or other gain'.[58] Its status protects it from dissolution on the basis of changes in taste; it was understood that the long-term value of works, like the long-term effects of exhibitions, cannot be seen at close range.

Art continued its ambassadorial role in the 1980s, even when it showed a view of Britain that was rather different from tourists' perceptions or that communicated dispositions of despair. Shifting geopolitical contexts prompted cultural sanctions as well as new opportunities. A Foreign and Commonwealth Office freeze on operations with China as a result of the conflict in Tiananmen Square, for example, saw a dramatic last-minute change of direction for a planned portrait exhibition in 1989, just as doors were reopening with Russia and Argentina.[59]

By the end of the decade, the parameters of the department had been expanded – not least by the new engagement with photography – and a change of name was instituted in 1990. What became the Visual Arts department provided intellectual, diplomatic, and operational expertise as an exhibition broker, negotiator, and organizer for major loans, as well as for Collection activity. A snapshot from one year in the mid-1980s, for example, reveals seventy-one art exhibitions on display in forty-one countries.[60] By the end of the decade, the British Council Collection included more than 5,500 items in ever-more diverse formats. These demonstrated adaptability, flexibility, and reach. Judicious early investments extended their value for money, while long-term artistic friendships enabled further purchases, loans, and collaborations. The Collection's ability to perform a range of functions, responding to Foreign Office direction as well as operating separately from it, gave it a unique dual vision, offering establishment prestige and cultural critique.

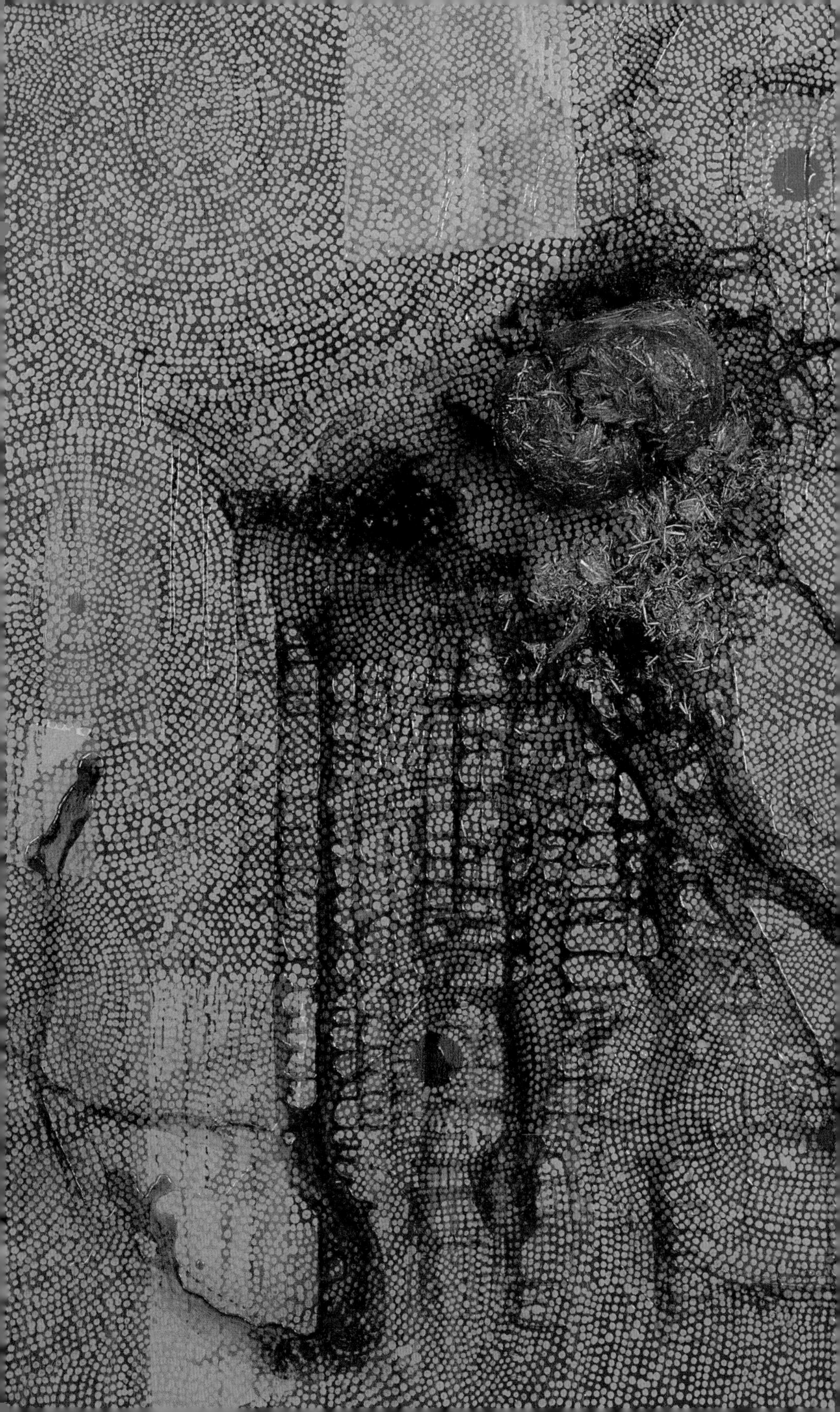

CHAPTER 6

A new generation

In 1995, art critic Richard Cork provided a snapshot of British art in the international context. 'Against all the odds,' he stated, 'British artists are now rejoicing in an extraordinary boom. Invitations to show their work arrive from all over Europe, America and beyond.'[1] While some of these opportunities were initiated outside the British Council, the Fine Arts department had played a key role in supporting, selecting, shipping to, and lending to many significant international exhibitions. This continued with the renamed Visual Arts department throughout the 1990s, in addition to leading on important displays and acquisitions of its own. With an emphasis on the new generation of Young British Artists, it presented art known for its irreverence during a period when cultural difference and national specificities played out in complex ways. As art historian Julian Stallabrass has observed, 'British art became more British throughout the 1990s.'[2] At the same time, however, the Council's exhibitions created the conditions to reflect on shifting understandings of multiculturalism and hybridity, on tradition and experimentation, and on the limits of nationalism in a globalized art world.

General Release: creating Young British Artists

In 1995, the Visual Arts department organized an exhibition in the Scuola di San Pasquale in Venice, on the centenary of the Venice Biennale. Designed to showcase emerging work, it brought together artists whose diverse character

Chris Ofili, *Painting with Shit On It*, 1993, acrylic and oil on canvas with elephant dung on linen, resting on two elephant dung supports, 182.5 x 122 cm (P6289) (detail)

Front cover of the catalogue for the exhibition *General Release*, held at the Scuola di San Pasquale, Venice, from June to October 1995, as part of that year's Venice Biennale

coalesced around age and place. Gregor Muir, author of the catalogue essay and a close colleague of many exhibitors, later stated that the shorthand 'YBA', which would endure as a title for the artists of this generation, was first coined for this show. 'YBA was not the result of the "Young British Artists" shows taking place at the Saatchi Gallery', he recalled; it was born of the British Council's Venice planning where 'the term referred to an all-encompassing phenomenon that included a number of different artists from a variety of backgrounds'.[3] 'YBA' would stick as a term, but the name of the exhibition went through several changes. The draft titles are instructive of the show's messages: there's a sense of foreboding in *Don't Look Now* (with its reference to the 1973 thriller film set in Venice of the same name); an association with upstarts in *Uninvited Guests*; an allusion to a cyborg generation in *Reared with Appliances*; and a promise of shock in the Italian *Vietato Ai Minori* (not suitable for children).[4] In grouping the artists under the final title, *General Release*, Andrea Rose, who had become the director of Visual Arts the year before, argued that their work shared a 'filmic quality', with disorientating images variously 're-played, re-iterated, spliced, edited and put onto a continuous loop'.[5] Such oblique perspectives came from fifteen artists, including Jake and Dinos Chapman, Fiona Banner, and Douglas Gordon, who would be bought for the Collection to supply the enormous international demand for the new generation of artists working in Britain.

Because of limited funds for acquisitions, the Council generally purchases works by artists at the beginning of their careers and rarely from those with established reputations. This financial necessity, combined with worldwide touring requirements, shaped its buying policies throughout the 1990s as it had done in previous decades. Large sculptures, outsize canvases, and installation works were rarely acquired for reasons of practicality, but such utilitarian criteria was seen to be limiting acquisitions in a period when art's parameters were expanding.[6] Art's new directions and forms informed the purchase of the Collection's first video piece in 1995. Glasgow-based Gordon's *10 MS^{-1}* reworked a fragment of a medical film from the First World War. A young male patient, physically fit and dressed only in underwear, appears to suffer the psychological effects of shell shock. On looped silvery footage,

Douglas Gordon, *10 MS^{-1}*, 1994, one-screen video installation, 10 min 48 sec (P6292)

Fiona Banner, *Top Gun*, 1994, bromide print, 19 × 55 cm (P6770)

silent and slowed down, in a technique previously deployed by the artist in *24-Hour Psycho*, his reinterpretation of Alfred Hitchcock's 1960 horror movie, the unnamed figure falls, contorts, and struggles to rise. Decontextualized and shown at cinematic scale, the subject is pitiful, and the film provides uncomfortable, compelling viewing. The work was shown alongside Banner's clinical transcription of the complete plot of the 1986 Hollywood military romance *Top Gun*, in dense, handwritten text across a vast canvas; Banner also produced a typed version of her work as a print. Each work is characterized by intensity and estrangement, and each pays close attention to the mediated cultures of war as seen on screen.

In *General Release*, artistic disorientations were styled as the product of social forces, primarily economic recession and political stagnation. The results – supplied through film, photography, drawing, painting, and sculpture – included flower arrangements in a bottle of urine (Cerith Wyn Evans), a bullet-holed blanket from a police firing range (Christine Borland), and a reconstruction of an etching from Francisco Goya's series *The Disasters of War* from 1810–20 using shop mannequins (Jake and Dinos Chapman). While many works in the show revealed shared interests across new technologies and popular culture, the abject and the everyday, the artists' age was the central pivot.

me are refuelling. There's an incredible noise as j
astically. 'Maverick and Goose!' In the sky a silver
urface of the sea is visible beneath them. Contact f
ougar, 'Cougar, I'm going head-to-head with him.' 'T
the target. Maverick fixes his missile lock on the
stuck to him. Cougar has him within range. He appea
gh and right and then completely inverts his aircraf
raft off, laughing and says 'gee, I crack myself up!
oblivious to them. Maverick's plane plane is coming
erly. His plane appears to be caught in some turbule
with me Coug. Hang on Cougar. You're all right ther
es fire, but he is not hurt. Below deck on the aircr
h other. Cougar turns to Maverick as he walks down
lose to Maverick and Goose, who stand bolt upright,
men, good luck.' They say in unison 'yes Sir!' Miri
naval aviators, the elite, the best of the best. We
nt Viper looks up and says 'In case your wondering w
n adds 'just remember when you're up there you're a
ou could get laid in a place like this, Goose.' Goos
rolled smile on his face. He doesn't look at all wo
children.' They look at each other and Maverick say
sn't. No she has not lost that loving feeling.' Mav
join in the singing. Finally they finish singing. Th
ou making it as a singer!' She walks off. Maverick
he leaves but as she re-enters the discotech she pa
a civilian so you do not salute her. Her call sign
s his eyes. He reaches for his dark glasses and put
g and looks over at Maverick and Goose who are whis
ant I have top secret clearance. The Pentagon sees t
was inverted.' Maverick says. Suddenly this seems a
ts 'communicating.' Maverick adds 'you know, keeping
he last to leave the classroom. As they walk down t
t weeks. Now I'm sure you can work that out Lieutena
u are flying against are faster, smarter and more m
faces are covered. Maverick says 'Goose, can you s
d. They lift again. It's as if they're flying in uni
directly towards a mountain range. Goose says 'watc
e says 'he's still there Mav. Come on Maverick, give
him at brake-neck speed, suddenly slams on his bra
t's like a roller coaster. Then they look left and s
the hard deck and return to base immediately!' Maver
he tower. It looks like he's going to clip it, but
and says 'Yeehaar, Jester's dead!' There is a gene
aren't you?' Maverick looks pissed off, he turns ro
e changing room. He crosses over to Maverick and Goo
r carrying a tray of tea. It spills all over his sh
eet. You knew it and you broke it. You followed Comm
to the window and continues speaking. 'Lieutenant Mi

Many were just a few years out of art school. According to James Roberts, writing in the catalogue, they were united in a 'wider generational consciousness'.[7]

The social conditions for this mood were mapped through a chronology provided in the catalogue that covered the previous five years of global politics, natural disasters, and domestic occurrences from the major to the minor. In 1990, for example, 'mad cow' disease was in the news along with the reaffirmation of Iran's death sentence for author Salman Rushdie. The Gulf War started in 1991, and in the following year an IRA bomb at the Baltic Exchange in the City of London left three dead and ninety-one injured. In 1993, Vaclav Havel became the first president of the Czech Republic, and the United Nations lifted economic sanctions against South Africa. These and other national and international news events were interspersed with domestic celebrity scandals and storylines from sport, pop music, and soap opera. In parallel, to suggest these events' interdependence with art, another chronology listed exhibitions by the Young British Artists, frequently in independent or non-art venues.

Venice exhibitions often form the basis for British Council Collection purchases, tours, and career-building, and *General Release* was no exception. All the artists had some exhibiting history, but few were well known beyond the art world at the time. The show thus provided a reputational boost and inspired future exhibitions. Most notable of these was *Brilliant! New Art from London*, held later in the same year at the Walker Art Center, Minneapolis, which reproduced aspects of *General Release*, including several of its artists. The exhibition was conceived by the Walker's American curator Richard Flood, while the Visual Arts department coordinated and funded the collection and shipping of works. It would play a major role in shaping how Young British Artists were understood in the United States.

Transatlantic culture clashes

Thirty years earlier, the Walker Art Center had hosted *London: The New Scene*. Described by American critics as the moment that 'the fog lifted on British art', the 1965 showcase, supported by the British Council, included the young Peter Blake, David Hockney, and Bridget Riley and was a key moment in the trans-

Tracey Emin, *I Came With the British Council*, 1992, paperboard and fabric, 7.7 × 6.6 × 0.2 cm

atlantic export of Swinging London.[8] Flood's 1995 show took *The New Scene* as its point of departure. Writing in the exhibition catalogue, critic Neville Wakefield noted that both generations of artists showing at the Walker used iconoclastic tactics. His catalogue essay – 'Pretty Vacancy' – drew another parallel, positioning the YBAs as neo-punks. In order to create a contrasting backdrop, he constructed an image of British art in destitution; its keepers were fuddy-duddies in flannels and boaters, and its products were endless figure studies and landscapes.[9] While hardly accurate, this characterization created a foil for the foul-mouthed incomers, obsessed with sex and death. Here were the revolutionaries storming the archaic institutions: *Épater les bourgeois!*

Brilliant! featured many artists centrally associated with the YBA grouping, from Damien Hirst and Rachel Whiteread to Tracey Emin. All had been recipients of British Council support, with works by Hirst and Whiteread purchased in the early 1990s. Emin received her first international funding through the Council's Grants for Artists scheme, for which she subsequently created a textile thank-you note, proclaiming '*I CAME WITH THE BRITISH COUNCIL*'. The promotion of the art and artists, however, was approached rather differently on different sides of the Atlantic and caused significant tensions.

The controversial front cover of the catalogue for the exhibition *Brilliant! New Art from London*, which opened at the Walker Art Center, Minneapolis, in October 1995 and then at the Contemporary Arts Museum, Houston, in February 1996

Flood assumed an artistic mentality of end times, which seems significantly overplayed in retrospect. 'It's hard to be content when you don't know that you're going to have a roof over your head, when issues of homelessness and early mortality confront you daily', he told *Minnesota Monthly*.[10] The perception prevailed that Britain was in existential as well as economic crisis, with the apocalypse almost at touching distance. Artists were characterized as living at the margins. The *Star Tribune* emphasized the scale of their struggle (or, rather, the scale of Flood's misunderstanding) by claiming, 'Several of these artists, mostly from the working classes, don't even have electricity in their lofts.'[11]

As critic Patricia Bickers observed of the view of British art abroad at this time: 'The English obsession with class is only matched by the obsession of the rest of the Europe and America with the English obsession with class.'[12] Not knowing how to be respectable, or not caring, was part of the package. Newspapers noted with glee that the artists in *General Release* had acted like drunken football fans in Venice.[13] In *Brilliant!*, the reliably provocative Chapman brothers stated, 'Our only export at the moment is hooliganism. The one thing that we're known for in Europe is football hooligans and that's something that's in us.'[14] In the mid-1980s, the British Council had viewed the export of culture as an antidote to negative images of the country prompted by continental football violence; a decade later the hooligans – or at least their mindset – had become the cultural product.[15]

Bickers observed 'appalling stereotypes' at the opening of *Brilliant!* Entertainment included a makeover room where guests could get a Margaret Thatcher hairdo and a photo booth that produced 'Your Face in the Tabloids'. British bobbies danced to jungle and The Beatles.[16] Clichés of stiff upper lips and teacups ran throughout reviews. The tone was reinforced by the catalogue, designed as a tabloid newspaper and printed on cheap newsprint, which shied away from serious analysis. It reflected the flippant, anti-intellectual tone of many of the artists. Rejecting art-historical language, moral certainty, and social responsibility was a deliberate ideological strategy. As a result, however, Young British Artists were sometimes perceived as uncritical, reinforcing chauvinist cultural stereotypes.[17]

The catalogue came in for public criticism because of its cover, which showed the devastation after the 1993 IRA bombing of Bishopsgate in the City of London, overlaid with a banner stating '*Brilliant!*' The lack of context – the photograph did not relate to any art on display – appeared to use the tragedy of terrorism as a superficial sales technique. This was certainly the attitude of the Visual Arts department back in London, which strongly criticized the choice of image. While Flood had directed the show and catalogue, the department's partnership role was credited in the first line. This led to accusations that the British Council was aestheticizing violence. Rose went to the press to separate the department from Flood's choices, on which they had not been consulted. 'England is quite a complex social structure', she stated. 'I think he's misunderstood it quite grotesquely. The whole package is a trivialisation that relies on outdated stereotypes.'[18]

Angry letters ensued between Rose and Flood. He defended his choices: 'The work in the exhibition is', he argued, 'soberingly nihilistic and obsessed with mortality. Even the most traditional-looking art in the exhibition is driven by end-game strategizing. I find these realities crucial to understanding the work and unique to its geography.' He continued: 'I know that you must have a somewhat kindred feeling as you included a social chronology running parallel to the art chronology in your *General Release* catalogue for the Venice Biennale. That social chronology was pretty relentless in its choice of unavoidably apocalyptic entries (Bishopsgate and Oklahoma City among them). The time we live in has everything to do with the art that the time produces.'[19]

Rose clarified that the image of another IRA bombing in *General Release* had been contextualized in social history and played a minor role, appearing at the back of the catalogue among twenty photographs in thumbnail size. In the run-up to *Brilliant!*, Flood had asked all exhibiting artists to send images that meant something to them. As Rose related, 'Mat Collishaw supplied this, together with several others, thinking Flood was producing a chronology similar to ours.'[20] Collishaw was dismayed that it had been used to represent the artists' art. Emin said none of them knew that the cover was to look as it did. She was personally appalled; the incident had been traumatic to those for whom the area was close to home. The nihilistic Chapman brothers, however, were predictably contrary. Jake noted, 'If anything unites the work it's that it's fractured, unreliable, irresponsible.' He continued, 'I thought the most interesting thing in the catalogue was the front cover. It seems hypocritical that the British Council should back essentially anarchic work, but as soon as that anarchism spills over into real life, to suddenly pull back.' As a final flourish, he added, 'Flood should plant a bomb in the British Council. You can quote me on that.'[21] Pushing at moral boundaries was as much a part of the artists' self-presentation as it was of their works.

James Hall of *Artforum* reflected that the dispute demonstrated 'the difficulties inherent in presenting much of the recent British art in a socio-cultural context'.[22] It was certainly commonplace to read the new generation as a product of political forces – almost all American reviews mentioned Thatcher

– but this positioning was then confused by the denial of social conscience by the artists. If they translated the social world, it was as a form of naturalism. As the *Star Tribune*'s correspondent put it, 'They aren't political. They present things as they see them, pure and simple.'[23] For some, the YBAs' irony made their work politically vacuous.[24] Many positioned the artists as oppositional rebels, yet what they were fighting for was unclear. Jeffrey Kastner wrote in *Art Monthly* that *Brilliant!* was a 'neo-apocalyptic free-for-all, with history and tradition as the enemy', with artists as 'vaguely bored guerrilla fighters ... skirmishing languorously in the cause of fuck-all'.[25]

Not all the work fitted into this category, however. Indeed, not all the work fitted in the Walker Art Center. Michael Landy's *Scrapheap Services* was part of the show but appeared off site at Soap Factory, a non-profit gallery in a nineteenth-century warehouse, the former home of the National Purity Soap Company. The location was fitting. Young British Artists had frequently created their own gallery spaces in former industrial sites; the work also imagined a fictitious company that hygienically disposed of unwanted people on an industrial scale. In the full installation, red uniformed mannequins with brooms appear alongside a shredder, dustcart, and bins, each bearing the corporate livery of a company that promises to 'rid society of its ills, so giving you a better quality of life'. In making 'a clean sweep' of 'people who no longer play a useful role', the mannequins process piles of human shapes cut from recycled product packaging.[26] In its factory setting, Landy's piece was convincing, offering a short imaginative leap from current cultures of disposability – those who fall outside employment and health-care structures – to a near future where inconvenient individuals could be conveniently destroyed in the pursuit of a more efficient, prosperous, and perfected world. As visitors walked through, they trampled cut-out people underfoot, becoming complicit in the process of disposal.

Landy's installation followed previous work by the artist that had considered value in consumer culture, including *Closing Down Sale* from 1991, which used the apparatus of retail clearance, from shopping trolleys to day-glo signs, to visualize the recession. It also preceded his best-known work, *Break Down* from 2001, where he systematically destroyed all his possessions in

a former department store on London's Oxford Street. The British Council owns items from each of these works, including a drawn post-mortem of *Break Down*'s conveyor belt of destruction, and refuse sacks of bagged 'people' from *Scrapheap Services*. The latter was included in *Dimensions Variable: New Works for the British Council Collection*, an exhibition that toured Croatia, Czech Republic, Finland, Germany, Hungary, Lithuania, Poland, Romania, Slovakia, Sweden, and Ukraine between 1997 and 1999.

Dimensions Variable: new forms and identities

Dimensions Variable launched around the same time as the seminal exhibition *Sensation*, which opened at the Royal Academy of Arts in London in September 1997 and showcased Charles Saatchi's collection of Young British Art. It was thus the moment that the YBAs achieved both public notoriety and institutional legitimation. By this time, the British Council had established a significant Young British Art collection of its own. The title of the show was used to

ABOVE Michael Landy, *We Love the Jobs You Hate*, 1995,
plastic refuse sack filled with metal cut-outs, 24 × 18 × 18 cm (P6366)

OPPOSITE Michael Landy, *Still from the video 'Scrapheap Services'*, 1995,
colour photograph, 40 × 50 cm (P6600A)

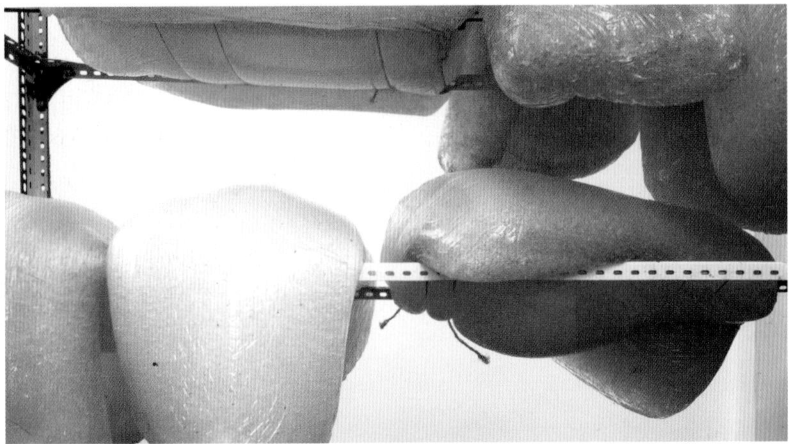

Vong Phaophanit, *Untitled*, 1995–6, painted steel, string, and industrial rubber, 154 × 27 × 230 cm (P6683)

communicate the shifting forms that such work took, embodied in a sculpture by Vong Phaophanit, where drooping rubber forms slowly descended through a framework of metal struts, shape shifting as they went. 'No photographs, no set of dimensions, no documentation can capture the work in its entirety', noted Rose, 'since its entirety only exists during the process of evolution.' *Dimensions Variable* also conveyed a nebulous mood, composed of 'the constantly shifting perspectives that new information, new technologies and new circumstances make evident'.[27]

These encapsulations by Rose were deliberately as broad as the work was diverse. Ann Gallagher, the show's curator, clarified the rationale: 'Young British artists have received a great deal of attention in the past three or four years and they have often been perceived as a coherent national grouping.' Yet, she continued, 'in grouping these works no new school or "ism" is being suggested nor is there any implication that this is a definitive picture'. As she observed, the range of new work 'is beyond the bounds of one exhibition or the limited purchasing resources of the British Council to represent it fully'.

Under the auspices of the British Council, the national identity of the individuals in the exhibition was inevitably a cause for reflection, yet this was not straightforward; the artists 'have a great deal in common with artists of their generation in many other countries'. Gallagher considered the complexity. 'All of the artists can be said to be British or live in Britain,' she noted, 'but a Britain made up of an admixture of cultures, influencing both individual subject matter and methodology.'[28]

What it meant to be a British artist in the 1990s was subject to recalibration. The British Council's representation had always been flexible, including artists who are resident in Britain but born elsewhere. There was no formal requirement to hold citizenship; Bombay-born but London-trained Anish Kapoor, for example, represented Britain at Venice Biennale in 1990, without the need of a British passport. There was increasing recognition – as summarized by Cork – that national artistic parochialism was over. At least, this was the aspiration. 'A significant number of foreign artists,' as Cork described them, 'including Vong Phaophanit, Michael Raedecker, Tomoko Takahashi and Wolfgang Tillmans, decided to make England their home after graduating from art school.' He continued:

> The British scene has long been energised by artists who, having grown up elsewhere in the world, settle in London and stay there. Lucian Freud, Frank Auerbach, Paula Rego, Susan Hiller, Gilbert Proesch, Mona Hatoum, Anish Kapoor and Shirazeh Houshiary are among the most notable of older emigrés, and art in London is now unimaginable without them.[29]

The crude characterization of 'foreign artists' and 'British artists' implies a delineation that was impossible to sustain in practice; nor, indeed, was it desirable. Multicultural Britain – within and beyond the art world – was increasingly a matter of pride, including in the broader work of the British Council where the celebration of Britain's cultural diversity became an objective, as was the ambition to 'challenge outmoded stereotypes of the UK abroad'.[30] It was no coincidence that these ambitions aligned closely with those of other official endeavours. Tony Blair, elected as Labour prime minister in May 1997, enthusiastically associated himself with a renewal in British youth culture that became known as 'Cool Britannia'. In the same year, political analyst Mark Leonard's influential book *Britain TM*, published by the independent think tank Demos, advocated refreshing national identity around creative and youth-orientated viewpoints. It explicitly promoted Britain as 'a hybrid nation'. The book aimed to adopt corporate branding to project a new sense of Britishness to secure an economic premium. While this agenda was separate from that of cultural relations, Leonard argued that the British Council should join forces with the Foreign and Commonwealth Office, the Department of Trade and Industry, and the British Tourist Authority to advance this shared vision.[31] Independent of these approaches, although sometimes in parallel with them, Council support for Young British Artists offered an opportunity to reflect on cultural character, on belonging and borders, and indeed, on multiculturalism as a policy object. The coexistence in the British art world of 'regressive neo-nationalism and multicultural normalisation', as cultural-studies scholar Kobena Mercer put it, could thus be explored and challenged.[32]

Pictura Britannica: postcolonial views

The most focused site for this engagement was the exhibition *Pictura Britannica: Art from Britain*, organized for Australia and New Zealand in 1997. Designed with the Museum of Contemporary Art in Sydney, the show was delivered as part of the NEWImages Festival, which aimed at producing 'perceptional change' between the United Kingdom and Australasia.[33] In Leonard's summary, Britain was seen by Antipodeans through a similar set of images to those held by Americans: 'croquet, teatime, Robin Hood, tweed, castles, Henry VIII, thatched cottages, stormy seas, Charles Dickens' London, pretty gardens, jaded aristocracy, James Bond, Beefeaters, Shakespeare and Eton'. To this was added dirt, darkness, and overcrowding.[34] In reverse, it transpired that British contributors to *Pictura Britannica* struggled to name any Australian contemporary artists.[35] The exhibition aimed to break down frontiers and upend clichés.

Front cover of the catalogue for the exhibition *Pictura Britannica*, which toured Australia and New Zealand from August 1997 to April 1998

British Council Australia had wanted 'Cool Britannia' in the exhibition's subtitle, but the curators would not have it.[36] The exhibition aimed to provide a corrective to platitudes; its heavyweight catalogue was the polar opposite of that produced for *Brilliant!*

In his 1999 demolition of Young British Art as 'a fast food version of the less digestible art that preceded it', Stallabrass stated that its stock-in-trade – British pop culture, seaside resorts, references to domestic television, and slang – seemed to speak to its own kind. He argued, 'all are matters that, if not entirely opaque to a foreign audience, are not likely to have for them quite the full effect'.[37] He also noted that international exports 'create a specifically British subject matter', that is, 'a distinct product that marks a readily consumable Britishness on the global scene'.[38] Both assertions can be tested through *Pictura Britannica*, which was less to sell a product than to start a dialogue; British subject matter also had a particular resonance in cultures with a shared European colonial legacy.

Take, for example, Mark Wallinger's video installation *Royal Ascot*. Four monitors, mounted on wheeled flight cases, show BBC coverage of members of the royal family waving from horse-drawn carriages at the annual Ascot horse-racing event in 1994. The fawning praise of the commentators and the highly choreographed performance show the absurdity of the rituals. The wheels mimic the royal means of transport, while the flight cases position the monarchy as a global export commodity. *Royal Ascot* could be seen as a nostalgic celebration – its message is deliberately ambiguous – but in the context of Wallinger's wider work, where he uses, for example, traditions of equine portraiture to highlight social Darwinist ideas of 'breeding' – more critical forces are at play. In shipping a work to Commonwealth countries, where the Queen functioned as a figurehead under Australia and New Zealand's constitutional monarchies, the royal family's ceremonial function and political purpose became an object of scrutiny from a dual perspective.

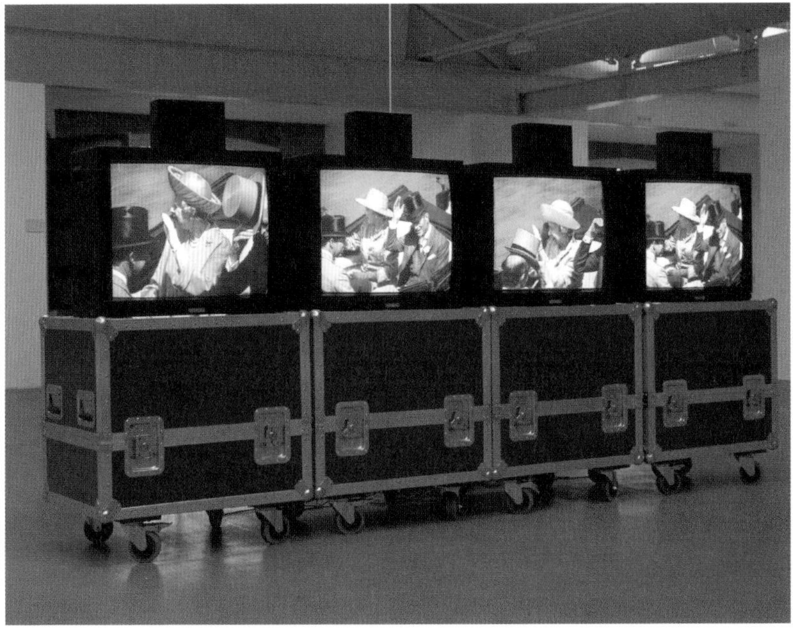

Mark Walllinger, *Royal Ascot*, 1994, video installation on four monitors with flight cases (P6682)

Maud Sulter, *Duval et Dumas*, 1993, C-type print, 76.2 x 101.6 cm (P6291/A)

Very little of the art in *Pictura Britannica* tackled national identity through conventional icons; Union Jacks and Big Ben appear rarely. As with all exhibitions under a national title, however, the contents were framed by cultural identity, and this was engaged with in relation to postcolonial studies. Bernice Murphy, chief curator of the Museum of Contemporary Art, Sydney, made the opening salvo: 'Most artists, understandably, abhor nationalism.' Nonetheless, she noted, it would be disingenuous 'to deny all reference to structures through which nations engage with each other culturally, and through which many international projects are directly funded'. More engagement is needed than the substitution of 'the international' and 'commonly shared values'. If national identity is 'too presumptuous, too narrow and too reductive', she argued, claims of universality are also too easy. New art coming from Britain 'is speaking in many contexts, and in voices from cultural backgrounds that have not gained utterance previously', she observed. These artists 'probe old closures and open fresh ground on which to build new vocabularies of representation'.[39]

Maud Sulter, *Duval et Dumas*, 1993, C-type print, 76.2 × 101.6 cm (P6291/B)

In this category Murphy included Maud Sulter, who engaged with occluded histories and reinterpreted historic systems of vision, providing new presentations of figures of African descent through historical photography. The diptych *Duval et Dumas* demonstrates her techniques in photomontage, splicing famous portraits with found imagery, including topographical postcards. With strategies borrowed from Surrealism, the methods are simple, but the messages are unsettling; they place stereotypes of Africa alongside European landscapes associated with racial purity to create new fictions cut from disrupted pasts. In the above image, Nadar's nineteeth-century photographic portrait of an unknown sitter is imagined to be Jeanne Duval, Charles Baudelaire's Haitian-born mistress and muse to the poet. This so-called 'black Venus' smiles through African masks and Alpine pastoral scenes. The novelist Alexandre Dumas, whose grandmother was a plantation slave, also sat for Nadar. At Sulter's hands, his image is intercut with an elephant and a snow-topped mountain; the geographical and cultural conjunctions compress space and time and disturb cultural certainty. The *Syrcas* series, of which this diptych is a part, looks imaginatively at black representation in European history, and specifically at its erasures. Sulter, born in Glasgow in 1960 of Scots and Ghanaian descent, was the British representative to the first 1995 Johannesburg Biennale, which took *Decolonising our Minds* as its theme and marked the opening up of South Africa to international arts activity after years of isolation and boycotts.

In the *Pictura Britannica* exhibition catalogue, Kobena Mercer reflected on political black British art of the 1980s and reviewed his perspective through new exemplars in the 1990s. He asked: 'How does the Britishness in British art ... relate to the beautiful chaos of the post-colonial convulsions?' For Mercer, black artists were moving away from fixed identity towards the recognition that, 'the necessary fictions we call our identities are constantly being altered and detoured by the unfinished stories of interculturation'.[40] These challenges provided a rich ground to explore people and place, and cultural identities in motion and migration. Perhaps the Young British Artist who engaged most mercilessly with these themes in the 1990s was Chris Ofili. Through beautiful yet controversial painted canvases rich with colour and detail, offset with embellishments and mounted on balls of elephant dung, Ofili confronts expectations about art and self. As he stated, 'I'm black and it's a very important part of what I am. I try to bring all that I am to my work and all that I experience. That includes how people react to the way I am – the prejudice and the celebrations.' He has noted that his art is double-coded; it is 'a criticism of the absurdity of making work about identity, but in some ways it *is* about identity, to the point of overload'.[41]

Ofili's biography famously includes a 1992 British Council-funded artistic residency to Zimbabwe, which he credits with fundamentally shifting his practice, not least in exposing him to dung as a medium. This trip has become a core part of how his work is contextualized, but Manchester-born Ofili subverts readings that try to apply a politics of origin to his interests.

Chris Ofili, *Painting with Shit On It*, 1993, acrylic and oil on canvas with elephant dung on linen, resting on two elephant dung supports, 182.5 × 122 cm (P6289)

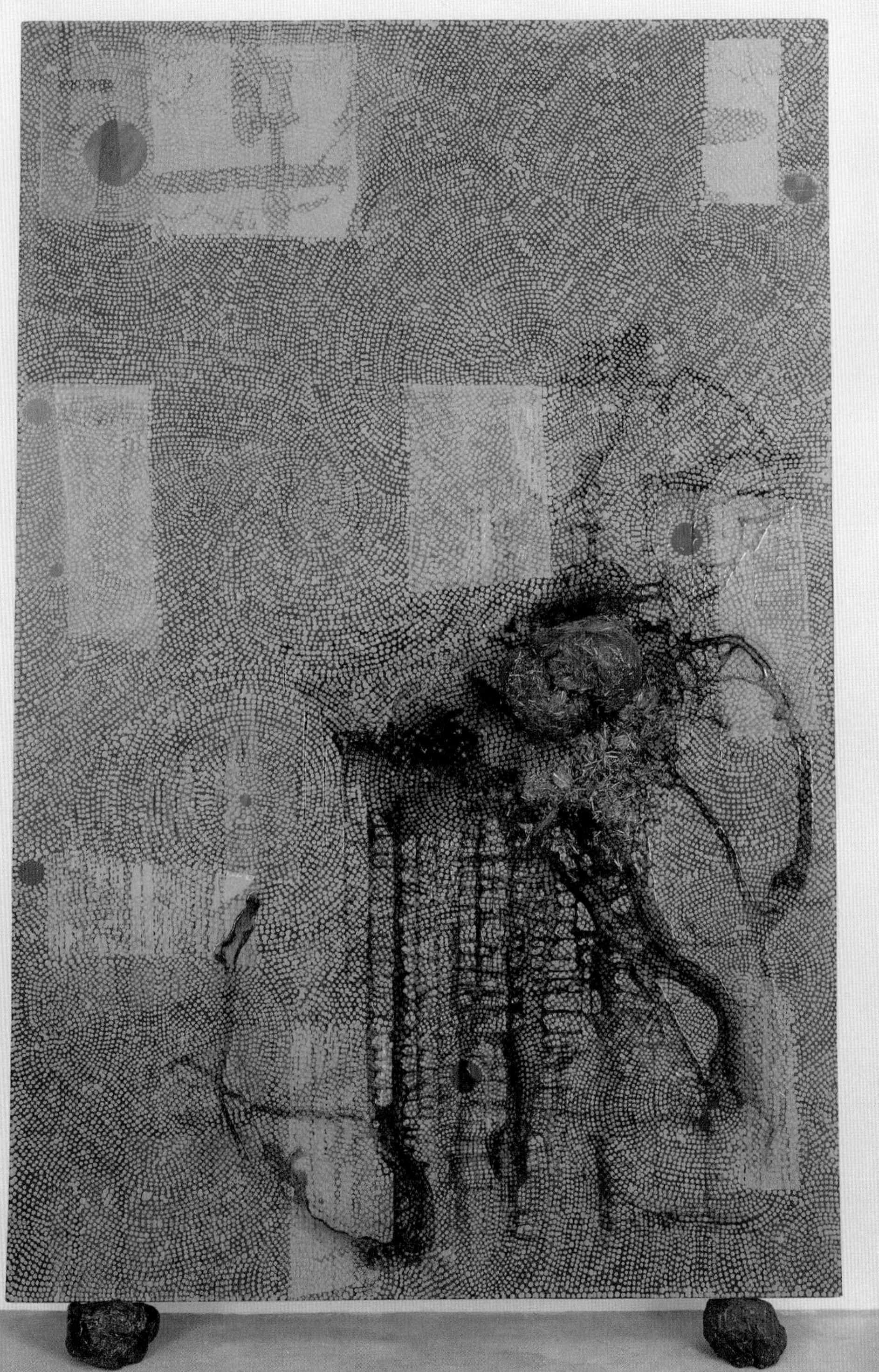

His work engages with white stereotypes about black artists, including assumptions that they tap into something essentially 'ethnic', such as expectations that there is some complex cosmology in his canvases. As such, his art combines the sacred and the profane, the sexual and the scatological, the beautiful and the base. As he put it, 'It's what people really want from black artists. We're the voodoo king, the voodoo queen, the witch doctor, the drug dealer, the *magicien de la terre*. The exotic, the decorative.'[42] In the British Council Collection, Ofili's *Painting with Shit on It* combines gorgeousness and outrage in geometric oranges and blues overlaid with earthy-brown splatters. The canvas rests provocatively on spheres of elephant shit, sourced from London Zoo.

Ofili's works have courted controversy; their combination of excrement and Christian iconography, for example, has led to public outcry, and his paintings have been defaced while on display. When Visual Arts planned to send some of the canvases to Australia, they were met with a further challenge, not in terms of their aesthetic message, but as a result of their material make-up. While the elephant dung was safely encased in polyester resin, the Australian government would not grant permission for the works to enter the country without assurances that the turds were fit to be imported. 'Faeces', a representative from the Museum of Contemporary Art in Sydney noted, 'is the only material that I have come up against that Quarantine "totally prohibits".'

The blockage over the excrement illustrates well some of the problems that can occur in the overseas shipment of art in unconventional formats, as careful but comical diplomatic discussions ensued between curators, customs officials, zookeepers, and the Australian Ministry of Food and Fisheries. The museum clarified the problem: 'These works of art cannot be imported into Australia unless we can provide written confirmation that the dung was from a UK-kept zoo elephant and what the animal/s have been fed on.' Might it be possible to find out if the elephants who supplied the materials 'are fit and healthy and only eat mashed veggies'? Clarrie Rudrum, the British Council exhibition organizer, wrote to London Zoo to ask, 'Whether you would be so kind as to provide me with a statement as to the medical history of your three elephants, "Gilberta", "Liang Liang", and "Mia", along with confirmation as to their diet. As a matter of great urgency, I would be very grateful if you could assist with this matter to ensure that this important exhibition of British art manages to travel intact.'[43] The outcome was happy: the London pachyderms were healthy, and the art was made mobile. The range of materials collected by the Visual Arts department in the 1990s pushed at boundaries in multiple ways.

A Changed World: transforming expectations

Logistical complexities marked another exhibition featuring Young British Art in 1997. Visual Arts organized a major exhibition for Pakistan, based entirely on works from the British Council Collection, in an event that raised specific challenges, including displaying art outside galleries and accommodating different aesthetic viewpoints in sensitive circumstances. That year marked the fiftieth anniversary of the partition of India and Pakistan, and the British Council staged exhibitions in both countries. For Karachi and Lahore, in order to 'forge links with the Pakistani artistic community' and to 'offer new ideas about creating art to younger and emerging artists',[44] it proposed 'a blue chip, sophisticated exhibition with all the big names'.[45]

The first challenge was to find appropriate locations. Exhibitions at this time were usually held at museums, galleries, and arts centres, or sometimes on British Council premises. Loan exhibitions needed to meet international display standards, including climate-controlled conditions and light levels, which had become more formalized by the 1990s. While the Visual Arts department always takes the highest level of care in the display and security of its exhibits, the purpose of the Collection is to travel widely, including 'to areas of the world where optimum environmental conditions cannot be guaranteed'.[46]

A Changed World is a good exemplar of how works from the Collection can be repurposed over time for a range of sites and needs. Initially formed as *40 Years of British Sculpture*, showing plinth-based works and drawings by British sculptors dating from 1939 to 1980, the exhibition travelled between 1981 and 1994 across Botswana, Canada, Cyprus, Egypt, Estonia, Greece, Jordan, Latvia, Lithuania, New Zealand, Philippines, Slovenia, South Africa, Turkey, Ukraine, Yugoslavia, and Zimbabwe. It included works by Henry Moore, Bernard

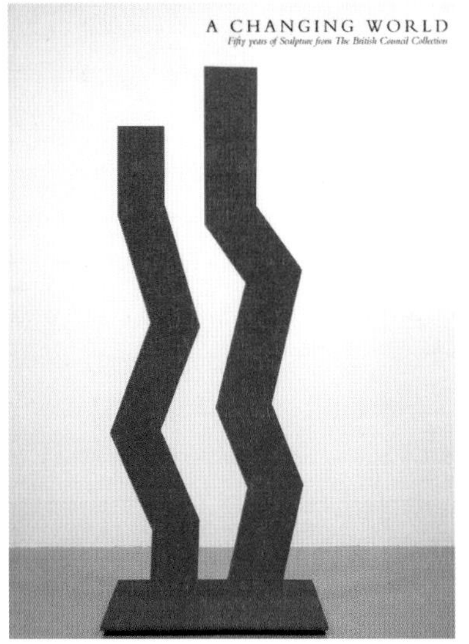

Front covers of the catalogues for the exhibitions *A Changing World*, 1994–6, and *A Changed World*, which opened in Pakistan in 1997

Meadows, Barbara Hepworth, Lynn Chadwick, Anthony Caro, and William Turnbull, among others. The show was then reformulated with updated content to mark the Queen's state visit to Russia in October 1994 and given a new name: *A Changing World: Fifty Years of Sculpture from the British Council Collection*. This expanded version now also included sculptures by Reg Butler, Eduardo Paolozzi, and Denis Mitchell alongside works by more recent practitioners such as Tony Cragg, Shirazeh Houshiary, Anish Kapoor, Richard Long, David Nash, Alison Wilding, and Bill Woodrow. It was shown first in St Petersburg and then Moscow, before heading to venues in the Czech Republic, Morocco, and Germany, where it concluded its tour in 1996 after almost two years. When planning a new version of the exhibition for Pakistan, the Visual Arts department nicknamed the project *A Changed World* and the title stuck. The third iteration focused mainly on floor-based works by British sculptors from 1965, and featured younger artists such as Damien Hirst, Douglas Gordon, Rachel Whiteread, and David Shrigley.

This was not the first time that the department's exhibitions had toured Pakistan. *Contemporary Artists' Lithographs*, assembled from the British Council Collection in 1948, travelled to seventeen sites over four continents on its thirteen-year tour, calling at Lahore in 1960. A Moore show of bronzes and prints, circulated worldwide from the mid-1950s to early 1980s, went to Peshawar in 1970. The 1997 exhibition was an undertaking of a different order, however, not least because of scale. The forty-nine works in the exhibition needed a thousand square metres of display space, and the weight of some of the sculptures required forklifts. Most Pakistan galleries were too small or had load-bearing issues. Because the exhibition was comprised entirely of the British Council's own works, other sites could be pursued.

Sheesh Mahal, also known as the Old Fort, in Lahore, and the Hindu Gymkhana in Karachi each offered large display spaces in distinctive settings. The Gymkhana was a historic building originally constructed as a cricket pavilion; it offered large white rooms, side galleries, walled gardens, and a decorative architecture of marble, minarets, and arched windows, but no air

The exterior of the Old Fort in Lahore, the location for the first iteration of *A Changed World*

Inside the vaulted galleries of the Old Fort, with Tony Cragg's *Canoe* on the floor

conditioning or lighting. Lahore's Old Fort offered similar opportunities and obstructions; a seventeenth-century building, it featured a large lower-ground-floor space with high arched ceilings. The setting was spectacular, with remnants of frescos, but it was plain enough to allow contemporary sculpture to make its statement. With no electricity and no drilling allowed, the exhibitions required enormous ingenuity to mount, including false walls, generators, and a creative lighting design provided by a local theatre workshop. Bureaucracy also added further complexity, not least that all import documents in Pakistan had to be signed by the minister for protocol or his deputy. As these officials travelled with the prime minister, when he was abroad, all trading ceased.[47]

British Council Collection policy of the 1990s reiterated that efforts should be made 'to minimise risks and to select exhibitions appropriate to local conditions'.[48] Mutuality is a core working method, and as such representatives from the Visual Arts department worked alongside Pakistani curators to take guidance on exhibits, although this coexisted with an ambition to stretch 'what has previously been considered acceptable and open up minds to new ideas'.[49] Pakistani partners pointed out 'the sculptures should be in accordance to the rules of the government i.e. nothing religiously objectionable can be displayed'.[50] The relationship between sensitivity and criticality is a consideration in any location; satirical works with Christian themes in *Pictura Britannica* had, for example, led to religious objections in New Zealand.[51] In Pakistan, these principles were enshrined in law, which meant that one new British Council Collection purchase, Mona Hatoum's *Prayer Mat*, comprising upturned brass pins in the form of a bed of nails around a central compass to locate Mecca, could not be included. Instead, works included Richard Deacon's outsize spinning tops wrapped in linoleum (*Boys and Girls Come out to Play*) and Tony Cragg's carefully arranged and colour-coded plastic detritus (*Canoe*). Sculpture by younger artists included Whiteread's imposing architectural plaster cast, *False Door*, and a sinister cage of toxic waste containers by Hirst, cryptically entitled *I'll Love You Forever*.

Tony Cragg, *Canoe*, 1982, mixed media (23 green pieces and 24 red pieces), dimensions variable (P4278)

Richard Deacon, *Boys and Girls (Come Out to Play)*, 1982, lino and plywood, 91.5 × 183 × 152.2 cm (P4276)

Mona Hatoum, *Prayer Mat*, 1995, nickel-plated brass pins, compass, canvas, and glue, 67 × 112 × 1.5 cm (P6468)

ABOVE Damien Hirst, *I'll Love You Forever*, 1994, painted steel, medical waste containers, gas mask, and padlock, 121.9 × 121.9 × 76.2 cm (P6401)

OPPOSITE Rachel Whiteread, *False Door*, 1990, plaster, 101.8 × 30.3 × 23.2 cm (P5919)

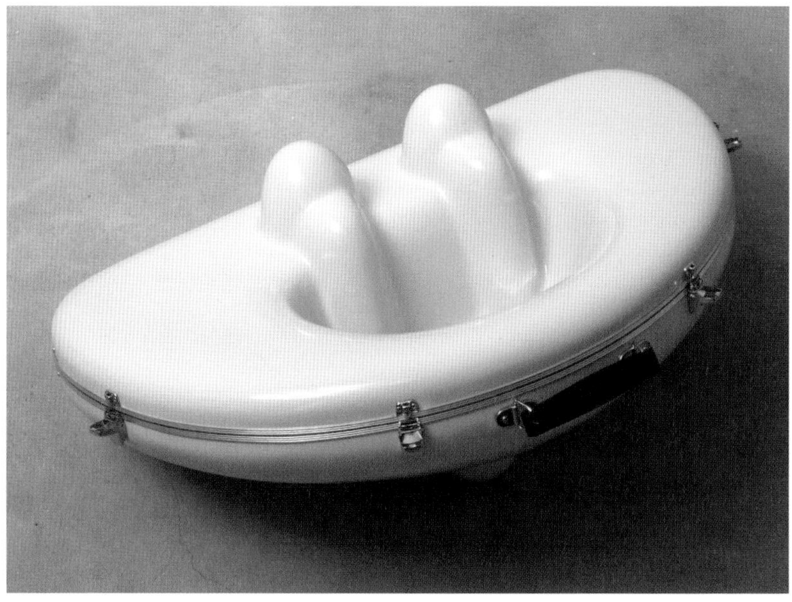

ABOVE AND OPPOSITE Hadrian Pigott, *Cadillac (Pink)*, 1996, upholstered fibreglass case, velvet, wash basin, 89 × 82 × 60 cm (P6681)

Hadrian Pigott, a Young British Artist just four years out of the Royal College of Art, was represented by a recently purchased work. His *Cadillac (Pink)* is a polished, pastel-pink, custom-built carrycase that snaps open to reveal, like a strange pearl in a shell, a puce-velvet interior containing a white washbasin, taps, soap, and plumbing fixtures. This impossible object, rich in sensual textures and surreal juxtapositions, suggests privacy and luxury, but also fetishism and fastidiousness. Displayed alongside concrete books and tin-can sculptures, its contradictions suited the exhibition dynamics. The works were both 'national treasures' – as described in press reports – and modest in manufacture.[52] Kitchen-sink realism met conceptual gesture in *A Changed World*, and contemporary forms were displayed in ancient settings. News articles made much of the exhibition's oppositions, in the dramatic differences between Mughal and postmodern styles, but also between the bullock carts that endured on the streets of Lahore and the sense of futurity in the artefacts on display inside.[53] The changing uses of the fort were also noted. Sheesh Mahal had been a torture cell for political prisoners under General Muhammad Zia-ul-Haq, the president of Pakistan from 1977 to 1988. Dr Iftikhar Elahi of the British Council Lahore stated, 'The Ministry of Culture has decided to convert all such notorious places into art galleries.' The transformation promised in the exhibition's title played out in its location.

Reviews noted the exhibition's potential shock factor, and the catalogue stated, 'It may not be to everyone's taste.'[54] Sculpture had, in fact, been chosen for Pakistan for strategic reasons. Rose noted, 'We are confident from

discussions with the local art constituency that an exhibition of sculpture, as opposed to work in any other medium, will stimulate a good deal of interest in a country where sculpture is still rarely practised and widely misunderstood.'[55] Peter Elborn, director of British Council Pakistan, explained that the country was 'just emerging from a long period when any activity in the arts was, at best, frowned upon, and frequently prohibited. The political climate has now changed and it is possible to do things which even three years ago ... would not have been possible.' The issue with sculpture was 'sensitivity towards Koranic laws and cultural attitudes towards representations of the human figure'.[56] The fact that few of the artists in the exhibition worked figuratively made the conceptual work on show permissible, if not always comprehensible.

While Elborn observed that sculpture suffered from the unfavourable political climate, he also noted that it was taught in 'a quiet, modest training programme' at the National College of Arts. Students from the college were trained as assistants and technicians for *A Changed World*. Meanwhile, Pigott was invited on a guest residency at the school. His subsequent report shows the value of bringing practitioners into cultural exchange; as a first-time visitor to Pakistan, his changed perspectives show how international dialogue can prompt self-questioning on both sides. Pigott was impressed by the expectations made of the exhibition by its visitors. The comments book contained many examples of its warm welcome, but there were also objections. 'The main criticism stemmed from Islamic condemnation of idolatry', he explained. 'I was assured by one journalist that this art work was dead, empty and meaningless in that society and culture, and questioned why this exhibition was here at all, and why I was there to defend it.'[57]

The exhibition challenged assumptions about what art was for, including for Pigott, who was struck by his comparative creative freedoms. Even in the relatively liberal context of the National College of Arts, where men and women mixed freely and the veil was optional, a hierarchy of art forms prevailed: 'Miniature painting is celebrated, painting in general accepted and

Anish Kapoor, *Void*, 1994, fibreglass and pigment, 110 cm diameter (P6528)

sculpture barely tolerated.' Sculptural expression followed a figurative tradition, problematic in the strict political climate. As Pigott saw it, 'Students are not able to work from the life model and so the work is entirely derivative, taken from pictures in books. Then once outside the tolerant confines of the college there is virtually no forum for figurative sculpture – no galleries will show it in the face of fundamentalist disapproval.'[58] This placed sculptors in an impossible position.

Contemporary artists in Britain, Pigott felt, 'take for granted the "expanded field" of sculpture, covering objects, photography, video, film, text, installation, performance'; they also took art's conceptual base as a given. He suggested, in Pakistan, 'If the sculptural form and content were to shift and change to encompass a diversity of materials and ideas then artists might find themselves under less pressure, and more free to express themselves. ... I am the last person to suggest that "West is Best",' he added, 'but it might be the freedoms available to contemporary artists in the West might allow artists in Pakistan to make work which would sidestep the censor's pen (or stick).' Metaphoric visual language, if adapted to local contexts, could enable the communication of a greater variety of concerns and ideas. The results might seem strange, he suggested, but they 'may not be seen as offensive or illegal'.[59] Pigott suggested further teaching and artistic exchanges.

The artist's reflections reiterate the importance of cultural dialogue rather than monologue. This is the promise of cultural relations, in opposition to cultural imperialism. From 1977 until 2001, the British Council co-sponsored (along with the Arts Council of Great Britain, the Crafts Council, and the Foreign and Commonwealth Office) the organization Visiting Arts, which facilitates incoming arts to Britain, ensuring cultural traffic flows both ways. 'Every creative or performing artist's standards, morale and career benefit from exposure in other countries', the British Council explained. 'It must be to Britain's benefit that its cultural life should be enriched by being made aware of other people's ideas, aspirations and achievements.'[60] In 1990, Visiting Arts supported more than 250 events at 465 venues.[61] In 1997, this included training, grants, bilateral exhibitions, and festivals.[62] *A Changed World* thus represents one example from a wide range of activities. At a moment of political flexibility in Pakistan and artistic flowering in Britain, it illuminates how the British Council Collection opens up new sites for exhibition, expands aesthetic horizons, and changes minds, including those of Young British Artists.

Productive provocations

Julian Stallabrass argued that Young British Artists of the 1990s sat ill with expectations that art could serve a social role. Their work, he claimed, was useless for this task; it was amoral and illiberal.[63] Critic and artist Matthew Collings made a related observation. Supported by Visual Arts to lecture in Latvia as part of British art events in 2001, he reflected on Young British Art in a cultural relations context: 'It was like a bizarre version of the old days when the British Council used to send Henry Moore sculptures to Europe after the Second World War.' Work sent overseas now, he observed, was not art 'that stands for peace and humanity, or for Man being in a good relationship with Nature, but for a kind of nutty, amusing, swimming, giddy feeling'.[64]

For all its black humour and interest in sex and swearing, Young British Art has been extremely productive for cultural relations, especially among young people. Art that attracts attention provokes dialogue. The work may not take a political stance – and in the case of the YBAs, it may take a deliberately apolitical position – but it is nonetheless born of particular social conditions. Young British Art's impudence captured the consciousness of the 1990s; it stimulated reflection about national clichés in the United States; it shifted perceptions in Australasia; it challenged tradition and encouraged experimentation in Pakistan. Since Moore, artists have come to be seen to be a nation's best ambassadors, yet latterly they have also operated as antagonists, provocateurs, and even self-styled cultural hooligans. Bombastic and iconoclastic, new art of the 1990s was as likely to provide rupture as reassurance. Logistically and conceptually complex, the variable dimensions, purposes, and consequences of Young British Art were mobile in meaning as well as in location.

CHAPTER 7

Art for a dangerous world

Early in the new millennium, following the attacks of 11 September 2001, the British Council announced a major reorientation and prioritized its funding to support cultural relations with the 'Islamic world'.[1] The Council had long had productive engagement with Arab countries, so this new focus was a continuation and enhancement, as well as an intensification, of existing practice. In a post-9/11 context, some of its activities would become increasingly sensitive, especially commissions of art works that examined individual or collective identities, and exhibitions in parts of the world previously hostile to a British presence. The organization's ambitions in the first decade of the twenty-first century, framed under the heading of *Arts for a Dangerous World*, tested the role of visual art in some of the most delicate of political situations, and in areas where the restoration of trust and the shifting of perceptions would prove to be a challenge. Over the same period, the structure and purpose of the arts within the British Council itself was reframed, with significant impact on how the Visual Arts department operated. Together, these changes cast a fresh spotlight on the department's activity, raising its public profile and resulting in a tighter remit for what a state-funded art collection could do for cultural diplomacy.

Anya Gallaccio, *Preserve Beauty (New York)*, 1991, red gerbera, glass, fittings, 247 × 130.8 × 6 cm (P7871) (detail of work after several weeks)

Finding common ground

Following 9/11, 'the need to address the gulf of understanding between communities in the UK and in the Arab and Muslim worlds' became the British Council's primary objective.[2] The organization's chair, Baroness Helena Kennedy, stated that there was 'lots of talk about the unfillable rift between Islam and the West'. She observed, 'All of us who know about the power of dialogue know that this is completely misconceived.'[3] The arts were understood to be an important and effective means of engagement, and initiatives worth more than £18 million were conceived for strategic locations. Under the title *Arts for a Dangerous World*, these projects initially focused on ten countries: Bangladesh, Egypt, Indonesia, Iran, Malaysia, Nigeria, Pakistan, the Palestinian territories, Saudi Arabia, and Turkey. In 2002, research conducted by the Foreign Policy Centre think tank among five thousand young people from these countries revealed what they called 'a push–pull dynamic at work in [them]: a desire to emulate the success and prosperity of the West but with a counter-current of antipathy towards its political agenda'.[4] In Baroness Kennedy's view, arts events, free from politics, would keep dialogue open.[5] Accordingly, the Visual Arts department organized major events in the 2000s, beginning with a photography exhibition, *Common Ground: Aspects of Contemporary British Muslim Experience* in 2003.

The purpose of *Common Ground*, whose planning long preceded the events of 9/11, was 'to explore the range and diversity of British Muslims' experience of life in the UK'. It was felt that there was too little existing material within the Collection from which to draw, so eight new bodies of work were commissioned. For the exhibition's curator, Sean Williams, two factors shaped the commissioning. Firstly, it was important that not all work should present solely 'positive aspects' of British Muslims' lives. Artists, it was observed, were uniquely able to offer this critical perspective as they, 'by their nature suggest in their work the complexities and ambiguities of human experience'.[6] Secondly, curators from countries hosting the exhibition were to be closely involved in the selection. Mutuality was required to ensure that sensitivities were handled appropriately, but also to create meaningful links with the places where the show was to travel, including the generation of new work in those locations.

Front cover of the catalogue for the exhibition *Common Ground*, which toured from July 2003 to December 2007

The eight commissions featured photographic explorations of the varied architecture of British mosques (by Rehan Jamil); celebratory portraits of Muslim dancers and musical performers (by the duo Amyandtanveer); and archival studio portraits of postwar immigrants in Bradford. Two series, by Suki Dhanda and Anthony Lam, were subsequently gifted to the British Council Collection by the artists.

Dhanda produced a study of teenage girls in the Whitechapel Muslim Youth Group in east London, working in particular with one fourteen-year-old subject, Shopna. Dhanda was interested in the role of clothing in the youngsters' lives, especially in relation to public discourses about the hijab, which were associated with orthodoxy and conservatism by non-Muslims and contrasted sharply with how young Muslim women, full of agency, independence, and confidence, felt about it. Shopna wore her hijab 'with attitude', combined with jeans and Nike sneakers; it was as much part of her daily existence as her tastes in music and make-up.[7] The head covering communicated cultural respect and personal identity. It also made her 'feel safe as a young girl living in a rough part of town'.[8]

Suki Dhanda,
Untitled, 2002,
C-type print mounted
on aluminium,
125 x 125 cm (P8160)

Suki Dhanda,
Untitled, 2002,
C-type print mounted
on aluminium,
125 x 125 cm (P8161)

Suki Dhanda,
Untitled, 2002,
C-type print mounted on aluminium,
125 × 125 cm (P8509)

To understand Shopna's world, Dhanda went where she went. The resulting large-scale portraits on aluminium offer an eloquent photo story of ordinary teenage experience in a globalized world. The girls drink Pepsi and eat burgers in fast-food restaurants; they cue up shots at the pool table in the youth club. The photographs aimed to show the normality of Muslim life. 'It is important to recognise that modern British Muslim girls have similar reference points and interests to any other British teenagers and are keen to expand their horizons beyond traditional social constrictions', Dhanda noted in the exhibition catalogue. 'This does not in any way undermine their devotion and loyalty to Islamic religious and cultural values.'[9] Dhanda also took photographs of Shopna at home, without her hijab, in a range of more contemplative moods. In one image, the young teenager gazes out of her bedroom window, her face suffused with natural light in a composition reminiscent of a seventeenth-century Vermeer oil painting. Shopna's profile is framed in a triangle, with her face and hair softly concealed under the net curtain's veil.

Anthony Lam, *Port of Call: Reintegration Assistance*, 2002, archival giclée print on rag paper, 60.9 × 83.8 cm (P8219)

Anthony Lam's 2002 photographic series *Port of Call* examines the psychology of borders, as perceived by asylum seekers, based on his experiences working with young male Bosnian and Somali Muslim refugees. The landscapes depicted in *Port of Call* are the locations around British detention centres and resettlement camps. Each is labelled with a phrase extracted from the bureaucratic language of the government's 2002 White Paper *Secure Borders, Safe Haven: Integration with Diversity in Modern Britain.*[10] Landscapes that might indicate openness and space are juxtaposed with terms of intervention and control. Rural and sea views suggest edges and limits. Closed shutters and smashed phone boxes show the difficulty of engaging in conversation. Phrases and places seem sinister and dehumanized.

'Reintegration assistance' in the official document relates to Home Office structures for those who fall under the category of 'voluntary assisted returns', that is, asylum seekers who wish to go home, as the report puts it.

Anthony Lam, *Port of Call: Further Representations*, 2002, archival giclée print on rag paper, 60.9 × 83.8 cm (P8223)

In Lam's treatment, *Reintegration Assistance* shows a bleak grey sky over the unrelenting body of water that must be crossed in order to leave. 'Further representations' relates to the additional levels of application required for asylum to be granted. In the government document, these relate to the 'statutory detention powers' and 'regimes' of 'reception centres'. In Lam's vision, *Further Representations* looms over a landscape marked by danger notices and warning signs, embodying the immigration policies that would later come to be known as the hostile environment.

Common Ground showed at three sites in Indonesia in 2003, before travelling to Bangladesh, Malaysia, Bahrain, United Arab Emirates, Saudi Arabia, Russia, and Germany. It was an invitation to dialogue, illustrated by the fact that the catalogue took the form of a set of loose leaflets that could be shuffled, added to, and subtracted from by its host curators to alter sequences and hierarchies. The displays were designed to be hung flexibly to emphasize different messages to suit each location. The exhibition was characterized by a diversity of textures, tones, and perspectives, and it necessarily had different resonances in different locations, indicating that there is no singular 'Muslim experience'. As it travelled, local artists – for example, in Jakarta and Riyadh – contributed further perspectives on what it meant to be Muslim.

In the latter city, the exhibition made a particular mark. As critic Judith Bumpus reported, six months of negotiation had been required to convince Saudi ministries 'that there was no hidden agenda beyond a desire for cross-cultural bridge-building'. Religious authorities censored two images containing crosses, but the rest was left to stand.[11] Saudi artist Manal Al-Dowayan exhibited in Riyadh, showing work from her two series *Look Beyond the Veil* and *The Choice*. Her prints, in lush silver-gelatin finishes, show, for example, a woman's henna-painted hand pushing a voting slip into a ballot box or slung across a steering wheel. This subject matter was provocative in Saudi Arabia at a time when free choices for women elsewhere were denied by law.

Saudi Arabia had rarely been in receipt of international contemporary art exhibitions, due to its aniconist traditions that make taboo the representation of bodies, and not least female bodies. According to journalist Arifa Akbar, *Common Ground* was 'the first significant collection to be imported from the West in more than three decades'. She stated that the impact of the exhibition could not be overestimated.[12] Reports show that it was received with eager curiosity, even though it presented significant challenges in form and content. At the all-female private view, Pola Uddin, Baroness Uddin, the first British Muslim woman to enter the House of Lords, encouraged Saudi women to keep pushing the boundaries of what was possible. A separate men's view, the following evening, was opened jointly by Prince Saud al-Faisal, the Saudi foreign minister, and Jack Straw, his British counterpart, who was in Riyadh for bilateral talks. Iyad Madani, the Saudi minister of culture and information, announced that Saudi Arabia was opening up; the cultural exchange of international ideas between international photographers embodied this new openness.

From a British Council perspective, it provided opportunities to learn. As Andrea Rose stated, 'this is an area of the world that we know very little

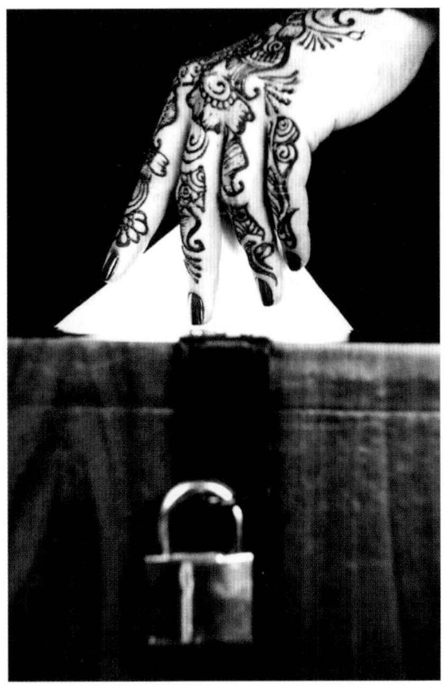

RIGHT Manal Al-Dowayan, *The Choice VI*, 2005

BELOW Manal Al-Dowayan, *The Choice 1*, 2005

about, apart from the stereotypes portrayed in the media'. She emphasized: 'Going to those countries encourages a more nuanced view.' *Common Ground*'s varied content also encouraged a different understanding of Britain. 'The fact that we could show reflective work', Rose noted, 'commanded respect, and showed that one positive aspect of being British is the ability to be self-critical. The exhibition was received much more readily as a true portrait of Britain as a result, not simply propaganda.'[13] German cultural-studies scholar Eva Ulrike Pirker also observed that the exhibition shed light on Britain: 'Not only Muslim identities are portrayed in *Common Ground* but also a nation in its process of finding an identity.' It underscored the nation as a construct 'made of fragmentary notions'. This is a significant difference from universalizing humanist messages of sameness; the 'common ground' acknowledges multiplicities of identity. At a time of what she described as rapidly rising Islamophobia, Pirker concluded that *Common Ground* provided a 'counter-weight to balance more simplistic, often damaging, representational practices'.[14]

How the exhibition was understood in Britain was also telling. Martin Davidson, chief executive of the British Council at the time, was challenged by parliamentarians about *Common Ground*; they were not happy about the 'less than rosy picture of Britain touring the world'. As with some earlier examples of exhibitions, artists critiqued government policy even as they were supported, in part, by government funds. Davidson was emphatic that the critical space was fundamentally necessary. 'The freedom to be self-critical, to uphold different views, and to underline our belief in the diversity – even perversity – of the individual voice ... are fundamental to the values of an open society. And such values are integral to the arts.'[15] Davidson was also confronted by one British exhibition-goer, who asked, 'Why on earth we were sending this show to what he called "repressive regimes in the Gulf".' Davidson felt that person-to-person dialogue is the bedrock of cultural relations; individual artistic voices could speak directly to people in a way that went beyond government-to-government discourse. While the British Council undertakes both forms of dialogue, exhibitions operated differently. 'Artistic engagement', he argued, 'provides an unmediated channel to individuals. It allows the individual to frame and often reframe their world view.'[16] *Common Ground* thus enabled a restatement of the British Council's aims in cultural relations: autonomy was essential for its credibility; exhibitions provide a forum for subjective viewpoints; individual conversations can challenge authoritarian messages.

Davidson entitled his observations to members of parliament as 'constructive engagement'. In using this title, he was adapting a foreign-policy term that refers to how one government might communicate with others that it does not support in every respect, but with which it wishes to have a dialogue. As such, 'constructive' (and 'creative') engagement offered a model for the British Council's work with Iran as relations between the two countries opened up in the early 2000s. British foreign policy towards Iran at the time was 'to support the reform process, while maintaining a robust dialogue on issues of concern. These issues include human rights, Iran's pursuit of a nuclear weapons programme, Iran's alleged support for terrorism and for groups seeking to undermine the Middle East Peace Process.' From a British government perspective, 'critical engagement enables us to put forward our views and concerns regularly and at all levels'.[17] In 1998, Iran lifted the fatwa on author Salman Rushdie, marking a shift in relations led by the liberalizing President Mohammad Khatami, a former culture minister who had taken power a year earlier. The following year, the United Kingdom and Iran exchanged ambassadors. In 2001, the British Council opened its first office in Iran since the revolution of 1979. Constructive engagement in cultural relations stood outside politics, but with visual arts in Iran, politics were never very far away.

British art in Tehran

With the easing of UK–Iran tensions, the Council's representative in Tehran began building connections. One was with Dr Ali Reza Sami-Azar, director of the Tehran Museum of Contemporary Art (TMoCA). Young, energetic, and educated in Birmingham, Sami-Azar was determined to develop artistic exchanges at his institution – the country's principal site for contemporary art – and was highly knowledgeable about British art. His personal passion was landscape photographs, so his first request was for an exhibition of Richard Long. Rose recalled,

Ali Reza Sami-Azar, director of the Tehran Museum of Contemporary Art from 1999 to 2005

'This was where the Collection came into its own; we could cover this.' She asked, 'When do you want it?' Sami-Azar said, 'In three weeks' time.' Unwilling to pass up the opportunity to work with a country with whom cultural relations had been closed for more than two decades, Rose said, 'Sure.'

With sixty-five per cent of the British Council Collection on loan at the time, however, Long works were committed elsewhere. Instead, Rose used the Visual Arts department's extensive connections to persuade artist Andy Goldsworthy's dealer to supply twenty-five photographs of his natural sculptures to be shown at TMoCA in an exhibition of contemporary European photography organized in cooperation with the European Union embassies in Tehran. As a result of the short notice, they arrived two days after the exhibition opening in June 2002, but, nonetheless, it represented the first showing of Western art in Iran since the thaw in relations. The gesture of willing marked the beginning of more ambitious projects between the two organizations. There were Moore sculptures on the museum's lawn, formerly owned by Mohammad Reza Pahlavi, the Iranian Shah, but left behind when he had to flee the country in the revolution. This prompted Sami-Azar to suggest British sculpture as a theme. As Rose put it, 'This seemed like a perfect place to start. Those sculptures had witnessed everything that had happened since that period.'[18]

Opened in 1977, TMoCA is a striking site of enormous cultural and political significance. Its cream stone and concrete cylinders and skylights surround a curving atrium inspired by the New York Guggenheim. It holds an exceptional art collection combining Iranian work with the largest collection of modern European and North American art outside those continents. As Iranian art critic Hamid Keshmirshekan notes, one of the state's cultural goals when led by the Shah between 1941 and 1979 was 'to fit into the currents of the Euro-American artistic scene'.[19] Queen Farah Diba-Pahlavi, the Shah's wife, was a collector of avant-garde art and TMoCA's patron. Her cousin, Kamran Diba, was the museum's architect and its first director.[20] Working with international advisors, together they built a world-class collection befitting the spectacular site.

Iran's art scene was marked by a flurry of activity in the 1960s and 1970s, with the establishment of new galleries, festivals, and international exchanges, but the moment did not last. As Iranian curator Rose Issa put it, 'Just when the country's privileged circles began to think that Iran was developing with some panache, the social turmoil that ended with the victory of the Islamic

Tehran Museum of Contemporary Art, with bronzes by Henry Moore on the lawn

Queen Farah Diba-Pahlavi and Andy Warhol in front of the artist's silkscreen portraits of her during a reception at the Waldorf Astoria Hotel, New York, July 1977

Revolution in 1979 brought artistic activity to a standstill. Most universities and galleries had to close, or reduce their activities to a minimum for at least a decade.'[21] Queen Farah was accused of being 'intoxicated' with the West, and she and her husband were forced to flee the country during the revolution, which brought regime change, a wholesale rejection of non-Islamic culture, and a reorganization of political structures around strict religious rules.[22] The revolution had enormous implications for art in Iran, including TMoCA, which had opened only months before the uprisings.

Art was subject to much stricter rules, as Issa has documented: 'Across every art form women's hair and male and female nudity were totally banned, and sculptures of human or animal form discouraged.' Many art collections were confiscated.[23] The TMoCA collection remained mostly intact, but a portrait of Queen Farah by Andy Warhol was symbolically slashed.[24] Revolutionary art, including 'large propaganda paintings, posters and murals commemorating the Islamic Revolution and revolutionary struggles', filled exhibition spaces instead.[25] The 1980–9 Iran–Iraq War ensued, resulting in a million deaths; together these events stifled contemporary art's former energy. As Issa notes,

The front cover of the catalogue for the exhibition *Turning Points*

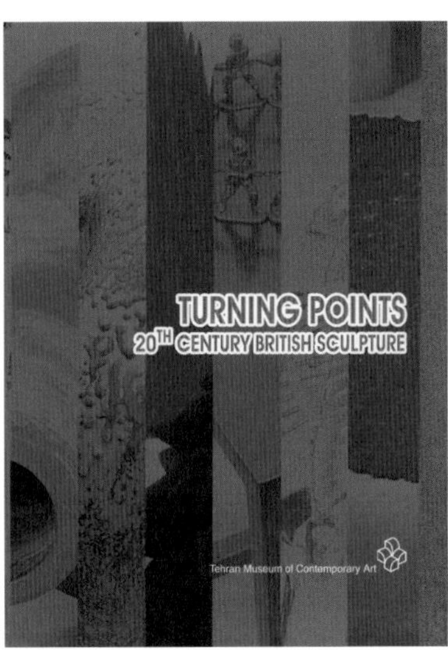

some ingenious youth circumvented 'the heavy hand of censorship', but it was not until the 1997 victory of the liberal wing of the Islamic Republic that greater freedom of expression arose, still within the confines of conservatism.[26]

Turning Points: opportunities and sensitivities

It was under Iran's cautious liberalization that TMoCA became the site for an exhibition of twentieth-century British sculpture named *Turning Points*. Co-sponsored by the Iranian Ministry of Culture, the exhibition could, the British Council believed, communicate 'the values of a tolerant and open society' by 'using the abstract and universal language of art'. It provided 'one way of elegantly side-stepping some of the most difficult problems in Iran today: how to talk openly about cultural difference in a monolithic religious state'.[27] Negotiations began in 2002, but were derailed by the Allied invasion of Iraq in 2003, which disrupted the Council's work more broadly, not least in the Middle East, where thirty-four offices had to close.[28] Communications with Iran continued, but museums became concerned about lending under such conditions. Works would have had to fly over battlefields to get to Iran and lenders were worried that the aeroplanes would be shot down.[29] Here the British Council Collection showed its versatility; it was built to travel where no other collections could go. Rose used it centrally in the show, but also wanted a wider range of contributors to ensure that the show was not perceived as purely diplomatic. *Turning Points* thus included loans from Arts Council England, the Henry Moore Foundation, and Tate, as well as artists and dealers. It was important that the exhibition displayed artistic quality and was good enough to stand up to scrutiny in Paris or New York. Care was taken to assemble a major statement.

Turning Points used TMoCA's collection as a point of departure. In response to the Moore sculptures outside, further works by the artist were to be provided. A key problem arose, however. Some of the finest works in the Collection, such as *Girl with Clasped Hands* (see page 84), depicted a naked female body. Even the semi-abstracted breasts of *Reclining Figure* (see page 83) were not considered suitable. Sami-Azar's personal tastes were adventurous, but he was aware that presenting religiously objectionable material would risk closing the project down. Abstract sculptural works were loaned instead. But there was also the issue that the meanings of artistic works shift according to their context.

Mona Hatoum's *Prayer Mat* (see page 263) was a potential contribution from the British Council Collection, but with its intersection of Muslim worship and pain – the carpet is constructed from thousands of steel dressmaking pins

Mona Hatoum, *Deep Throat*, 1996, table, chair, television, glass plate, fork, knife, water glass, laser disc, laser disc player, 89 x 85 x 130 cm

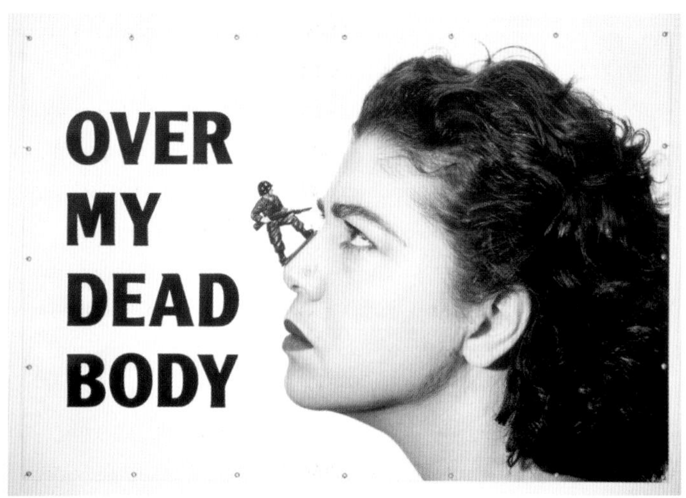

Mona Hatoum, *Over My Dead Body*, 1988–2002, inkjet on PVC, 3050 x 2050 cm (P7872)

– local advisors felt that it might be interpreted 'as a British sponsored satire on Iranian sensitivities'.[30] Other works by Hatoum, whose sculptural speciality is to make strange domestic objects through sinister strategies, included a wheelchair whose handles were ferocious serrated knife blades, and a pair of crutches incongruously made of flaccid rubber, giving the appearance of supports that have failed when most needed. While these had been constructed in different places with different intentions, it was noted by Iranian colleagues that they could insult those injured in the Iran–Iraq conflict, which was considered to be a Holy War; those who participated were considered heroes and martyrs. Alternative works were found from Hatoum; these were no less challenging.

Deep Throat, for example, showed an endoscopic video of the artist's digestive system, projected onto a dinner plate on a table laid for a meal. This visceral work provides a stomach-turning self-portrait. Its disconcerting content and its title, referencing a sexual act, did not offend, however; the exterior of the artist's body was not shown. Much of Hatoum's work is concerned with dislocation, and her biography is shaped by war. As a child of Palestinian parents, born and brought up in Lebanon, Hatoum has stated that displacement ran through her early life. This came to the fore when war broke out in Lebanon while she was on a trip to London in her early twenties and she was unable to return. The enforced circumstances led to her enrolling in art school in Britain and consequently developing a career in the British art world; much of her output reflects on exile, estrangement, and oppression, although often in elliptical ways. A major work from the British Council Collection depicts the artist in profile, staring down a toy soldier advancing – gun in hand – up the bridge of her nose. Printed onto a PVC banner at billboard scale, the work declared 'Over My Dead Body' as a direct statement of anti-war feeling in *Turning Points*, making a provocative pacifist gesture in the middle of the Iraq War then being led by the United States and the United Kingdom.

Gilbert & George were a part of the TMoCA collection; their sixteen-panel picture *Mental No. 6* from 1976 shows them in a series of isolated postures in juxtaposition with images of London streets, around a central blossoming tree viewed through a saturated and oppressive red filter. The Visual Arts department had long supported the artists, with works from the 1970s onwards bought for the British Council Collection, but providing state-funded endorsement for artists keen to cultivate controversy had also formed a point of debate. When the British Council co-organized the artists' 2001 exhibition in Greece and Portugal, George claimed, 'Every time we do a show in a foreign city, the British ambassador is suddenly called away at the last moment. Either his mother is ill, or this time it was an emergency in Crete.' With titles of pictures such as *Bent Shit Cunt* and *Black Jesus*, the artists saw embarrassing those in authority as a necessity and a badge of honour, claiming that they 'will never compromise' and will never become 'establishment'.[31] *Mental No. 6* is one of the artists' more palatable pieces, excluding the monumental turds, curses, cocks, and arses that are the pair's iconography in other works. Its inclusion challenged what could be considered sculpture, but not public taste.

Sami-Azar was keen to include Damien Hirst. The artist offered a new work, *Resurrection*, which showed his recent interest in Christian themes. It was a coup to secure this major new sculpture, but the subject matter caused concern to the Visual Arts department. Would it be too challenging in a strict

Gilbert & George, *Mental No. 6*, 1976, 247 × 206 cm.
Tehran Museum of Contemporary Art

RIGHT Damien Hirst, *Steak and Kidney – The Last Supper*, 1999, silkscreen on paper, 153 × 101.5 cm (P7217)

OPPOSITE Visitors to the *Turning Points* exhibition look at Damien Hirst's *Resurrection*, 1998–2003, glass, paint and human skeleton, 213.4 × 213.4 × 213.4 cm

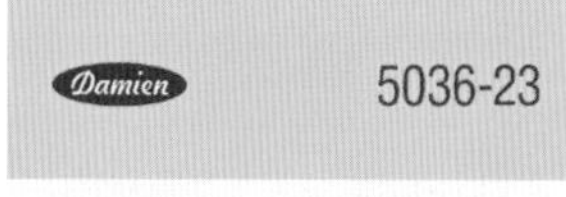

Islamic setting? Comprised of a human skeleton suspended on cruciform glass panels, this work included human remains and made explicit religious references. Sami-Azar was adamant that it would not carry any negative connotation. Iranian experts observed that crucifixion was not exclusive to Christianity.[32] Art historian Sabiha Al Khemir also pointed out that, 'resurrection itself is not a problem for Muslims, who believe in life after death'.[33] In installation, *Resurrection* was surrounded by thirteen further works by Hirst from the British Council Collection. Entitled *The Last Supper*, the satirical screenprints present meals – many traditional to Britain, from steak and kidney pie to chips and beans – in the style of medicine packaging. Combining Hirst's interests in pharmaceuticals with an irreverent approach to transcendence, the embodiments of Christ's disciples offered a fitting foil for the skeleton, positioned at the entrance of the museum. Sami-Azar acknowledged that its location was 'provocative'; it was displayed close to, but screened off from, the permanent portraits of Ayatollah Khomeini and Ayatollah Khamenei, guardians of Islamic virtue. Nonetheless, it did not 'cross the red line'. He stated: 'Artists should be allowed to express their own opinions. As long as it doesn't offend against religious sensibilities or display explicit eroticism, then it can be shown.'[34]

The department was particularly keen to include the work of Shirazeh Houshiary. The Iranian-born sculptor trained in London in the 1970s and came of age in the 1980s as one of the generation of New British Sculptors, which included Richard Deacon, Tony Cragg, Anish Kapoor, and Bill Woodrow, each of whom are well represented in the British Council Collection. Houshiary's works combine the formal language of minimalism with references to Sufi poetry, sacred geometry, and calligraphy. Examples in the Collection include an abstract copper sculpture, *The Pen and the Ant*, which travelled extensively in the exhibitions *A Changing World* and *A Changed World*. As the Iranian curator and scholar Fereshteh Daftari has put it, of Houshiary and diaspora artists who combine Islamic and non-Islamic visual forms, they refuse to represent their cultures within a Western framework and 'shun homogenization into a purely Western aesthetic language'. Instead, they 'speak in a multivocal polyphony marked with a mixture of accents'.[35]

Objections and risks

Houshiary's major contribution to British sculpture and her British-Iranian status made her important to *Turning Points*, but the artist had second thoughts. She wrote to Rose expressing concerns informed by her passionate political beliefs about Iran and about the importance of human rights, democracy, and freedom of speech. Like Barbara Hepworth in relation to Portugal in the 1960s, she wanted to withdraw her work and she urged the British Council to boycott the country and the exhibition.[36] Rose, however, felt that the show should go ahead despite the difficult conditions, and the pair had further correspondence. Houshiary wanted to hear from someone with current knowledge of the Tehran art scene and consulted Daftari as an Iranian curator based overseas but who returned home each year. Daftari's perspective was that 'the situation is not black and white. Unfortunately in Iran art has never been free of governmental interference.' However, she noted that Iran had also been cut off culturally: 'How can you be part of the world when the doors are closed?' In her opinion,

Turning Points could thus be an important development. It could be 'of special significance not only because it is a project carried out by professionals but especially because the inclusion of people like Mona Hatoum, Anish Kapoor and Shirazeh Houshiary who complicate essentialist notions of nationality while at the same time offering perspectives relevant and useful to the Iranian public'. She felt that the exhibition could be a powerful opportunity for exchange, but cautioned that great care should be taken that it was not hijacked by political forces, whether those of sender or receiver, where it might risk becoming 'no more than a political feather in someone's cap'. Her principal concern was with 'young Iranians who are hungry as a sponge. ... They are intelligent. They deserve to be treated as such.'[37] Following these discussions, Houshiary decided to participate, contributing a work that had personal and spiritual resonance. Her four-channel video and sound work *Breath* showed a rhythmic misting of four screens marked by the exhalation of vocalists chanting prayers from Buddhism, Christianity, Sufism, and Judaism. Houshiary is interested in breath as a metaphor for presence and as an embodiment of form and formlessness: it can capture an essence, 'transcending name, nationality, cultures'.[38]

Shirazeh Houshiary, *Breath*, 2003 (remastered in 2012/13), four-channel video, nineteen-inch HD screens. Museum of Modern Art, New York

Boundaries and limits

After two years of sensitive negotiations and political disruptions to UK–Iran relations, *Turning Points* opened at TMoCA in February 2004 with sixty-one works by fifteen of Britain's most celebrated sculptors. The opening, which was attended by thirteen hundred guests, came four days after controversial national elections in which conservative Islamists took power. The complexity of the exhibition's organization made its realization all the sweeter. Bill Woodrow and Richard Deacon gave artist talks; Stephen Deuchar and Tim Marlow – at the time, directors of Tate Britain and White Cube, respectively – gave lectures on art history. Michael Muller, long-time assistant to Henry Moore, provided conservation training using the museum's neglected sculptures by the artist; and Mary Moore presented the museum with an etching by her father. The bilingual catalogue – bookended with the dedication 'In the Name of God' – drew parallels between the messages of the works and the wider political turning point. Sculptors were seen to embody a search for renewal and reinvention, a willingness to experiment with different ideas and materials, and 'the acceptance and assimilation of new thoughts from cultures outside the mainstream Christian west'. Rose stated in a short text, 'Not conforming is one of the prevailing themes.'[39] Elsewhere she wrote that 'change and the

LEFT Anya Gallaccio's *Red on Green*, 1992–3, at the opening of the *Turning Points* exhibition

OPPOSITE Anya Gallaccio, *Preserve Beauty (New York)*, 1991, red gerbera, glass, fittings, 247 × 130.8 × 6 cm (P7871)

process of change is embodied in works in the exhibition'.[40] This was particularly the case with the ten thousand red roses that carpeted the floor of the museum for *Red on Green* by Anya Gallaccio. Gallaccio's monumental sculptural works in ice, salt, burning candles, and cut blooms – including the British Council Collection work *Preserve Beauty (New York)*, which is constructed from five hundred red gerberas pressed under glass and remade anew each showing – communicate impermanence and unpredictability.

International press coverage of the exhibition included the *New York Times* and the *Wall Street Journal*. There was surprise expressed at the daring showed by the organizers and the permissiveness of the Iranian mullahs. Some British critics and artists, including Andrew Renton and Gavin Turk, felt that boundaries should have been pushed further, saying that by removing works perceived as offensive, the British Council had 'sanitized' or 'erroneously pruned' the selections.[41] It is clear from a close reading of the exhibition correspondence, however, that boundaries were pushed as far as they could go; any further and

Anish Kapoor, *The Chant of Blue*, 1983, mixed media and pigment, 61 x 61 x 61 x 76 cm (P4362)

the show would not have taken place. Works were vetoed, but this was in the context of high diplomatic tension: several participants had visas refused or withdrawn without explanation in the midst of proceedings, including the director of the British Council in Iran. Sami-Azar said that he 'could be sacked at any moment'. As he explained, 'Everyone looks for some excuse to take advantage of a situation and to make political capital out of it. There are those who don't like the relatively open atmosphere we have managed to build up here.'[42] Western press created a divide between 'risky' British art and Iranian conservatism, but the biggest risk was taken by the staff of the TMoCA, who drove the aesthetic decisions.

Continuing a movement

Western press coverage also underplayed aspects of the cultural situation. Exhibition attendees were highly educated. Bill Woodrow was astonished at how much people knew of his work, which had never been exhibited in Iran before. A journalist asked: 'Why do you have such low expectations of Iranians' cultural knowledge?' Woodrow said he held 'an image of Iran constructed by the British and international press'.[43] That image positioned Iran as culturally regressive, but as the Middle Eastern art journal *Bidoun* noted, '*Turning Points* was not the alien imposition on a tabula rasa many have imagined.' In Tehran:

> it is not uncommon to encounter art students deconstructing the history of the realist tradition in French cinema or the influence of [Aby] Warburg's *Mnemosyne Atlas* on conceptions of contemporary photography. While access is limited, a hyper interest in the surrounding world, combined with enhanced access to Internet and satellite television, has further tied Iranians into an international fabric that defies trite images of isolation and naiveté, artistic or otherwise.

From the journal's perspective, *Turning Points* represented 'an extension of movements already in progress'. These included new Iranian work in photography, installation, and performance that defied expectations of decorative, religious, or 'ethnic' art. Exhibitions were abundant under Khatami, and art and design magazines were 'ubiquitous'. As such, Tehran 'may be turning traditional notions of center–periphery on their collective heads'.[44]

Iran's appearance at the 2001 Venice Biennale for the first time in more than two decades was a marker of this international artistic flowering. An unprecedented number of exhibitions of Iranian contemporary art took place in Britain, including major shows at the Barbican in 2001 and at Christie's in 2003. TMoCA began making international loans from its extraordinary collection, including an important (and sexually explicit) Francis Bacon triptych, *Two Figures Lying on a Bed with Attendants* (1968). This work was shown at Tate Britain in 2004 in an exchange facilitated by Visual Arts via a reciprocal loan to *Turning Points*. It had been bought directly from the artist's studio shortly after it had been produced and had never been previously exhibited, certainly not in Iran, where homosexuality was (and remains) illegal, now punishable by death. A major conference, 'Contemporary Iranian Art: Modernity and the Iranian Artist', was held at the University of Oxford in 2004, and new English-language publications reconsidered the dominant art-historical narratives that had positioned art produced outside of the West as being also outside of modernism.

The prehistories of *Turning Points*

As part of these historical reconsiderations, Fereshteh Daftari has looked back to the pluralist potential of modernist art practices in Iran before 1979 to argue that its artists were 'forerunners of later diasporic conditions'.[45] British art historian Anthony Downey has similarly noted that it is wrong to assume that Iranian cultural production operated in a closed world view. Iranian art was displayed in the 1867, 1873, 1878, and 1900 world fairs in Paris and Vienna, for example, and 'cross-cultural propagation' featured in Iranian art in the early twentieth century, including through its educational institutions, such as the Academy of Fine Arts, established 1911 by Kamal al-Mulk, who studied in Europe.[46] The British Council played a role in some of these historic international artistic dialogues, taking several exhibitions to Iran, including a Barbara Hepworth show that visited Tehran in 1966 and Isfahan in 1969. *Maquette for*

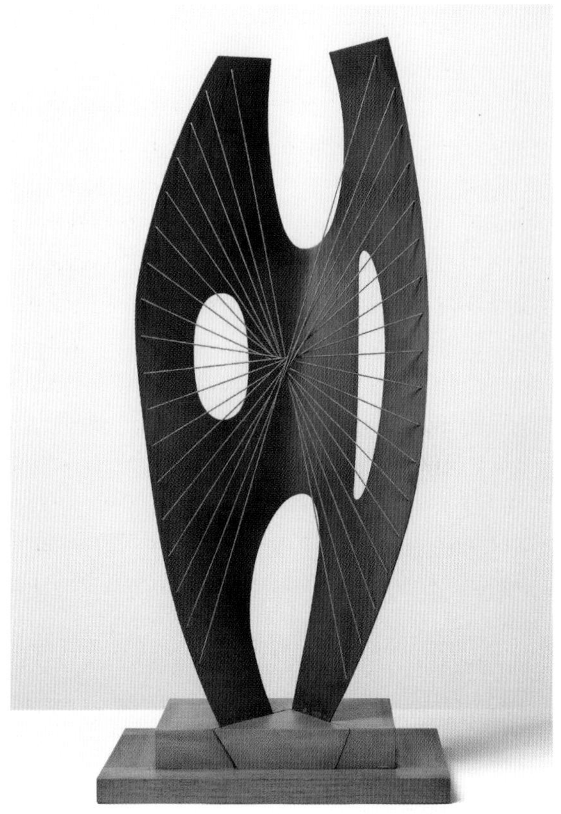

Barbara Hepworth, *Maquette for Winged Figure*, 1957, brass with cotton strings, 29.5 × 63.7 × 24.3 cm (P313)

Winged Figure from 1957, a string-and-brass sculpture evoking the yearning for freedom that Hepworth described as a 'universal dream', was among works on display in that exhibit. Four decades later, the sculpture returned to Tehran for *Turning Points*. As Jenny White, former head of the Visual Arts Programme poetically observed, works in the British Council Collection lead lives separate from their makers. As she put it, 'They have seen some sights.' About Hepworth's *Maquette*, which saw Tehran on both sides of the Islamic Revolution, she exclaimed, 'Oh, the conversations it has heard!'[47]

Henry Moore, *Working Model for Knife Edge Two Piece*, 1962, bronze, 47 × 71.8 × 23.5 cm (P398)

Henry Moore's *Working Model for Knife Edge Two Piece* from 1962 is another British Council Collection work that has travelled twice to Tehran. The first time was as part of *Henry Moore: An Exhibition of Sculpture and Drawings*, which visited three Iranian cities in 1971, and from which the Shah's purchases of the large-scale sculptures outside the museum were made. The second time was for *Turning Points*. *Working Model for Knife Edge*'s bronze forms suggest figures in relation, but their flowing shapes are curves and planes rather than recognizable bodies. Figurative sculptures welcomed in pre-revolutionary times could not be more different from the aesthetic of *Turning Points*, where none were permitted. Installation photographs from 1971 show suited men handling Moore's nude *Falling Warrior*, legs akimbo, into position. Further photographs record young Iranian women clustered around the works in loudly patterned mini-dresses and fashionably middle-parted long hair. These images are

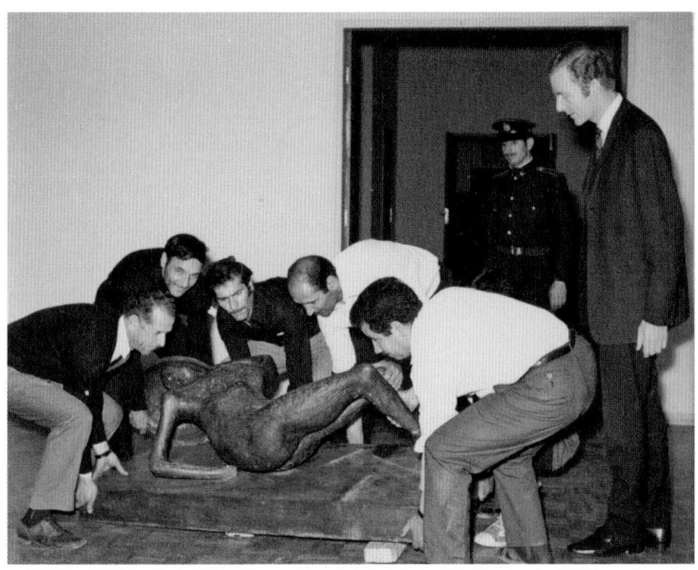

TOP Installing the touring Henry Moore exhibition in Iran in 1971

ABOVE Visitors to the Henry Moore exhibition in Iran in 1971

striking for the distance they signal from the compulsory hijab instituted for women after the revolution. The 1971 exhibition was assembled at the National Museum of Iran with the help of Changiz Shahvagh, an internationally exhibited Iranian sculptor who was the husband of celebrated painter Mansureh Hossaini. Shahvagh enthused about the significance of the exhibition for him and for international art exchange, describing it as one of the biggest moments of his life. 'He's my teacher', he claimed of Moore. 'He's the greatest sculptor in the world. ... This is a wonderful time for Tehran.'[48]

The aftermath of *Turning Points*

If international exhibitions mark peaks in cultural relations, they also mark its limits. The 2004 exhibition signalled a different kind of turning point as relationships between Iran and the UK declined when conservative hardliners took power soon after. Khatami was replaced by President Ahmadinejad in 2005 on the back of his promises of 'reviving the early revolutionary principles', including combating 'western cultural invasion'.[49] Under the new regime, for young Iranian artists who work in idioms perceived as Western, Keshmirshekan notes, 'there is a limited chance for showing their work in official venues such as the Tehran Museum of Contemporary Art'; instead they focus their attention outside the country.[50] The shift in political direction also led to a termination of British Council operations. In January 2009, staff were summoned to Ahmadinejad's office and were 'forced to resign'.[51]

At the time of the *Turning Points* exhibition, the press captured some immediate local impressions, such as the statement made by Helia, a postgraduate art student: 'In a country like Iran where everything is really limited politically, art is something without boundaries. And having relations with other countries and cultures is too important to me to speak about. It is having an enormous effect and I want it to continue.'[52] A decade on from *Turning Points*, the Visual Arts department looked back at the exhibition to assess its effects, interviewing key players from Iran. Anahita Rezvani, formerly of the TMoCA International Office, described how Iranian art teaching had been limited by tutors' inability to travel; their knowledge was 'a bit old-fashioned', she said.

The fact that the newest of internationally famous contemporary artists showed in *Turning Points* was 'a really big deal'. For Rezvani, the exhibition was transformative. She accompanied the Bacon triptych loan to the Tate and stayed on to study at Chelsea College of Art and Design and the Courtauld Institute of Art; she then became Bill Woodrow's studio assistant. She was struck how, in the United Kingdom, 'people were so ignorant about Iran, the position of women and the art they make, the way young people live ... Yes, we can drive and yes, we can go to university and get jobs.' The lack of knowledge worked both ways. Britain 'has a really bad reputation in Iranian minds, so to get past all of that and have a big exhibition in one of the national museums is a big deal. To have the ambassador or cultural attaché come and open the exhibition, and nothing happens – no demonstration outside, nobody brings the walls down – that is all a big deal.' The change of government in 2005 put TMoCA's international art works into storage, and the international department closed down. Nonetheless, 'when you open some doors, you can't go back after that'.[53]

Payam Parishanzadeh, also formerly of TMoCA's International Office, noted that *Turning Points* 'was special because of the political implications – it wasn't just an ordinary art exhibition', she reflected. 'It was as much political as artistic.' Parishanzadeh was emphatic: 'Cultural organisations like the British Council can play a role in providing a platform for people to start a dialogue ... to go beyond politics and make politicians listen to them.' Echoing Martin Davidson's argument that culture can speak to people on an individual level, and thus enable meaningful subjective engagement, she stated, 'People have never had problems with other people; it's governments that create trouble.' Despite this, an exhibition on display for just forty days, even with six hundred visitors per day, can do only so much: 'A single exhibition is not enough to create harmony between people on both sides. More work needs to be done to break the stigma and bring Iranian people closer to British.'[54] That work continues. In 2017, for example, the British Council hosted *Critics and Criticism: Reflections on Iranian Contemporary Art* at its London headquarters, in collaboration with the Iran Heritage Foundation.[55] Works from the British Council Collection may not currently be able to travel to Iran, but the conversations carry on.

Visual Arts in danger: restructuring risks

As the British Council made key changes to its geopolitical priorities in the 2000s, it also reorientated its structures at home. This had significant implications for the arts. One change, outside Council operations, was the restructuring of the Government Indemnity Scheme. This had provided comprehensive insurance for art travelling internationally under the care of the Council. With the rapid rising of art values and the governmental capping of financial risk, the upper limit was significantly reduced in 2003. This not only immediately affected loans to *Turning Points*, but also had a bigger implication for the large-scale loan shows that had long been a key part of the Visual Arts department's activities.

Matters first came to a head in 2002 with the organization of a show of work by John Constable for Paris, selected by Lucian Freud. The valuation of the paintings in the exhibition was £400 million. With such a huge figure to be insured, Rose recalled, 'We had to make a request to the Foreign Office, and the Foreign Office had to make a request to the Treasury, and there had to be a parliamentary minute to allow it to be approved.' The chief secretary of the Treasury said, 'We could build a hospital with this amount of money.' Rose countered, 'Well, yes, but we aren't going to lose any of the art.'[56] The exhibition took place, but afterwards the government reduced the British Council's upper limit for indemnity. The effect was to limit major loan exhibitions for an organization used to dealing with high value works of art and producing up to sixty exhibitions a year. By the early 2000s, national museums were developing international touring programmes of their own, so this aspect of the Visual Arts department's activity was reconsidered, particularly in view of the British Council's plans for a major institutional restructure in 2007.

Previously, the Visual Arts department received an independent annual budget from the Council to use as appropriate, under the guidance of its advisory committee. Still constituted of heads of national museums and galleries and other senior expertise, this connection enabled the department to work with other institutions' exhibition and collecting plans, and sustained the relationships required for loans. The list of advisors from 1935 to 2007 is a roll-call of extraordinary quality, including curators, academics, and critics of the highest calibre. In 2007, following the body's restructure, the separate arts departments of the British Council lost their independent funding and needed instead to apply to regional budgets. Advisory committees were dissolved and plans were made to dismantle specialist departments, covering drama, dance, film, literature, design, and visual arts, under a proposed merger of the disciplines.

The structural shift, and its associated loss of specialism and expertise, seemed to undo a sixty-year success story. A public outcry ensued, similar to the one that had taken place in the early 1980s, when arts activities in the institution were threatened by a major budget cut. Outraged international press notices highlighted the value of the Visual Arts department. In Britain, these included Richard Dorment's article in the *Telegraph*, 'British Council: These crass bureaucrats are placing the arts in real danger'.[57] An open letter to the *Guardian* was signed by more than one hundred of the country's most celebrated artists, from Bridget Riley and David Hockney to Gilbert & George and Jake and Dinos Chapman, alongside leaders of major art institutions, including the Royal Academy of Arts, Tate, and the National Portrait Gallery. The declarations of support showed the affection in which Visual Arts was held, but also the scale of what was at risk. The message was clear:

> Although best known here for its participation in the Venice Biennale, the department's programme of over 60 exhibitions a year, shown everywhere from national museums to local galleries worldwide, would be an inexplicable and, indeed, tragic loss. These exhibitions, whether in Moscow or Beijing, Tehran or Maputo, represent Britain in the best possible light. The links and collaborations involved are surely the very essence of cultural relations.
>
> Our trust in the department's professionalism and expertise has been built up over many years. It is partly the result of their work that contemporary British art is held in higher regard internationally than ever before. Why, without any consultation, does the British Council seem intent on abandoning the best proven means of conducting cultural relations through the arts?[58]

Restating purpose

The result of this public outcry was an urgent consultation and a restatement of the value of the arts in cultural relations. In immediate terms, the proposed merger of the separate departments was halted. Acknowledging that the United Kingdom's 'creative sector expressed grave concern over the future of the British Council's arts work', the Council published *An Action Plan for the Arts* in 2008. It committed to redress the decline in quantity, to maintain specialist departments, and to increase the arts budget. 'Because all of the British Council's arts and creative work is developed through partnerships,' the report recognized, 'without the full confidence of the sector it loses viability and legitimacy.'[59] As such, a new advisory committee was put in place, with a broader remit to cover all arts areas.

The *Action Plan* also enabled the British Council to restate what it was for, and what art could do within it. 'The arts have been privileged over time to act as a representation of the beliefs and values of most cultures and societies', it stated. 'The UK government understands and values the role of the arts in international cultural diplomacy.' That said, there were wider changes that the British Council operated within. 'Almost all cultural agencies and many larger cultural organisations in Britain now have international strategies', they noted. These organizations 'focus on one-way presentation, income generation, talent migration and the international enrichment of the arts for their own sake'; none, however, focused on cultural relations. This showed the institution's unique purpose and key aim: 'The British Council does not offer support to arts and creative economy work that is unlikely to contribute to the development of cultural relations between the UK and the rest of the world.'[60]

Repairing trust

The *Action Plan* reiterated art's value in reconstructing 'broken trust with UK and the West'. This 'creative engagement' was said to 'hold up a mirror to regimes and encourage the development of alternative social models'. Arts work 'supports liberal values and encourages societies to internationalise'.[61] These ambitions continued at the close of the decade.

Thomson & Craighead, *Decorative Newsfeeds*, 2004, data projection (P7954/0)

Flicker: A Visual Intervention into the Cityscape of Damascus, for example, took twelve video works from the British Council Collection in 2009 to a variety of sites in the capital of Syria, from screenings at Damascus University and Mustafa Ali Gallery to projections onto shop shutters on city streets at night.[62] Collection artists Thomson & Craighead travelled to accompany the projection of their digital data work, *Decorative Newsfeeds*, which gathered rolling news from the BBC website and programmed it to undulate in snaking forms across a screen in ever-shifting configurations. Its real-time view of the endless flow of information embodies all the urgencies and disorientations of constant updates and global connectivity. As such, it is a perfect fit for a British Council presentation, utilizing data from another editorially independent public body to result in an elliptical, alluring, but never-finally-fixed travelling message. The opportunity to work with Syrian students to develop film screenings and media

Tim Hetherington, *Vital Structures: Water Towers, United Arab Emirates*, 2008, lightjet print, 42 × 42 cm (P8439)

production skills came at a brief and fragile moment. It followed the opening up of diplomatic relations between the country and Europe, but preceded the 2011 uprisings that closed all British Council offices in Syria in 2012.

My Father's House: The Architecture of Cultural Heritage travelled across Oman, Bahrain, Saudi Arabia, United Arab Emirates, Qatar, and the United Kingdom from 2009 to 2011. Curated by Sean Williams, it commissioned new work by five Middle Eastern artists and three British photographers to explore how cultural identity emerges through local forms. Slideshows and films, photo-

Tim Hetherington, *Vital Structures: Minarets, United Arab Emirates*, 2008, lightjet print, 42 × 42 cm (P8440)

montage and pinhole cameras recorded and displayed the humble homes of Yemeni street cleaners, the historic alleyways of Jeddah, the cinema architecture of Qatar, and the abandoned apartments of the relentlessly modernizing United Arab Emirates. Around twenty-five thousand people attended the exhibition or took part in the related events and photographic competitions.[63]

In *Vital Structures*, the award-winning British photographer and filmmaker Tim Hetherington examined overlooked architecture in the United Arab Emirates and Yemen, including gas stations at night. These he displayed alongside similarly illuminated mosques. Each was given a lush, large-scale treatment as a spectacular unpopulated subject. The visual strategy, evocative of Ed Ruscha's early photographic surveys, adds cultural status to the vernacular design of gas stations, which feature decorative arches and inscribed prophecies among their regional architectural motifs. Hetherington's nine-part grids of water towers, mosques, and minarets show the typologies of parallel forms in a flat style evocative of the German conceptual artists Bernd and Hiller Becher.[64] He paid the same cool attention to architectural details depicted in pale stone against bright blue skies. In drawing parallels between infrastructures for water and petrol and those for worship, Hetherington expanded the category of cultural essentials in a location with distinctive characteristics of climate, wealth, and religion.

Threats and promises

My Father's House was touring in 2011 when Hetherington was killed in Misrata, Libya, struck by shrapnel from a shell fired by government forces while he was photographing the civil war in the country. *Arts for a Dangerous World* argued that art had important work to do for cultural relations at risk of conflict, and the opportunities to test this during the first decade of the twenty-first century were abundant. Risk characterized the Visual Arts department's activity at that time, whether the risk was safety and security or moral and aesthetic. The arts were perceived to be in danger as a result of new approaches to management and money, but they also operated where there was a genuine threat to collections and persons, where rights and freedoms were under pressure from political forces.

The effects of the Visual Arts department's' activities can be mapped through attendance numbers and other statistics, but they are perhaps felt most closely through their legacies in individuals' lives. These attest to the value of sustaining relationships in difficult times. The British Council's aim, especially in conditions of war, has been to operate as an 'instrument of peace'.[65] In relation to the role of the British Council Collection, curator Jenny White emphasized, 'The lending of an authentic, and sometimes highly valuable, work of art demonstrates trust. We recognise that art can't do all of the work required – that would be naïve – but it can make a powerful contribution.'[66] The examples discussed in this chapter attest to this potential.

Art in the British Council, as reiterated in the 2000s, serves a very particular purpose. Gemma Hollington, former director of programmes, described this aim more recently. 'As a cultural relations organization,' she said, 'we have a set of things that we need to do. Art is the means by which we do it.'[67] For this set of things to be done with integrity, to engender trust and international understanding, to enable genuine exchange, they need to take place, as Martin Davidson has argued, in 'an operational space distinct from that of policy advocacy'.[68] Davidson quoted the British Palestinian academic Sultan Barakat on this point: 'If the British Council simply parrots what the Embassy says about Britain, we are not interested. But there's a Britain we'd like it to show us – the Britain of the million marchers against the war in February 2003.'[69]

Art provides a way to offer this alternative vision; its promise is that it can hold a space apart from politics even in highly politicized contexts. As Baroness Kennedy explained, because the organization is 'independent and outside the political fray', at best it can 'build relationships that reach beyond the immediate. Sometimes poetry finds consensus when politics cannot.'[70] *Arts for a Dangerous World* argued that these forms provide 'a fundamental way of reaching out across cultural divides'.[71] Whether this took place through photographs in Riyadh, sculptures in Tehran, or video in Damascus, art exhibitions in the 2000s contested official narratives, opened personal dialogues, and challenged preconceptions through the making of temporary safe spaces in dangerous times.

CHAPTER 8

Rehang, relate, reprise

To mark the seventy-fifth anniversary of the British Council, five exhibitions were displayed at London's Whitechapel Gallery in 2009 and 2010, each drawing exclusively on the Collection, as seen through the eyes of a guest curator. As the Collection was formed to undertake cultural relations work overseas, this was a rare opportunity to showcase its holdings in Britain. Those who curated the selections brought their visions to bear on a body of works that, with almost nine thousand items, has enormous potential to be reconfigured in a wide variety of ways. In the past decade, the Collection has seen a number of such reinterpretations, not least through the processes of co-curation, collaboration, and co-working that have characterized the Visual Arts department's activity over that period, and that deliver on the principle of mutuality. As an organization that uses its art works for international dialogue, the Council's sharing of authority has enabled new forms of inclusion and innovations in exhibition-making. These developments have shaped recent acquisitions that correspond with the earliest purchases in fascinating ways.

Passports and after: five new views

The Whitechapel series began with *Passports: Great Early Buys from the British Council Collection*, selected by the artist Michael Craig-Martin, whose work was first bought by the Council in 1973. His interpretation focused on two aspects. First – and unusually for an exhibition – he highlighted the prices that had been

Laura Aldridge, *Mean (Mean)*, 2014, fabric, wood, metal, string, 80 × 249 × 6 cm (P8548) (detail)

paid for the works. Cost, he noted, is often seen as irrelevant to the understanding of art, and is usually mentioned only when excesses are under scrutiny. But with work that was bought at strikingly low prices, with public funds, and that went on to have exceptionally busy exhibition lives (the second of Craig-Martin's emphases), the reflection on purchasing decisions was an opportunity to consider art's material and use values side by side, as well as to showcase the Council's prescience in anticipating trends and building artists' careers. Craig-Martin asked, 'What normally happens to a work of art after it is purchased?' It often meant a shutting away: 'Most disappear into private collections and live quiet lives, only occasionally disturbed, perhaps for inclusion in a retrospective. Even those in public collections spend much of their lives in storage, only occasionally seeing the light of day on exhibition or on loan.'[1] In contrast, works in the British Council Collection rarely get to put their feet up. The list of tour dates in the accompanying catalogue were in some cases as long as the essays.

Notable works in *Passports* included Henry Moore's *Girl with Clasped Hands* (1930) and Barbara Hepworth's *Rhythmic Form* (1949), as early purchases with lengthy display histories. Later examples reinforced the department's acuity in consolidating reputations. Richard Hamilton's 1970 chromed plastic reliefs were bought as the artist moved into slick forms that mimicked packaging, showing the museum as a site of artistic consumables as well as a consumable product. Gilbert & George's *Intellectual Depression* (1980), a two-metre-high yellow and black gridded piece, depicts the results of another cultural relations exercise: a fragile, silhouetted tree in Finsbury Circus gifted to Britain by the Japanese government as reparation after the Second World War. A Sean Scully abstract, *Red Light* (1971), can be read geographically and biographically, as it anticipated the artist's move from Newcastle to New York, trading Tyne bridge girders for skyscrapers. It also showed how the Council bought work by artists on the cusp of recognition. Scully produced *Red Light* a year after his degree show, and it secured him a 1972 John Moores Painting Prize. The Damien Hirst spot painting *Apotryptophanae* (1994) was painted and purchased in the year between Hirst being nominated for the Turner Prize (1993) and winning it (1995). This was when, as the catalogue put it, Hirst was 'dicing with institutional sanction'.

A view of the exhibition *Passports: Great Early Buys from the British Council Collection*, held at the Whitechapel Gallery from April to June 2009

ABOVE Sean Scully, *Red Light*, 1971, acrylic on canvas, 274.3 × 183 cm (P1588)

OPPOSITE Richard Hamilton, *Guggenheim (Black)*, 1970, vacuum-formed acrylic and cellulose, 60 × 60 × 10 cm (P1538)

Damien Hirst, *Apotryptophanae*, 1994, household gloss on canvas (three-inch spot), 205.7 × 221 cm (P6271)

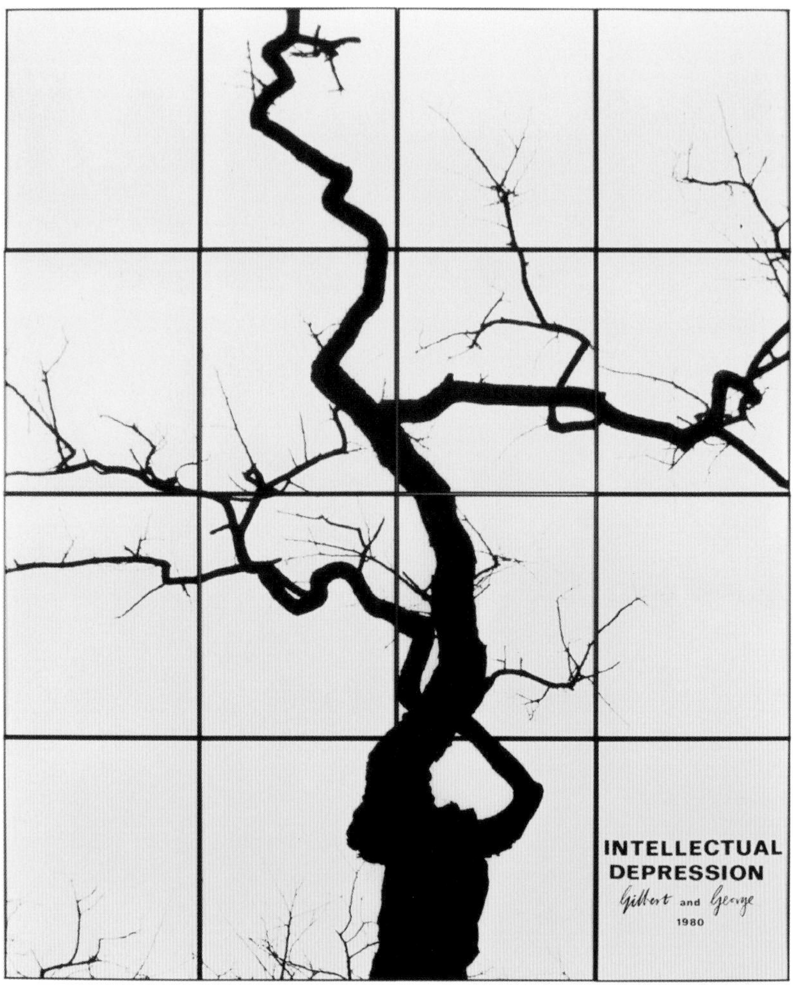

Gilbert & George, *Intellectual Depression*, 1980, 242 × 202 cm (P3963)

LEFT Gerald Leslie Brockhurst, *Adolescence*, 1932, etching, 37 × 26.5 cm (P2406)

OPPOSITE Jake and Dinos Chapman, *Painting for Pleasure and Profit: a piece of site-specific performance-based body art in oil, canvas and wood (dimensions variable)*, 2006, oil on canvas, 30.5 × 25.3 cm (P8037)

Other displays in the Whitechapel series provided different perspectives. *Thresholds* by Paula Rego brought the artist's love of fine printing, the grotesque, and the fabulous to a very personal selection that paid little attention to the highly celebrated or financially valuable. Rego, born in Portugal but living and working in London from the 1950s until her death in 2022, is well represented by more than forty works in the British Council Collection. Her international reputation is built on her substantial body of figurative work exploring psychodrama and storytelling, often with a strong thread of black humour. Her selections for *Thresholds* continued in this line, looking back to the earliest of the Wakefield prints and creating arresting configurations with more recent Collection acquisitions. Gerald Leslie Brockhurst's meticulous 1932 etching *Adolescence*, for example, is full of sexual desire for its teenage subject, with whom the middle-aged artist eloped. Katherine Woodward, the life model in question, contemplates her naked body in a dressing-table mirror and is depicted with a formality that had fallen out of fashion. The etching travelled to the New York World's Fair in 1939, but had not appeared in exhibition since 1949. Could its maker have ever envisaged that it would end up on display, seventy-five years after its production, alongside the strange daubs and deliberate distortions of Jake and Dinos Chapman? The oil selected by Rego from the Chapman brothers' portrait painting booth of 2006 is full of playful disdain for its sitter, who is part alien and part monster, with outsize ears, goofy teeth, and swastika antennae. These against-the-grain pairings, bringing together the beautiful and the ludicrous, the academic and the anarchic, the celebrated

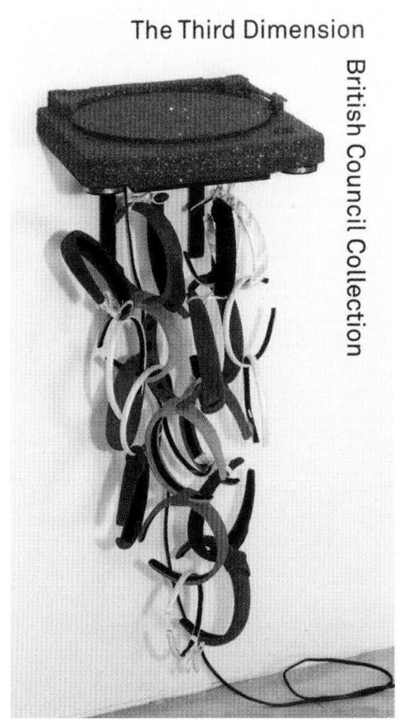

Front covers of the catalogues for the second and third exhibitions in the series at the Whitechapel Gallery, *The Third Dimension* and *My Yard* in 2009

and the forgotten, created new textures only possible in a collection comprised of so many layers, visions, and voices, accrued across time by so many hands, and designed to travel far beyond its original location and meaning.

Tim Marlow, at the time a director at the commercial gallery White Cube, brought his own predilections to the British Council Collection with a survey of sculpture's dematerialization, *The Third Dimension*. Collaborating artists Jeremy Deller and Alan Kane offered an idiosyncratic take on domesticity in their display, *My Yard*. Following these four selections by well-known figures, the final exhibition resulted from a competition, *The Fifth Curator*. The call encouraged new views from aspiring curators under the age of forty and from outside the United Kingdom, noting that fresh perspectives were 'vital to ongoing debates about British art in an international context'.[2] From 161 applicants across 47 countries, the winner was twenty-six-year-old Swedish curator

Theodor Ringborg, with a proposal to explore war and conflict. Observing that as 'an outsider, coming from Sweden', and thus from a location 'that has remained "neutral" for almost two hundred years', he felt that 'the endeavours and conflicts that Britain has engaged in remains somewhat foreign'.[3] Ringborg noted that British public space was regularly punctuated with war memorials. The representation of conflict in the British Council Collection, however, was much less monumental. Among the century-wide selections that he made was Stephen Dixon's decorated earthenware pot *On the Brink*, created in 1990 in response to the Gulf War. Making reference to the long British historical tradition of satirical ceramics, but representing the technologies of modern conflict among its decorative motifs, Dixon modelled the allegorical warring figures of

Stephen Dixon, *On the Brink*, 1990, lead glazed earthenware, press moulded lidded vessel, with sprigged and modelled details, height 40.7 cm (P5971)

Tim Head, *Fall Out*, 1985, cibachrome print, 123.5 × 93.5 cm (P5832)

East and West, mounted on elephant and camel, locked in a battle of aggressive futility on the lid of a fragile vessel designed to hold a plague of insects. Tim Head's *Fall Out*, which formed the exhibition's title piece, provided another example of how war can be figured laterally. Head's gaudy colour photograph, a dense display of eye-popping plastic children's toys, features play missiles and fighter jets in gold, pastel pink, and baby blue. As appealing as sweets, the pretty little symbols of destruction show the normalization of war in everyday life and its penetration into the imaginative spaces of the youngest members of society.

New interpretive codes

The scale of the British Council Collection, alongside its varied material textures from ceramics, prints, and painting to sculpture, installation, and new media, enables such rich re-readings. Added to this, the welcome extended to curators outside the organization to create new interventions from different perspectives showed the Visual Arts department's willingness to share authorial direction. In this, it was part of a contemporaneous movement among cultural institutions more broadly to open up their art collections for new interpretations. As Tomoe Takagi of newspaper *Asahi Shimbun* has noted, this pattern was particularly prominent with institutions 'under criticism for placing too much emphasis on Western historical perspectives and for having fortified their privileged status as authorities on art'. Institutions that welcomed this self-critique, inviting in curators from 'non-Western cultural regions', as he put it, 'are not merely attempting to reject the canonical art history code, but are anticipating a breakaway'. While Takagi observed that many museums were inviting new 'interpretive codes' for their collections, for most, he argued, it was little more than a temporary interlude in a dominant narrative that upheld the status quo. How it could be done meaningfully was modelled by the British Council, he argued: 'Whether its exhibitions are organised by the collection holders or "the Other", they are always temporary exhibitions and visitors understand that any code will be replaced with a different one in the next exhibition. By happening not to have a permanent exhibition facility,' Takagi concluded, 'the British

Front cover of the catalogue for the exhibition *Private Utopia*, which toured Japan in 2014. The cover features the distinctive blue packing cases that are used to transport British Council Collection works around the world.

Council is able to avoid some of the dilemmas that plague other art institutions.'[4] The necessity to regularly remodel meant that exhibitions could be more responsive to changing ideas.

Takagi was writing in particular about *Private Utopia*, an exhibition of contemporary art selected from the Collection for four cities in Japan in 2014 and 2015. This show gathered one hundred and twenty mostly recent acquisitions by thirty artists, and was assembled by Japanese curators who came to London to view the Collection and to visit artists' studios in preparation. From this stimulus, they developed their themes – around artists' individual world views – and built narrative structures, including 'Myself / Yourself', 'Landscape / Mindscape', 'Quotation / Appropriation'. The *Private Utopia* show built on the British Council's long exhibition history in Japan, dating back to the early 1950s, and on cultural relationships that had been especially productive since the 1980s, resulting in significant purchases of British contemporary

Front cover of the catalogue for the exhibition *Aspects of British Art Today*, which toured from February to October 1982

art for the country's developing museum sector and major artistic educational exchanges. In earlier exhibitions of contemporary British art – *Aspects of British Art Today* (1982) and *British Art Now: A Subjective View* (1990) – Jenny White, a former arts officer in Japan, noted, Japanese curators always expressed their own preferences.[5] And as Richard Riley, a former curator in the Visual Arts department, adds, more dialogic ways of co-working developed with the exhibition *Real / Life: New British Art*, which was held in five cities across Japan in 1998 and 1999, where the artists and final list of works were determined solely by the Japanese curators, paving the way for the equal exchange demonstrated in *Private Utopia*.[6]

These models also set the template for other collaborative exhibition-making in Asia, such as *Aftershock: Contemporary British Art 1990–2006*, which toured two museums in China in 2006 and 2007, with contents selected by Chinese curators working closely with the Visual Arts department and British

Council colleagues in China. As the first institutional showing of works by the YBA generation in that country, it marked a milestone in a period of prolific activity there, which included a large-scale Henry Moore show in 2000–1 and *Made in Britain: Contemporary Art from the British Council Collection 1980–2010*, a major 2011–12 survey exhibition that toured four cities and was selected wholly by Chinese curators.[7]

Authority and mutuality: historical shifts

While mutuality has been cited as a 'cardinal principle' since the early days of the British Council, debates about authority and excellence, collaboration and competition, exchange and reciprocity reveal shifting attitudes over time.[8] The efforts made in recent years to co-work on more equitable grounds contrast with some earlier practices. Value judgments about cultural differences, communicating hierarchical attitudes about cultural superiority and inferiority, occur periodically through archival papers, especially in the Fine Arts department's first decades. These expose the challenges of doing cultural relations while maintaining a rigid set of standards about what is 'good' and 'bad' as tastemakers. The department saw its role as an arbiter of quality and a voice of authority; this led to practices of gatekeeping that could sometimes be exclusionary.

In the days of Lilian Somerville's directorship, there were anxieties about sharing decision-making powers, especially in relation to exhibitions put together by others; these included shows assembled by commercial dealers, but also those by esteemed professionals, such as the Royal Society for British Sculptors. There was a blanket rule, communicated by Somerville with characteristic certainty in 1953: 'The Council's reputation for the discrimination and excellence of its selection would only too easily be lost if the Council's name were associated with exhibitions, the selection for which it was not responsible.'[9] In its early incarnation, the Fine Arts department brokered British art overseas, often for the very first time, and sometimes as the only possible channel. By retaining sole authority over what was shown under its official imprimatur, they kept a tight handle on 'quality' and 'prestige'.

These issues of control also included matters of interpretation. When Moore was to be shown in Greece in 1951, there were concerns about sharing the introduction to his works with local arts professionals. The British Council representative in the country wrote back to London: 'Mr [Angelo] Procopiou, Professor of Fine Arts at the Athens Polytechnic and a valuable British Council contact, has suggested that he himself should also write an introduction to the catalogue in order, as he says, that "Moore's work be initially presented to the Greek public by a Greek as well as a British art critic".' The representative was hesitant. 'Mr Procopiou is probably the leading art critic in Greece,' he admitted, 'but we ourselves doubt whether this would be advisable.'[10]

The cautions about sharing authority with international critics seem hard to square with other practices that model equal cultural relationships. In the same year, for example, the British Council declared that Britain had become 'a pioneer in broadening the scope and technique of what in old-fashioned terms was known as "cultural propaganda" and in transforming it from at best a minor form of national self-advertisement and at worst a form of intellectual imperialism into a serious branch of a country's external relations, conducted on a basis of exchange and equality'.[11] Cultural dialogue underpinned many mid-twentieth-century British Council practices; some employees, however, seem not to have received the memo. In the case of Moore in Greece, despite hesitations, local painters, sculptors, and critics were central to the shaping, delivery, and interpretation of his work. Procopiou wrote the preface and lectured to an audience of six hundred. The organizing committee included the Greek painter Nicos Hadjikyriakou-Ghika and sculptor Michael Tombros, who 'lent his own pedestals, personally repaired the base of one of the works, interpreted to many students and visitors the meaning of Moore's sculpture and was instrumental in getting the services of art students as voluntary attendants'.[12]

Mutuality in the British Council has long aimed to ensure that sender and receiver are equally invested in the project and that both sides are partners in decision-making, and this is core to its activity. From its very beginning, the Fine Arts department liaised with their overseas counterparts; the cultural knowledge of British Council representatives, as country residents and specialists, and close colleagues of local art contacts, would also inform practices. They shaped the exhibitions that were sent, where they were displayed, and how they were engaged with. Sometimes, however, in the early days, overseas partners might be limited to saying 'yes' or 'no' to the offer of a preselected exhibition, already designed and constructed, and sometimes already on tour. In some cases, representatives – who originally were more likely to be a British overseas posting than a locally born employee – perpetuated clichés about the country they purported to represent.

For example, in relation to propositions to travel Moore internationally in the 1940s and 1950s, the director of the Latin America department reinforced stereotypes about national tastes. Modern art was used as a yardstick by which to measure cultivation: 'I do not know if the Jamaicans would take to Henry Moore', he reflected. 'As for the Mexicans, I think they are sophisticated enough. ... They would also be flattered by the choice. But whether they would prefer him to water-colours is a question which might have to be referred to the Representative. My own feeling', he stated, 'is that they would prefer Moore drawings.' He claimed, 'I have never noticed that Latin-Americans are greatly attracted by water-colours, unless they are unusually violent.'[13] The representative in Greece made similar assertions in 1951 in relation to the cultural sophistication of the locals. 'The unsophisticated country Greek has a natural good taste,' he pronounced, 'but this is largely lost in the towns. Furniture and domestic architecture has to give ornate evidence of real or imagined wealth, when it does not go in for a barren jazz-cubism.'[14]

These characterizations betray hierarchical cultural judgments in an organization premised on principles of equity. Structurally, in British Council parlance and practice, well into the 1960s, the world was categorized into 'developed' and 'undeveloped' countries.[15] These were not descriptors based on economic and industrial measures, such as 'the developed' and 'the developing world' – commonly used by the United Nations, the Organization for Economic Cooperation and Development, and others, but still contested terms – but were instead used to signal levels of cultural advancement, which European countries were seen to possess, while non-Western countries did not. These rigidities were not, of course, exclusive to the British Council in this period, but it is worth noting that dialogue and mutuality in the early decades took place in a circumscribed context of cultural supremacy.

Shared ambitions

Given some former limitations, the dialogical and intercultural practices of recent years most fully realize the relationship-building ambitions that underpin the British Council's promise. International partnership working and co-production are all important characteristics of the Visual Arts department's recent development, and they form the basis for the ways the British Council Collection is now used. Past and present members reflected on shifting mutuality. Brett Rogers, for example, described some historic exhibitions sent internationally as akin to 'care parcels'. She said, 'Over time, it became obvious that this strategy had problems. It was very one-directional. Curators who were recipients began to ask why they couldn't make the curatorial selections; it was very colonial.'[16] Andrea Rose also observed the absolute necessity for dialogue. She argued, 'You can't just transfer current taste in British culture and expect it to work anywhere in the world. This is the worst thing that could happen.'[17] Nicola Heald, the current manager of the Collection, agrees: 'It would be arrogant and paternalistic to assume that London can prescribe what is wanted and needed.'[18]

In Rogers' recollections, core shifts in collaborative exhibition-making began in the 1990s; and the show *To be Continued ... / Jatkuu ...* in Helsinki in 2005 offers a model for how such partnerships could work. Focusing on contemporary photographic artists, as a joint initiative between the Hippolyte Gallery and the British Council, the exhibition had a Finnish co-curator and included equal numbers of Finnish and British artists. The themes explored were shared by practitioners regardless of geography and, as such, embodied the exhibition's aim 'to transgress national, linguistic and international boundaries'.[19] The art sometimes spoke of familiarity and strangeness, and could thus communicate the uncertainty of identities. *Them #1*, a photographic work by Danny Treacy bought for the British Council Collection, for example, is a self-portrait of the artist wearing fragments of found clothing scavenged from marginal places,

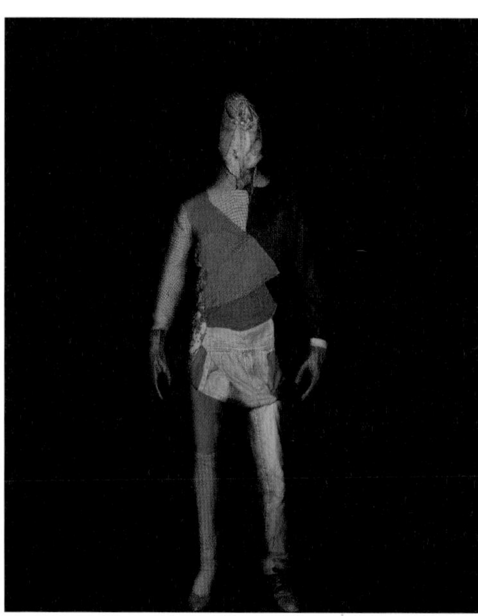

Danny Treacy,
Them #1, 2002,
Lambda print,
250 x 200 cm
(P7956)

including derelict buildings and roadsides. These have been refashioned into a strange full-body costume that communicates the illicit behaviours and interrupted practices that led to the clothes being abandoned. The figure performed is an unhomely outsider; from the title outwards, the image embodies and critiques categories of 'us' and 'them'.

Collaborative practices help counteract paternalistic attitudes about the dissemination of culture that might be read into some earlier exhibition models. The advancements of the last decade have happened in several ways: through sharing exhibition design and delivery, through bringing new voices to bear on the British Council Collection from outside Britain, and through themes of identity and location, self and other. *Homelands: A 21st Century Story of Home, Away, and All the Places in Between* brought these three methods together in a show that toured India, Pakistan, and Sri Lanka in 2013 and 2014, using more than eighty British Council Collection works by twenty-eight artists. The exhibition

Front cover of the catalogue for the exhibition *Homelands: A 21st Century Story of Home, Away, and All the Places in Between*

was conceived by Delhi-based curator Latika Gupta, a finalist in *The Fifth Curator*. As Rose observed in the catalogue, opening up the Collection in the curatorial competition had been sobering. 'From all over the world, we learned how others see us.'[20] The insights were too good to waste, and Gupta developed her ideas for Delhi, Kolkata, Mumbai, Bengaluru, Lahore, Karachi, and Colombo.

Identities in motion

The themes of *Homelands* fitted a world characterized by migration and transition. 'Today many of us move with ease across inter/national boundaries', Gupta noted. 'We are born in one country, we make another our home. In the resulting crisscrossing of political, social and cultural borders, we live our lives through hyphenated identities: belonging here and there; inhabiting multiple places – both physical and metaphorical.'[21] The concept adapted Salman Rushdie's notion of 'imaginary homelands of the mind'.[22] As such, the works

ABOVE Grayson Perry, *Village of the Penians*, 2001, glazed ceramic, 50 × 24 cm (P7486)

OPPOSITE Cornelia Parker, *Meteorite Lands on Buckingham Palace*, 1998, maple boxed frame map of London revealing burn mark left by the meteorite in various locations, 54 × 69 cm (P7273)

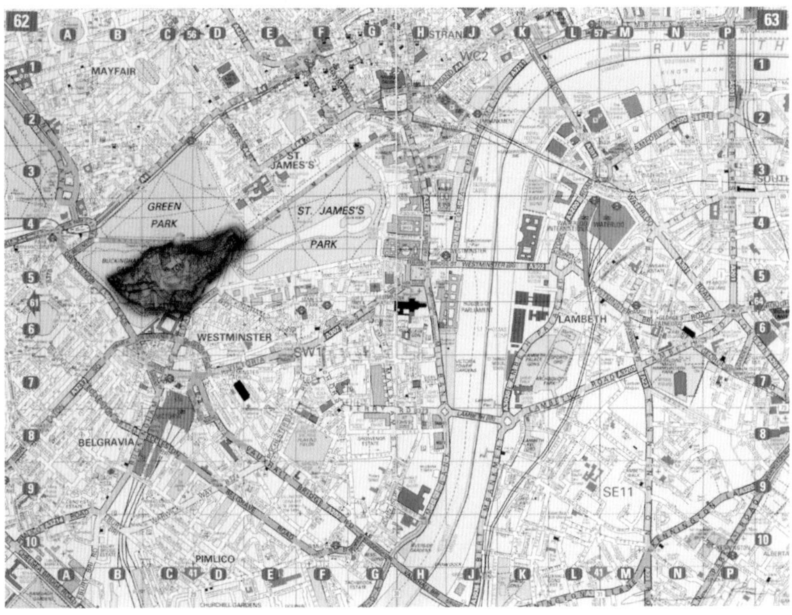

in the exhibition – none previously seen in India, Pakistan, or Sri Lanka – drew on real and imagined spaces and reflected on belonging and alienation in direct and indirect ways.

In *Village of Penians*, for example, Grayson Perry invented a parallel universe where the erect penis – whose depiction is a visual taboo in Western polite society – is a kind of folk deity. In this preposterous world-turned-upside-down, the phallus is the most common of sights and features as a decoration on an elegant vase. It figures in flowers and food, in hats and shoes, and as repeat patterns on every surface. It is simultaneously everywhere and nowhere, venerated and banal in Perry's surreal ceramic utopia. In a more bleak and apocalyptic vision, Cornelia Parker provided scorch marks on atlas pages as evidence of imagined devastation. Buckingham Palace and the Houses of Parliament are among the obliterated locations that Parker burns off the page using a heated meteorite, embodying the fear of the alien unknown. More literal

Tim Hetherington, *Alpha kamara, 97 Pademba Road, Freetown, Sierra Leone*, 2004, C-type colour print, 42 × 42 cm (P8182)

George Shaw, *Scenes from the Passion: The Blossomiest Blossom*, 2001, Humbrol enamel on board, 43 × 53 cm (P7370)

depictions come from Tim Hetherington's study of the Creole board houses of Freetown, Sierra Leone; bricked-up windows and bright but peeling paint show vernacular buildings persisting despite a century of poverty and neglect. George Shaw's *Scenes from the Passion: The Blossomiest Blossom* depicts a humble home on the other side of the world, on a suburban Coventry council estate. Shaw's moody paintings, incongruously constructed with glossy modelmakers' paint, show loving views of sometimes unlovely locations as bittersweet paeans to a childhood place to which one can never return.

Also in *Homelands*, Anthony Haughey's photographs from his 1991–2 series *Home* showed Catholic family life in Northern Ireland. The prints were produced as a result of deep immersion into domestic experience; Haughey

Anthony Haughey, *Untitled*, 1991/2, from the series *Home*, C-type colour print, 61 × 50.8 cm (P6137)

camped in the living rooms of five homes for a year. The resulting images show personal expression and belief as well as 'objects and images that referenced historical antagonisms and the world outside'.[23] Homes are always microcosms of world views. Belonging and identity have figured throughout Haughey's socially engaged practice, which explores citizenship and disputed territories across Europe, including a 2007 British Council-funded project in a refugee camp in Malta. As Haughey states of migration: 'We are all immersed in this culture, we choose whether to embrace, ignore or reject the Other.'[24]

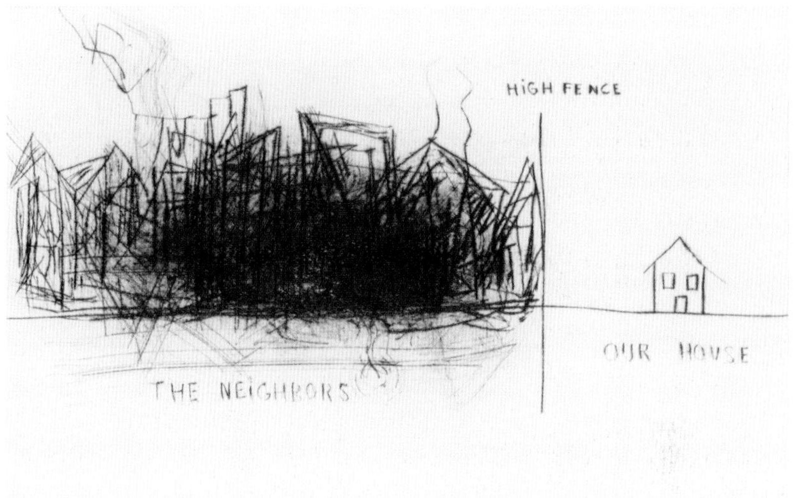

Jimmie Durham, *Our House*, 2007, drypoint on copperplate, 29.7 × 42 cm (P8102)

In a similar vein, *Our House*, a drypoint print by Jimmie Durham – an artist whose own identity and homeland, as an American-born but European resident who claims Cherokee ancestry, has been the subject of art and of public contestation – explores personal relationships marked by proximity and distance. An immaculate line drawing of a house sits alongside a frantic tangle described as 'The Neighbors'. The two characterizations, positioned on either side of a dividing fence, provide a reflection on prejudice that can apply to many spaces and times. It also neatly embodies an early British Council statement of purpose. In 1949, the organization stated its aim: not 'blind Anglomania but a neighbourly understanding'.[25]

The understanding that Gupta hoped would develop was delivered as the *Homelands* exhibition travelled across India, Pakistan, and Sri Lanka:

> With one of the tribes in Bombay, because the museum is located in a Muslim area, a lot of the work had to do with the state of Islam or religion or worship or cultural markers in other societies. In Calcutta

> people were coming and talking about the conflict between East Bengal and West Bengal, refugee settlements along the border, what it means to be a refugee, what immigration may mean and what it's like to be a migrant between two places. So people were taking regional histories and local histories into their viewing experience.[26]

On taking the show to Pakistan, Gupta noted: 'The reviews which came out of it were so personal'; they were 'less to do with the exhibition from the point of view of art, and more to do with how all of this spoke to them'. In the context of the historic divisions, she observed, 'we talk about the conflict and how we're two different places ... yet the responses were entirely personal and exactly the same'.[27] Curator Rattanamol Singh Johal, writing in *Art India*, claimed the 'real triumph' of *Homelands* was 'its ability to create an open-ended dialogue between a set of works emerging from the United Kingdom and its audiences halfway across the globe'. This was attributed to its origins in 'a national collection that embodies many of the contradictions and complications of our contemporary condition'. Together, 'the colossal cacophony arising out of the sheer range of voices and perspectives on offer informs us about the futility of borders'.[28]

The national–international interrelationships of the British Council's work necessarily prompts debate about frontiers. As the director of British Council India noted, the organization 'exists not just to promote international cultural relations but to interrogate it'.[29] Varied voices add to the conversation. The Collection belongs to a British institution, but 'British' artists in *Homelands* were variously born in America, Lebanon, France, and Hong Kong and had diverse cultural heritages. The catalogue included contributions by Tibetan poets alongside Palestinian and Pakistani scholars. In the closing words, Gupta drew on Indian cultural theorist Homi K. Bhaba. He argued it is 'politically crucial ... to think beyond narratives of origin and initial subjectivities and focus on these movements or processes that are produced by the articulation of cultural differences. These in-between spaces', he suggests, 'provide the terrain for elaborating strategies of selfhood – singular or communal – that imitate new signs of identity and innovative sites of collaboration, and contestation in the act of defining the idea of society itself.'[30] *Homelands* materialized these ambitions through a new optic on the British Council Collection.

Regional revisions: Wider Europe

Art Connects Us, the British Council's five-year arts strategy published in 2016, reasserted art's value in cultural relations:

> The arts offer an approachable way to reach people who might not otherwise engage with complex issues, presenting an accessible way for audiences to become part of a community and talk with others about what they have seen. Art can create and represent distinct identities for our nations and regions, articulate the voices of all our communities, and influence the way others see us and the way we see ourselves.[31]

Within this strategy, the newly named 'Arts for Social Change' approach stated a long-standing ambition much more explicitly. Every such restatement of institutional aims enables a refreshed view of British Council objectives. The language and geographical priorities may change over time, but there are consistent underpinnings. Over the decades, the layering of practices, especially in revisited tour circuits, creates echoes and reflections. Indeed, the British Council's exhibition history now provides a significant resource for reflecting on the legacies of international cultural relations. The partnerships that the Visual Arts department has developed over the last decade in the region that the British Council categorizes as Wider Europe (Albania, Armenia, Azerbaijan, Bosnia and Herzegovina, Georgia, Israel, Kazakhstan, Kosovo, Macedonia, Montenegro, Russia, Serbia, Turkey, Ukraine, Uzbekistan) show this in action.

The Council's cultural relations activities are currently clustered by regions rather than individual nations, and the Wider Europe grouping of fifteen countries covers some 335 million people. Within such a vast territory, including former Soviet republics and states once part of former Yugoslavia, the region is marked by significant borders within as well as without. Exhibitions travelling to this region have been enacting principles of art for social change and international collaboration throughout the organization's history, regardless of the region's shifting names and frontiers. In the Second World War, for example, the British Council ran what it called 'national houses' for allied nationals from the occupied territories, such as Yugoslav House in London, which were social, educational, and cultural clubs serving those living in exile. The Council's support included the display of their art. 'While it is not the Council's duty to show the achievements of other countries to the people of Britain', it was stated that 'an exception can be made for those nations whose countries the enemy has over-run'.[32] As such, the British Council organized wartime exhibitions of Allied artists alongside displays of, for example, the arts and crafts of Yugoslavia.

Yugoslavia was, in turn, the site for a travelling postwar exhibition of sculpture and drawings by Henry Moore in 1955 (see page 94), which took Collection works to Skopje (now in Macedonia), Zagreb (now in Croatia), Ljubljana (now in Slovenia), and Belgrade (now in Serbia). It was the first major British art exhibition in Yugoslavia since the war, and forty-five thousand visitors attended. Sculptor Petar Hadzi Boskov saw the exhibition at Skopje and credited it with a transformation in his artistic practice from academicism to modernism. He was later the recipient of a British Council scholarship that enabled him to study at the Royal College of Art and the Slade School of Fine Art. His first solo show in Britain, at London's Grabowski Gallery in 1960, was opened by Moore and marked the first showing of Macedonian sculpture in Britain. Boskov shared his story during the 2013 Skopje leg of the travelling exhibition *Henry Moore – The Printmaker*, which toured eleven sites in Wider Europe during 2013–15.[33] Nearly seventy years on, this experience embodies what Richard Hoggart described as the profound long-term effects of arts in cultural relations.[34]

Perhaps the most moving reflection during that exhibition tour came from the Albanian artist, architect, and writer Maks Velo, who was imprisoned for eight years under Albania's Communist regime for his 'modernist tendencies'. Velo had been given a book of Moore's sculptures in 1972, but even owning reproductions of Western 'decadent' art was deemed subversive. He was arrested in 1978 and interrogated for six months. Being inspired by

Moore was part of the case against him, in which Velo was proclaimed as a 'pseudo-artist' whose art was a product of his 'political and moral degradation'. In addition to his imprisonment, Velo's collection of paintings and sculptures were destroyed and the Moore book was confiscated. As *Henry Moore – The Printmaker* travelled to Tirana in 2013, the exhibition gave Velo an opportunity to reflect on the personal and political potency of art in Albania and beyond.[35]

Artistic dialogue

Henry Moore – The Printmaker marked the first of several Wider Europe exhibition projects. A Damien Hirst show, *New Religion*, travelled to Bosnia, Macedonia, Serbia, and Kazakhstan in 2015 and 2016. This was followed by Grayson Perry's *The Vanity of Small Differences* in 2017, comprising an eight-city tour of six Wider Europe countries organized by the British Council and linked to a nine-city UK tour organized by Arts Council England. The art, exhibition, and tour demonstrate a different aspect of co-working, but continue to show the adaptability of the British Council Collection to be repurposed and shared.

The Vanity of Small Differences showcased six large-scale tapestries by Perry, co-owned and co-managed by the British Council Collection and the Arts Council Collection. The tapestries depict a latter-day satirical narrative, directly inspired by William Hogarth's eighteenth-century moral tale *The Rake's Progress*. Hogarth's prints formed an integral part of the original Perry exhibition. Both sets of works show the decline and fall of a dissolute spendthrift, but its handling by the two artists adds different perspectives. The Hogarth etchings entered the British Council Collection in 1964 as a partner for David Hockney's *A Rake's Progress* 1961–3, the semi-autobiographical account of the artist's experiences in New York. Across sixteen sparsely marked, two-colour etched aquatints, the bespectacled figure arrives, sells prints, dyes his hair blonde, runs out of money, turns to drink, marries inadvisably, and loses his individuality. Hogarth's rake took a different journey through debt and debauchery, ill-chosen relationships, and insanity, but the conversation between the works, more than two hundred years apart, shows how an enduring moralistic narrative can travel across time and place.

Grayson Perry, *The Annunciation of the Virgin Deal*, 2012, wool, cotton, acrylic, polyester and silk tapestry, 200 × 400 cm. Edition of 6 plus 2 artist's proofs.

Steve Jobs
Bill Gates
PLASTIC
Bourgeois and Proud
Allotment Organic Home-Made Local
BAKEWELL SELLS TO VIRGIN FOR £270m

William Hogarth, *The Rake's Progress*, Plate 4, 1735, etching, 35.5 × 40.7 cm (P794)

Travel it certainly did. The exhibition *The Rake's Progress: William Hogarth and David Hockney* visited twenty-eight countries on its unbroken tour from 1966 to 1993, and Hockney's rake has continued his picaresque journey across six continents. Hogarth's rake, meanwhile, found a new sparring partner in Perry's *The Vanity of Small Differences*, whose central character, Tim Rakewell, traverses through the British class system of the twenty-first century across technically impressive and highly detailed panels as beautiful in form as they are biting in message. Perry's tapestries were produced as a result of conversations with members of the British public as part of an enquiry into class and its communication through material goods. These social studies were then transposed into allegorical textiles. *The Annunciation of the Virgin Deal*, for example, shows economic expansion via a vocabulary of British middle-class taste preferences and art-historical motifs from the Renaissance artists Carlo Crivelli, Robert Campin, and Jan van Eyck. The exhibition opens up conversations about inter-

David Hockney, 'The Wallet Begins to Empty', *A Rake's Progress*, Plate 6a, 1961–3, etching, aquatint, 41 × 30.5 cm (P751)

national mobility, and its reach in Wider Europe has been significant, breaking attendance records at Novi Sad in Serbia, for example.

Institutional co-working

Perry's tapestries also communicate other forms of co-working as they represent the first joint purchase between two institutions pooling their resources, aided by financial support from other partners, including Channel 4 and the consultancy company AlixPartners. The British Council and the Arts Council have long had close relations, operating as domestic and international counterparts where required, especially in the postwar period, with the Arts Council historically managing incoming international exhibitions, while the British Council handled outgoing ones. Although they have separate remits, their respective collections – one focused on UK exhibitions and loans and the other on overseas – have collaborated together at home and abroad. In 2011, following parliamentary suggestions that public art-collecting organizations may not be providing value for money, a review was launched into the purpose and management of the British Council Collection, the Arts Council Collection, and the Government Art Collection, which serves the British government with historic and contemporary works for display on its estate. David Lee of the *Jackdaw* magazine complained to ministers that artists who were not British-born should not represent British art, and that public institutions should show art that was popular, such as works by Jack Vettriano and Beryl Cook. Finally, he claimed, 'there is no point in the British Council having 8,500 works that have been accumulated over 60 years ... if they don't show them and nobody knows where they are'.[36]

The review was an opportunity to examine the three national collections' purposes, connections, and distinctions. None of them, it was observed, had its own dedicated exhibition space. While this may be an advantage in some respects, the review noted that it has led to ignorance about what the collections are for, exemplified by Lee's statement above. On the other hand, it showed that they are 'perceived by artists, UK and overseas curators, gallery and museum directors, ambassadors, Ministers, and civil servants to be of immense value. As art collections, they represent the achievements of successive generations of British artists, both to international and national audiences, including those with whom the British government works.'[37]

The review provided the British Council Collection with an informative snapshot of its usage. It was hardly unknown and unseen. Nearly half of the works were on display at the time, primarily overseas, in a mix of touring exhibitions and in British Council premises. The financial base was also outlined: British Council offices overseas seek commercial sponsorship towards local costs of Collection exhibitions, and recipients meet the costs of transport, insurance, installation, and marketing. Working with international curators was noted as good practice, while joint acquisitions were highlighted as a positive step to cost-efficiency. The review's conclusions were resoundingly positive about the British Council Collection and its 'tangible benefits'. For a cultural relations organization whose international influence has been described as a 'glittering intangible',[38] the Collection stands as a materialization of its aims. It is a valued tool in British Council arts practices, reaching an audience of more than five million across twenty-four countries since 2015.[39]

Equality and inclusion

One recent focus of Wider Europe activity has been *Perceptions* in the Western Balkans, which saw five different exhibitions bring British Council Collection works into dialogue with art from the region. As Emma Dexter, director of the Visual Arts department since 2014, explained, 'Our Council colleagues in the region, and the partner galleries they wanted to work with, were aware that together we'd done exhibitions by Moore, Hirst, and Perry back-to-back. So they wondered if we could now focus on women artists' work.' The resulting project enabled curators from five countries to develop collaborative exhibitions that drew on art by women in the British Council Collection. As Dexter continued, the project is infused with mutuality:

> The core of the exhibition of twenty-four works from the British Council Collection, which travelled from museum to museum, was selected by curators at those museums. The Visual Arts team in London did not create the list. We might have introduced them to certain works we thought might be interesting, but together they made the final selection collectively – curators from Kosovo, Bosnia, Macedonia, Montenegro, and Serbia all working together. At each venue, the works borrowed from the Collection have been augmented and integrated with works from the host institution's own holdings or borrowed directly from the locality. Wherever the show happens, it is in dialogue with local influences, voices, and histories.[40]

The selected items from the Collection included images by the interwar colour-photography pioneer Madame Yevonde; works by British artists with established reputations, such as Tracey Emin, Sarah Lucas, and Rachel Whiteread; and recent purchases by young artists Laura Aldridge and

Madame Yevonde,
Violet, Baroness von Gagern as Europa, 1935, archival pigment transfer print, 50.7 × 40.6 cm (P6649)

Celia Hempton, in the form of wall hangings and expressionist portraits in oil, respectively. The varied textures and forms of these works, as well as their mixed messages, communicating desire and torment, bodies and dress, performance and resistance, entered into new conversations with contributions from the region, among them the earliest known portrait by a woman in Serbia (Katarina Ivanović's 1837 painting of the strikingly self-possessed Anka Topalović) and, in Montenegro, Gordana Kuč's 2017 suggestive explorations of graphic forms and voids constructed with fishnet tights stretched over canvas. *Self-Portrait with Fried Eggs* by Lucas makes visual reference to a British slur about women's bodies, but the artist's take-no-prisoners demeanour speaks to women who face down sexism everywhere. Madame Yevonde's aristocratic women as classical goddesses represent a different demographic, as seen in the golden-robed Baroness von Gagern, who drapes herself across a garlanded bull's head as Europa. The surrealist performances of these women's dream selves, however, evoke archetypes that speak beyond their time and place.

Sarah Lucas, *Self Portrait with Fried Eggs* 1996, 1999, Iris print on watercolour paper, 80 x 60 cm (P7242)

ABOVE Celia Hempton, *Raul, Serbia, 2nd June 2014*, 2014, oil on canvas, 25 × 30 cm (P8545)

OPPOSITE Laura Aldridge, *Mean (Mean)*, 2014, fabric, wood, metal, string, 80 × 249 × 6 cm (P8548)

The five *Perceptions* exhibitions, organized by the collections manager Nicola Heald, were on sequential display in 2018 and 2019. They began at the National Museum of Montenegro in Cetinje, which displayed Collection works alongside Montenegrin counterparts under the title *Why Have There Been No Great (Wo)Men Artists?* In Serbia, *Women Tailored to Society* brought in work by female artists from the Gallery of Matica Srpska at Novi Sad. The title of the exhibition at the Kosova National Gallery in Pristina, *Burrneshat*, translates as 'sworn virgins', referring to women in the Albanian mountains who are said to live a man's life. The word is also used to compliment a woman who shows decisiveness and strength.[41] *The Beauty of a Flower is in the Picking*, in Banja Luka in Bosnia and Herzegovina, was named after a folk proverb that is also the title of a work by Sandra Dukić, the first female artist in that city's Museum of Contemporary Art of Republic of Srpska.[42] The Museum of Contemporary Art in Skopje followed with *Engendered*, in combination with Macedonian artists. The project continues, with further Western Balkans collaborative exhibitions planned.

In each case, the organizing curators chose their own titles and themes. As Dexter reflected, 'It is all about authorship. If you want your partners to really engage with a project, they have to own it.' As a curator, she admitted, 'When we first started working on projects like this, I would think, "Can we really do that? Can we let go?" Now, I know it's the only way to work.'[43] It was also important to reshape exhibitions at each site, as social conditions vary widely in the Western Balkans, a region whose title is a geopolitical grouping rather than a geographical cluster. Different countries not only have their own art histories, but also diverse attitudes to the position of women in society and in the art world, as well as to their representation in art. Serbian women artists, for example, had long been active in the Serbian art scene and are well represented in the Serbian national collections, but in Kosovo the first woman graduated from art school only in the 1970s when women's production was limited to needlework.[44]

Women's rights remain, of course, a live issue across the globe and in many sectors, and that includes the arts. Gender imbalance had been a characteristic of the earlier Fine Arts department, which, despite Somerville's leadership through the 1950s and 1960s, had been male-dominated from the outset. As with other British arts organizations, this situation began to shift in the 1980s, and today the Visual Arts department's workforce is strongly female. Even so, diversity of representation was not considered relevant to the British Council Collection's collecting criteria until comparatively recently, and it still has fewer works by women than by men (although its mix is better than some other collections). Gender equality is a key objective for the British Council as a whole; the empowerment of women and girls has been a consistent theme of its global programming for a number of years. For the Council, cultural and political issues are never far apart, and the proximity of the *Perceptions* exhibitions to the 2018 Western Balkans summit hosted in London was planned. That event brought together heads of governments with European Union leaders to facilitate political cooperation, strengthen regional security, and increase economic stability with a view to the region's future European integration.[45] Gender equality is one of the values that must be demonstrated by countries wishing to gain entry to the European Union. In the case of the *Perceptions* tour in the Western Balkans, therefore, government policies, British Council agendas, and Visual Arts practices aligned, enabling projects that are meaningful to communities wishing for social change.

A museum without walls

One key purpose of the establishment of the British Council Collection was to make it easier to lend art to parts of the world where other works could not travel. It has also been used as a tool to communicate with artistic communities overseas, including, in the British Council's parlance, aspirants, influencers, and leaders,[46] but this still relies on the existence of institutions to display the work. How can the Collection reach those who do not have easy access to museums and galleries, or who might not feel comfortable entering such a space, or for whom there may be an impediment to doing so? The belief that the arts are not a luxury is core to the British Council's strategy *Arts for All*, which seeks to pioneer practices of inclusion, the representation of marginalized voices, and widening of access. To address these issues in the context of new digital possibilities, the British Council Collection has been used to create new online innovations.

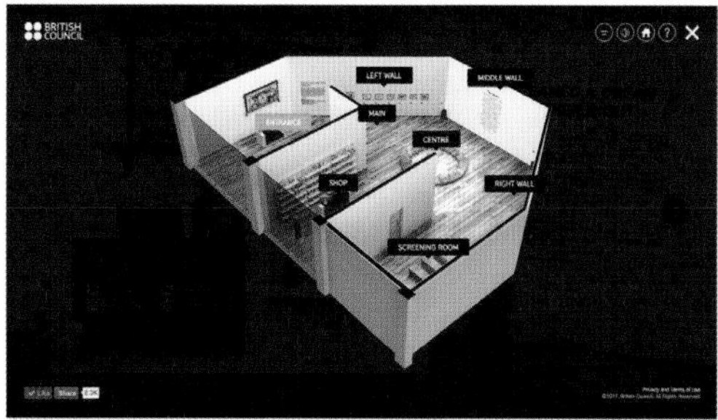

LEFT AND OPPOSITE
Screenshots from the digital exhibition *I Dreamed a Dream the Other Night*, 2017

In 2016, the Turkish curator Elif Kamışlı was selected to curate the first *Museum Without Walls* digital exhibition. This was a five-year project initiated by Turkish colleagues to develop new curatorial talents. Kamışlı had a short research visit to London to see the Collection and also undertook training at Whitechapel Gallery, provided by the British Council Cultural Skills team. Following this, she constructed a digital exhibition of British landscape and sculpture, entitled *I Dreamed a Dream the Other Night*. The Visual Arts department has long provided digital supports for exhibitions in the form of accompanying web resources; *I Dreamed a Dream the Other Night* offered something further, creating digital versions of art works, including a version of Richard Long's *Spring Circle* that particularly pleased the artist.[47] The exhibition's accessibility was enhanced by dual-language narratives and audio descriptions. The end result attracted visitors from more than one hundred countries, and won 2017 Website of the Year in Istanbul.

BRITISH
COUNCIL

BRITISH
COUNCIL

BRITISH
COUNCIL

Screenshots from the digital exhibition *Dancing with Witches*, 2019

Pinar Yolaçan, *Untitled* from the *Perishables* series, 2004
Digital C-print,
81.3 x 101.6 cm

The next digital exhibition in the series was *You Look Familiar* in 2018 – a portrait exhibition reflecting on the power of the form to disrupt stereotypes.[48] The exhibition was curated by Ulya Soley of the Pera Museum in Istanbul, who was chosen, like Kamışlı before her, from an open competition. Curator Mine Kaplangi curated the third exhibition in the series, *Dancing with Witches*, which explored representations of powerful women across painting, print, photographs, sculpture, video, and historic posters. Here the website was designed as a haunting, immersive space in the woods, and storytelling works by Peter Blake and Paula Rego, for example, are enhanced by disembodied whispers and animal cries. *Dancing with Witches* also integrated the work of Turkish contemporary artists, such as Pinar Yolaçan, whose older female subjects present noble expressions despite being dressed in pale, bloodless animal parts. Nearly five million Turkish citizens have at least one disability; additionally, a billion people experience disability worldwide.[49] Together, these *Museum Without Walls* projects created easy-to-open gateways to the British

Council Collection; by 2019, approximately nine hundred thousand visitors had engaged with the exhibitions.[50]

The *Museum Without Walls* concept, drawn from André Malraux's 1965 French text of that name, which imagined globally democratized access to art collections, serves as a fitting description for the British Council Collection's activities.[51] The term captures its flexibility and its ambitions to push at boundaries. The phrase also formed the basis for an artistic commission in 2012; Ed Hall produced two large-scale appliqué textile works in the mode of trade union campaign banners. Each depicts key pieces from the Collection. One of them is foregrounded by blue appliqué squares signalling the British Council Collection's packing crates used to transport the works around the world. These fabric squares are a tiny gesture of recognition of the enormous intellectual labour and practical expertise that underpins the shipping of fragile and valuable art to every corner of the globe.

Dissonance and dissent

Hall's banners were a particularly appropriate commission as his work forms a major part of Jeremy Deller and Alan Kane's *Folk Archive*, whose 280-plus items – including joke-shop displays, ceremonial costume, prisoners' drawings, and cigarette art – belong to the British Council Collection. Its unruly public record of everyday responses to life in Britain was originally created in counterpoint to the vision of the nation that the artists feared would populate London's Millennium Dome.[52] It is therefore fitting that it travels at the service of the British Council, whose status as a non-departmental public body encapsulates a similar set of official-unofficial locations. The forms of *Folk Archive* bear some resemblance to Muriel Rose's *Exhibition of Modern British Crafts*, and both projects raise similar questions about their humble materials. What did hand-crafted teapots and table mats, ashtrays and armoires, corn dollies and cushion covers embody when they travelled three and a half thousand miles to the United States, under conditions of war? And what cultural purpose does it serve for the British Council to carefully conserve, crate, and fly embroidered underpants, false nails, and plastic turds five and a half thousand miles to South Korea?

Ed Hall, *British Council Collection Banner*, 2012, cotton drill, fabric paint, 194 × 358 cm (P8393)

Ed Hall, *British Council Collection Banner*, 2012, cotton drill, fabric paint, 194 × 358 cm (P8394)

ABOVE Ed Hall, *Brixton Bomb Protest Banner*, 1999, part of Jeremy Deller and Alan Kane, *Folk Archive: Contemporary Popular Art from the UK*, 2005 (P8028)

LEFT Tom Harrington, Cumberland and Westmoreland Wrestling Champion, Egremont, Cumbria, 1999, part of Jeremy Deller and Alan Kane, *Folk Archive: Contemporary Popular Art from the UK*, 2005 (P8028)

OPPOSITE Installation view of Doc Rowe and Jill Pidd's *Burry Man*, part of Jeremy Deller and Alan Kane, *Folk Archive: Contemporary Popular Art from the UK*, 2005 (P8028)

Two views of the exhibition *The Art of Dissonance*, Seoul Museum of Art, 2017

Bob and Roberta Smith's hand-painted protest placards in *The Art of Dissonance* exhibition

The Art of Dissonance, the 2017 exhibition in Seoul in which *Folk Archive* featured prominently, encapsulated many of the shifts in politics and culture in British Council practices of recent times. Jointly curated by Claire Feeley of the Visual Arts department and Gahee Park of the Seoul Museum of Art, the exhibition provided a forum, according to Choi Hyo-jun, the then director of the museum.[53] With Hall's appliqué campaign banners suspended above protest placards by Bob and Roberta Smith proclaiming 'Art Spreads Messages' and 'Art Saves Lives', the exhibition literally figured protest, but it also signalled more lateral strategies for dissent embodied by states of mind. As Alan Kane stated in an accompanying film, 'If an artist is doing their job properly, they are always going to be challenging something or other. Challenge is almost built into the job description.'[54] Lubaina Himid was represented in the show by three painted portraits, entitled *Lost Election Posters*, where she imagined an alternative black political history. Himid uses this work 'to remind people that they have agency'.[55] The imagined figures, whether from 1792 or 2015, prompt

An installation view of *The Art of Dissonance* shows Mona Hatoum's *Prayer Mat* on the right and Lubaina Himid's *Lost Election Posters* in the background

viewers to exercise and treasure their power at the ballot box. Himid describes her practice as 'political activism in paint'.[56] Lived political activism was reiterated in John Akomfrah's three-screen 2012 video installation examining the life and social context of black British critical theorist Stuart Hall (1932–2014). Entitled *The Unfinished Conversation*, the film's form and content demonstrated Hall's conception of identity as multiple, dialogic, and ongoing, in an exhibition dealing with similar themes.

Throughout the British Council's history of presenting art overseas, exhibitions have operated as messengers. The historic nature of its state funding, and now with its financial sponsorship from partners, and earned income, means that the works inevitably travel in the service of agendas to a greater or lesser extent. These agendas shift over time and alter according to the Council's priorities, the subjects of the exhibitions, and the particularities of place. One key finding that emerges from this study of almost nine decades' worth of exhibitions is that what is communicated is always about identity.

ABOVE Lubaina Himid, 1792, 2015, acrylic on canvas, 45.3 × 64 × 2 cm (P8600)

FOLLOWING PAGES John Akomfrah, *The Unfinished Conversation*, 2012, three-screen video with high-definition colour projections and surround sound, 45 minutes (P8519)

It may often be national identity, but it can also be personal identity, autonomy, and agency, the individuality of artistic vision and the freedom of expression to challenge norms, aesthetic or otherwise.

Political art that looked political was formerly the British Council's nemesis: not only was it too didactic and thus smacked of totalitarian regimes, but it also made culture political, and the British Council has always insisted that culture operates as a space apart. *The Art of Dissonance* included contemporary practice that intertwines art and activism, but it did more than provide a neutral presentation. It also suggested that art has political work to do in the world. Clearly this message has resonance in an exhibition only thirty miles from the border with North Korea, and that opened in the same month as North Korea tested a hydrogen bomb. The right to protest was communicated in the British ambassador's statement at the opening: 'Artists often present us with viewpoints that can be at odds with authority or challenge tradition. The freedom to create and present work in this way', Charles Hay noted, 'is fundamental to any society that values diverse opinions and the right to express these.'[57] The British Council's current arts strategy makes the same point: 'Artists in the UK have long reflected traditional values as well as questioning, mocking or undermining them.'[58] Artistic critique is a benefit of the form; the challenge and mockery it promotes are the values that it can spread.

New purchases: identity reprised

Since the 1930s, the British Council has been purchasing art to furnish its growing collection. This work continues. To bring the story full circle, I explore some recent additions. The Acquisitions Advisory Committee Steering Group – comprising directors and curators of museums and galleries in the United Kingdom – advises on purchasing plans; a collection policy ensures that it meets institutional requirements of transparency and diversity.[59] Moira Lindsay, the head of the Collection, notes that the central criterion is to collect the best of artistic practice: 'This is always the top priority. Work may align with British Council principles, but it would never be acquired solely to meet Council objectives.' Purchases reflect current concerns – such as new collaborative ways of working – as well as innovations in materials and form. 'There are debates in the team about the acquisition of works that have the potential to shock', Lindsay adds. In an echo of earlier generations of the department, she feels that, 'the Collection exists to showcase what Britain has to say around the world, and it is important to represent what British artists are saying. The Council is not a government organization, and this gives us a certain level of freedom to create its messages. That said,' she cautions, 'all work needs to be usable.'[60]

Diversity, equality, and inclusion are all key British Council agendas, and the Acquisitions Advisory Committee Steering Group, working closely with the Visual Arts team, has worked hard to ensure that the Collection represents, as much as possible, the range of work produced in contemporary Britain, including acquiring works by artists who had previously been overlooked, even as the remit and budget of the Collection does not allow exhaustive or encyclopaedic coverage. Purchases since 2015 have included Donald Rodney, Lubaina Himid, Claudette Johnson, and Rasheed Araeen, all of whom have contributed significantly to British art, including as part of the Black British Art Movement of the 1980s, but none of whom had been purchased before. These shifts take place in the context of wider debates about diversity and decolonization in museum collections, but have particular resonance in a collection rooted in a national frame. How to represent identities, however, is tricky in visual art; artists may not want to be identified as a representative of a particular aspect of gender, sexuality, ethnicity, religious belief, or (dis)ability. The communication of identity can be more subtle. As I have argued throughout this book, art in the British Council Collection, because of its context, becomes more or less about identity of some kind whenever it travels for Council purposes. Sometimes, however, a work is all about identity, and this is the case with two recent purchases.

Untitled by Hardeep Pandhal features the artist's first-class fine-art degree certificate at its centre, overpainted with motifs from a cult movie and Sikh iconography. A gun-toting Al Pacino appears in a drawing from the final scene of *Scarface*, in which his character leads an impossible shootout and continues to stand triumphant despite being gunned down from all sides.

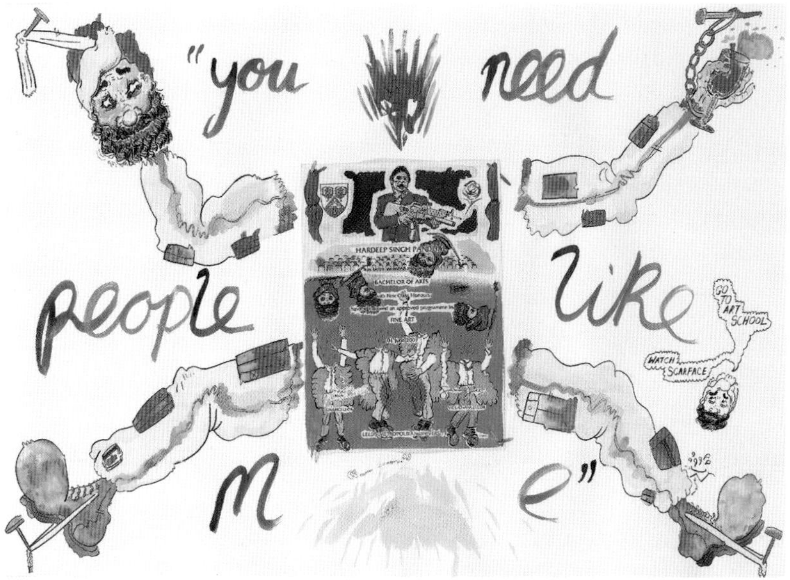

Hardeep Pandhal, *Untitled*, 2014, Indian ink, gouache, and BA (Hons) Fine Art degree on paper, 42 × 60 cm (P8679)

Beneath this, turbanned heads spin off decapitated graduates, making reference to Baba Deep Singh, the eighteenth-century Indian Sikh martyr who was said to have continued to avenge the desecration of a temple by the Afghan army despite being beheaded on the battlefield. According to legend, he held his head in his left hand and swung his sword in his right. Baba Deep Singh appears as a recurrent motif across Pandhal's practice, often as a superhero, not least when featured on knitwear made by his mother.

Pandhal learned about postcolonial theory during his degree and links its ideas to his Sikh Punjabi family heritage, his experience of racism, the monoculture of his art education, and his tastes in pop culture. The statement 'you need people like me' that surrounds the certificate takes a joyful swipe at positive ethnic discrimination in the arts, even as Pandhal believes its necessity in the building of a fairer world.[61] Complex issues, bundled into a rich iconography of symbols and signs, characterize Pandhal's witty works. Their visual strength and the proximity of his themes to the concerns of the British Council made him a top priority for purchase. There was discussion about cultural sensitivity; the team in Visual Arts wanted to be certain that his irony would travel. They were interested in his collaborative family working methods and his use of materials from textiles to video, but they selected a piece that spoke of British history, cultural identity, pop culture, student life, and art institutions. 'When one work can communicate such a lot,' Lindsay explained, 'it is highly adaptable for exhibition purposes.'[62]

Another recent buy is *What We Don't Know Won't Hurt Us? (Self-Portrait)* by Delaine Le Bas, a cross-disciplinary artist and member of the Romany traveller community in southern England. Made of a shamanic mask and a ribbon-embellished dress with a central embroidered panel, the wall piece is one of two works bought in 2019 directly from the artist, who has been making art, both singly and as half of a partnership with her late husband Damian Le Bas, since 1984. She mixes media with a bricolage methodology, gathering objects from disparate sources and grouping them into banners, altars, and other assemblages. Combining personal references from family photographs with images from mass media, she constructs a layered world. Central to the mix is the romanticization and demonization of Romany Gypsies. In *What We Don't Know Won't Hurt Us?*, Le Bas depicts the shadows lurking beneath the picturesque landscape by picking apart Victorian ladies in crinolines from embroidered tablecloths, and skeletal forms from fashion accessories. On a pink party dress, the work evokes poisoned fairy tales and the painful truths behind pastoral myths.

This was the artist's first work to be purchased by a national collection; she has exhibited overseas more than in her own country. When considering the acquisition, the Visual Arts team highlighted Le Bas's production techniques; collections care and conservation issues also informed the selection, since the artist works with fragile and ephemeral materials. As the British Council Collection travels extensively, such questions are also part of purchasing decisions.[63] In particular, the department was interested in the way that Le Bas communicates as a woman, wife, and mother. Her work makes international references through the material that she has gathered on her travels, and it speaks about marginalized communities, not least as she reflects on her Romany background. The multiple alignments between Le Bas's messages and the objectives of the Council mean that the work can reach a wide range of groups around the world.

Multiple visions

Acquisitions made in 2019 might seem a very long way from the beginnings of the British Council Collection, but the multiplicity of voices within its holdings leads to echoes and refrains. As a native other, raised in small-town Sussex, Le Bas channels her rage into representations of the rural, and reads history against the grain, showing the elements that it chooses to omit or ignore. Inevitably, the latest works return us to the first. Duncan Grant's *Charleston Barn* from 1942 (see page 74), the first painting listed in the acquisitions ledger, might seem to embody such romantic omissions. Journalist Geraldine Bedell has described it as 'chocolate-boxy' and 'inward-looking' and dismissed it as 'a bucolic idyll of a certain kind of Britain' that is 'not the one the British Council wants to promote any more'.[64] In another reading, however, the rural Sussex site that Grant represented was painted in wartime by a conscientious objector, when locations within ten miles of England's south coast were on the front line of the expected invasion.[65] The painting depicted a vulnerable country in troubled times, framed by international conflict. It is the British Council Collection's multiple visions, by a variety of artists living in Britain over many generations, that make it such an extraordinary resource to review what British art means. Each work casts new lights and shadows on the others; they operate in collaboration. Debates about national identity and isolation, federation and unity have never been louder. Who we are in the world remains hard to see and important to picture; multiple viewpoints are needed.

Delaine Le Bas, *What We Don't Know Won't Hurt Us? (Self Portrait)*, 2006–18, mixed-media sculpture, 293 × 54 cm (P8680)

What we don't Know Won't

CASE No. 1
83 x 79 x 104 CMS
66 KGS
HT35S
CASE No.
CMS
P6594
HT1S4
CASE No. 1
77 x 66 x 75 CMS
81 KGS
HT46
CASE No. 1
77 x 66 x 75 CMS
81 KGS
P7S70
P7S70
CASE No.
90 KGS
FULL
IN
CASE No. 1
98 x 66 x 103
179
Mtec
BCV-EQUIPMENT 2019/1
BRITISH COUNCIL VENICE
TOOLS AND ENGINEERING EQUIPMENT 2019
BIENNALE
98 X 66 X 103 cm 179kg 1 OF 3

CONCLUSION

An ongoing journey

This book has examined the practices of the British Council's Fine Arts and Visual Arts departments and the development of the British Council Collection over nine decades. There are many possible tales to be told during this long and rich period, with fascinating personalities, extraordinary art, and a complex world history. Inevitably, with such a texture of times, voices, places, works, and exhibitions, I can tell only some of those stories here. The fact that there is so much more to be said is testament to the depth and richness of the Collection and its use. As an outsider to the organization, I have looked beyond the bureaucracy to find the most telling of moments, objects, and encounters, exploring challenges and successes. Where I have highlighted controversies, these illuminate the passionate investments made of art in cultural relations.

Through an exploration of international exhibitions, and particularly the establishment, development, and use of the British Council Collection, the book has charted several themes. These include art in cultural relations, and its various roles as projection, persuasion, protest, and partnership; the intersections between art and national identity, including the Britishness of British art, its inclusions and exclusions, and its increasing hybridity and multiplicity; and the shifting purpose of the British Council itself, from international competition to global collaboration, and from early certainties to later self-critique, all played out against changing objectives and geopolitical context.

The blue packing cases used to transport the British Council Collection works

The chronological format enables a view of a project in development. As the work continues and the Collection expands, the book's core questions remain pertinent: What kinds of engagement can international art exhibitions allow? What parts can art reach that other means of communication may not?

As I have shown, while the art in the British Council Collection may not be individually propagandist in message, it is nonetheless used to serve specific agendas. This leads to another key question: does the use of art in cultural relations amount to its political instrumentalization and thus reduce its value? The answer depends on whether culture and politics are seen as separate spheres or necessarily interconnected; whether one believes in 'art for art's sake' or in art's socially productive capacities. It also depends, of course, on how one defines both art and politics. As art historian Anthony Downey has argued, art may be understood as an inherently social act that engages audiences, participants, and institutions in critical discourse; as such, it always has a socio-political dimension.[1] At its most critical, art explores the parameters of these discourses, as well as producing them. 'Doing art means displacing art's borders', the French philosopher Jacques Rancière has noted in *The Paradoxes of Political Art*, 'just as doing politics means displacing the borders of what is acknowledged as the political.'[2] As the book's title acknowledges, art has the capacity to resist and reframe any boundaries put around it; as it travels across geographical frontiers, it has the capacity to do the same work in the world.

Art in the British Council Collection was formed to serve British Council objectives in international cultural relations, and it continues to travel, extraordinarily widely and frequently, now supported by the Council's own financial resources, external sponsorship, and earned income. The Council has variously operated as a charity, a commercial entity, and a state-funded agency at different times and places. Its purposes have been reframed and re-emphasized over its long history, but in relation to the visual arts, these have been underpinned by three core principles: to promote British art abroad for the purpose of reputation-building and to create public benefit; to align with or otherwise support diplomatic policy agendas; and to enable meaningful international exchange to stimulate interconnection and mutual understanding. Some of these agendas may not always have been explicit, and at times they may run in counterpoint to one another; at other times, however, they sit together as neatly as a set of nesting tables.

The use and reception of the Collection overseas may complement or challenge the agendas of government, but in the spirit of the British Council's arm's-length structure of independence, it has its own autonomy. Its potential to provoke is what draws the crowds and creates the headlines, yet the arts are much more than a straight messaging system. The way that they inspire imaginations and encourage creative responses make them potentially sites of profound engagement but also slippery containers of meaning. Art's significance can be complex and ambiguous. Its messages can clarify, but also complicate. The Collection's capacity to start debate is part of its risk, but also its central appeal.

Art is a highly invested category that can evoke strong emotional reactions. It may create powerful feelings of identification or repulsion in subject matter or form; its meaning may baffle or illuminate. As objects that are prized culturally and valued financially, as fragile objects transported with great care across vast distances sometimes at enormous risk, the British Council Collection embodies trust, investment, and commitment. Art in the Council's cultural relations work is understood to be a means of peacekeeping and of producing social change. There are many things art cannot do, of course, and it would be naive to expect exhibitions to resolve conflict. However, art can communicate and model liberal values, including equality, democracy, tolerance, freedom of speech, pluralism, and humanism, even if, in the case of works in the British Council Collection, they rarely depict these explicitly. The way that art opens up conversations about cultural purpose, value, and identity means that art exhibitions can become productive sites of international intercultural encounter and debate about similarity and difference, self and other, home and abroad. This capacity has been shown repeatedly through almost ninety years of British Council examples, and the potential of the Collection to promote fresh thinking through new forms and formats is far from exhausted.

While the component works of the Collection are individually interesting, a fascinating aspect, which adds fundamentally to its richness, is the variety of uses to which it can be put. The exhibitions in which its works appear, whether in part or whole, have been aesthetically diverse and geographically ambitious. There is no official national style and no singular message; instead they show art's variety and endless capacity for recoding. Mixed messaging may happen in distinctive ways when the art is non-figurative, but a range of possible readings can also happen when figurative works making seemingly clear statements are put into new thematic conjunctions. These reinterpretations shift the meanings, which change also in different places and times.

The reasons that art was collected by the British Council can be traced through archival records, but its purpose is not static; works are rethought with every rehang. The authority that they carry as embodiments of artistic quality is reinforced by the reputations built as they travel. Most interestingly, however, the uses to which such art works have been and can yet be put are multiple and open ended. More than 8,700 works by in excess of 1,250 artists operating in 110-plus countries over more than 80 years: numbers alone show the enormous scope of possible configurations. When fresh perspectives are added in the form of interpreters from outside the organization and beyond the Collection's country of origin, the potential to refresh meanings is expanded even further.

The British Council is not the only conduit through which British art and artists can travel overseas. Expanded networks for art, sophisticated gallery infrastructures, and advanced shipping logistics have all facilitated international artistic exchange. British Council work in the visual arts, however, has primed the ground. The relationships established between senior cultural figures and major institutions over nine decades have created a basis on which others can build. The Collection is a material and visual history of these endeavours and a fertile base to form new directions. As works move across the globe, they witness the complex and changing circumstances of world history and, in their own way, contribute to and leave a mark upon them.

What art is for in the British Council is not the same today as it was in 1934; an audience's interpretation of a work's meaning is not necessarily the same as that of its maker or purchaser; those who receive exhibitions do not always view them as was intended by those who conceived them. Its capacity to engender multiple, layered messages in diverse sites and contexts – and the regular and provocative ways in which this happens all over the world – shows the enormous potential of the British Council Collection, not only as a body of British contemporary art for the purpose of international cultural relations, but also a means to reflect upon what those terms can mean and what those objects can achieve.

NOTES

Introduction

1 The British Council, <https://www.britishcouncil.org/>, accessed 27 August 2019.

2 'Report on the Council's Work, For the year ended 31 March 1943', *British Council Annual Report 1942–3*, 1943, p. 5.

3 Harold Nicolson, 'The British Council 1934–1955', *British Council 21st Anniversary Report*, 1955, p. 5.

4 A. J. S. White, *The British Council: The First 25 Years 1934–1959* (London: British Council, 1965), p. 2.

5 Harold Nicolson, 'The British Council 1934–1955', op. cit., p. 7.

6 'Report on the Council's Work, For the year ended 31 March 1943', op. cit., p. 5.

7 'Report on the Council's Work, For the year ended 31 March 1945', *British Council Annual Report 1944–5*, 1945, p. 9.

8 'Report on the Council's Work, For the year ended 31 March 1943', op. cit., p. 5.

9 Philip M. Taylor, *The Projection of Britain: British Overseas Publicity and Propaganda 1919–1939* (Cambridge: Cambridge University Press, 1981), p. 125.

10 Harold Nicolson, 'The British Council 1934–1955', op. cit., p. 11.

11 'Introduction', *British Council Annual Report 1946–7*, 1947, p. 9.

12 Fine Arts Committee minutes, 22 October 1936, p. 4.

13 Fine Arts Committee minutes, 29 September 1938, p. 3.

14 Nicholas J. Cull, 'Overture to an Alliance: British Propaganda at the New York World's Fair, 1939–1940', *Journal of British Studies*, Vol. 36, No. 3 (July 1997), p. 341.

15 Public Record Office, Kew, Foreign Office 371/20651, A2378, Ronald Lindsay to Anthony Eden, No. 247, 22 March 1937, quoted in ibid., p. 330.

16 Fine Arts Committee minutes, 26 October 1939, p. 1.

17 Nicholas J. Cull, 'Overture to an Alliance', op. cit., p. 339.

18 Ibid., p. 352.

19 Marco Duranti, 'Utopia, Nostalgia and World War at the 1939–40 New York World's Fair', *Journal of Contemporary History*, Vol. 41, No. 4 (October 2006), pp. 663–83.

20 Fine Arts Committee minutes, 25 November 1937, p.2.

21 Andrea Rose, 'Introduction', *The British Council Collection 1984–1994* (London: British Council, 1995), p. ix.

22 Fiona McCarthy, *Eric Gill* (London: Faber and Faber, 1989).

23 Penelope Hughes-Stanton, *The Wood Engravings of Blair Hughes-Stanton* (Pinner: Private Libraries Association, 1991).

24 *British Council Annual Report 1942–3*, op. cit.

Chapter 1

1 Major Alfred A. Longden, letter to Muriel Rose, 25 April 1941. Muriel Rose archival papers 8b.1387. Crafts Study Centre, Farnham.

2 Eric Maclagan, 'Introductory Note', *The Exhibition of Modern British Crafts* (London: British Council, 1942), p. 5.

3 Ibid., p. 6.

4 Muriel Rose, 'Curriculum Vitae', 20 December 1945. Muriel Rose archival papers 8e.1438, Crafts Study Centre, Farnham.

5 'Miss Rose's Report to be read at Fine Arts Committee', n.d. (*c.* 1945). Muriel Rose archival papers 8e.1437, Crafts Study Centre, Farnham.

6 Ibid.

7 Ibid.

8 Letter to Muriel Rose from Allan Eaton, director of the Arts Department of the Russell Sage Foundation, New York (quoting Mr Constable, curator at Museum of Fine Arts, Boston; director of the Toledo Museum; and a press report from *Telegram*, Worcester), 1942. Extracts from Letters and Reports 1942–3, 8e.1433, Muriel Rose archival papers, Crafts Study Centre, Farnham.

9 Ibid.

10 Charles Marriott, 'Preface', *Exhibition of Modern British Crafts* (London: British Council, 1942), p. 9.

11 Extracts from Letters and Reports 1942–3, 8e.1433, Muriel Rose archival papers, Crafts Study Centre, Farnham.

12 Vanessa Vanden Burghe, *Oliver Hill and the Enigma of British Modernism in the Interwar Period*, unpublished PhD thesis, University of East London, 2013.

13 Oliver Hill and Muriel Rose, 'Exhibition of British Craftsmanship 1490–1940', Muriel Rose archival papers 8c.1393, Crafts Study Centre, Farnham.

14 Extracts from Letters and Reports 1942–3, 8e.1433, Muriel Rose archival papers, Crafts Study Centre, Farnham.
15 'Notes for a planned exhibition', Muriel Rose archival papers 8c.1392, Crafts Study Centre, Farnham.
16 H. J. Massingham, 'Preface', *Exhibition of Rural Handicrafts from Great Britain* (London: British Council, 1945), pp. 7–10.
17 Ibid., p. 9.
18 Bernard Leach in 1928, quoted in Tanya Harrod, '"The Breath of Reality": Michael Cardew and the Development of Studio Pottery in the 1930s and 1940s', *Journal of Design History*, Vol. 2, No. 2/3 (1989), p. 145.
19 Kate Woodhead, 'Foreword', in Jean Vacher (ed.), *Muriel Rose: A Modern Crafts Legacy* (Farnham: Crafts Study Centre, 2006), p. 5.
20 Charles Marriott, 'Preface', *Exhibition of Modern British Crafts*, op. cit.
21 Simon Laurence, *Dunbar Hay Ltd 1935–40 and the Achievements of Cecilia Dunbar Kilburn* (London: The Fleece Press, 2016).
22 James Noel White, 'The Unexpected Phoenix I: The Sutherland Tea Set', *Craft History*, Vol. 1 (1988), pp. 49–64.
23 Ibid.
24 Extracts from Letters and Reports 1942–3, Muriel Rose archival papers, 8e.1433, Crafts Study Centre, Farnham.
25 Tanya Harrod, 'Outbreak of Talent', review of Andy Friend, *Ravilious & Co.: The Pattern of Friendship* (London: Thames & Hudson, 2017), *Literary Review*, No. 452 (April 2017).
26 Simon Olding, 'Muriel Rose: An Introduction', *Muriel Rose: A Modern Crafts Legacy* (Farnham: Crafts Study Centre, 2006), p. 13.
27 'The Craft Collection', *The British Council Collection 1984–1994* (London: British Council, 1994), pp. 121–2.
28 The Wedgwood ceramic carpet bowls were transferred as a gift to the Potteries Museum & Art Gallery in Stoke-on-Trent in 2007. Other ceramic items were donated to the Crafts Study Centre in Farnham in 2006 and to University of Wales, Aberystwyth, in 2007.
29 Craft activities, including the current British Council commissioning project *Crafting Futures*, now sit within the remit of the British Council's department of Architecture, Design and Fashion (ADF). Craft and design (including architecture) came in and out of the remit of the Fine Arts Department (renamed Visual Arts in the 1980s), throughout its life. In 2000, the department was briefly renamed Art, Architecture, and Design. ADF was later created as a standalone area.
30 Reports on British Council Exhibitions Abroad, Tate Archive, TGA200317/2/232.
31 *Home for Orphaned Dishes*, Tokyo, <https://home-for-orphaned-dishes-jp.tumblr.com>, accessed 25 August 2020.

Chapter 2

1 The offer and selection of these works took place in 1946, according to minutes of the Fine Arts Committee. The Acquisitions Register lists the works as coming into the Collection permanently in 1948.
2 Fine Arts Committee minutes, 24 July 1946, p. 3.
3 Fine Arts Committee minutes, 29 May 1946, p. 4.
4 Paul Nash, letter to *The Times*, quoted in 'Unit One', Tate, <https://www.tate.org.uk/art/art-terms/u/unit-one>, accessed 23 June 2019.
5 Fine Arts Committee minutes, 28 March 1946, p. 4.
6 *British Council Annual Report*, 1946–7, 1947, p. 71.
7 Alfred Munnings quoted in Andrew Brighton, '"Where Are the Boys of the Old Brigade?" The Post-War Decline of British Traditionalist Painting", *Oxford Art Journal*, Vol. 4, No. 1 (July 1981), pp. 35–43.
8 Letter from H. C. Travell Stronge to the Director of Fine Art, 9 October 1956, TGA 200317/5/1.
9 Letter from H. C. Travell Stronge to the Director of Fine Art, 20 November 1946, TGA 200317/5/1.
10 Michael Middleton, 'Points arising from the reception of the current exhibition of British Painting in Sweden', April 1948, TGA 200317/5/1.
11 Translations of Swedish newspaper reviews, TGA 200317/5/1.
12 Michael Middleton, 'Points arising from the reception of the current exhibition of British Painting in Sweden', op. cit.

13 Ibid.
14 'Art and Palmerston North', unknown source, n.d., n.p. Newspaper cuttings, TGA9712/2/47.
15 Ibid.
16 Tom Bolster, 'Will British Art Jolt Auckland Too?', *Auckland Star*, 12 June 1953, n.p.; 'Art Exhibition "Trash"', *Birmingham Mail*, 4 June 1953; 'Art '"Trash" from British Council', *Yorkshire Evening Post*, 5 June 1953. Newspaper cuttings, TGA9712/2/47.
17 'Art and Palmerston North', op. cit.
18 Ibid.
19 Sybil A. A. Ferguson, Hon. Secretary and Members of the Palmerston North Art Group, letter to the New Zealand Representative, British Council, 9 June 1953.
20 Members of the Palmerston North Art Group, 'Correspondence: City Council and British Council', unknown source, n.d., n.p. Newspaper cuttings, TGA9712/2/47.
21 Fine Arts Committee minutes, 2 December 1947, p. 4.
22 Pauline Rose, *Henry Moore in America: Art, Business and the Special Relationship* (London: I. B. Tauris, 2014), p. 55.
23 'Henry Moore: Reclining Figure, 1939', Tate, <https://www.tate.org.uk/art/research-publications/henry-moore/henry-moore-om-ch-reclining-figure-r1147454>, accessed 23 June 2019.
24 Lyndsey Morgan and Rozemarijn van der Mole, 'Henry Moore's Approach to Bronze', Tate, <https://www.tate.org.uk/art/research-publications/henry-moore/lyndsey-morgan-and-rozemarijn-van-der-molen-henry-moores-approach-to-bronze-r1151468>, accessed 23 June 2019.
25 Sebastiano Barassi and James Copper, 'Henry Moore and Stone: Methods and Materials', Tate, <https://www.tate.org.uk/art/research-publications/henry-moore/sebastiano-barassi-and-james-copper-henry-moore-and-stone-methods-and-materials-r1151462>, accessed 23 June 2019.
26 Clive Phillpot, 'Introduction', in Sophie Bowness and Clive Phillpot (eds), *Britain at the Venice Biennale 1895–1995* (London: British Council, 1995), pp. 11–13.
27 This term was repeatedly used in relation to Moore by his supporters. Andrew Stephenson locates its earliest use by Nikolaus Pevsner in 1945. Andrew Stephenson, 'Fashioning a Post-War Reputation: Henry Moore as a Civic Sculptor *c.* 1943–58 in *Henry Moore: Sculptural Process and Public Identity*, Tate Research Publication, 2015, <https://www.tate.org.uk/art/research-publications/henry-moore/andrew-stephenson-fashioning-a-post-war-reputation-henry-moore-as-a-civic-sculptor-c1943-r1151305#fn_1_105>, accessed 5 November 2019.
28 Henry Meyric Hughes, 'The Promotion and Reception of British Sculpture Abroad, 1948–1960: Herbert Read, Henry Moore, Barbara Hepworth, and the "Young British Sculptors"', *British Art Studies*, No. 3 (July 2016), <https://www.britishartstudies.ac.uk/issues/issue-index/issue-3/1945-1960>, accessed 23 June 2019.
29 Herbert Read, catalogue essay. Papers relating to the Henry Moore Exhibition, Greece, 1951, TGA9712/2/48.
30 Lilian Somerville, letter to British Council representative in Athens, 9 October 1950. Papers relating to the Henry Moore exhibition, Greece, 1951, TGA9712/2/48.
31 Henry Moore Exhibitions of Drawings in Guadalajara, Jalisco, Mexico, February-March 1950, TGA9712/2/39.
32 Geoffrey Grigson, catalogue essay. Papers relating to the Henry Moore Exhibition, Mexico, 1950/1, TGA9712/2/38.
33 Ibid.
34 Ibid.
35 Lola Vidrio, 'Reflections on the Opening of an Exhibition', 9 June 1950, unknown source. Papers relating to the Henry Moore Exhibition, Mexico, 1950/1, TGA9712/2/38.
36 M. G. Field (administrative officer, Mexico), report. Papers relating to the Henry Moore exhibition, Mexico, 1950/1, TGA9712/2/38.
37 Mathias Georitz, letter to Henry Moore, 19 February 1950. Papers relating to the Henry Moore exhibition, Mexico, 1950/1, TGA9712/2/38.
38 Ibid.
39 *Sunday Times*, 4 March 1951. Papers relating to the Henry Moore exhibition, Greece, 1951, TGA9712/2/48.
40 W. G. Tatham

(representative, Greece), letter to Lectures Department, 17 March 1951. Papers relating to the Henry Moore exhibition, Greece, 1951, TGA9712/2/48.

41 Mr Lidderdale (representative, Greece), report. Papers relating to the Henry Moore exhibition, Greece, 1951, TGA9712/2/48.

42 Report on the Henry Moore Exhibition in Athens, 4–22 March. Papers relating to the Henry Moore exhibition, Greece, 1951, TGA9712/2/48.

43 W. G. Tatham (representative, Greece), 12 April 1951. Papers relating to the Henry Moore exhibition, Greece, 1951, TGA9712/2/48.

44 Ibid.

45 *Annual Report, Greece*, 1950–1. Papers relating to the Henry Moore exhibition, Greece, 1951, TGA9712/2/48.

46 Translation of article in *Aimos*, 18 April 1951. Papers relating to the Henry Moore exhibition, Greece, 1951, TGA9712/2/48.

47 Moore itinerary. Papers relating to the Henry Moore exhibition, Greece, 1951, TGA9712/2/48.

48 'Henry Moore's Exhibition', *Kathimerini*, 12 March 1951. Papers relating to the Henry Moore exhibition, Greece, 1951, TGA9712/2/48.

49 *Ethnos*, 14 March 1951.

50 Larraine Nicholas, 'Fellow Travellers: Dance and British Cold War Politics in the Early 1950s', *Dance Research: The Journal of the Society for Dance Research*, Vol. 19, No. 2 (2001), p. 97, quoted in Verity Clarkson, *The Organisation and Reception of Eastern Bloc Exhibitions on the British Cold War 'Home Front' c. 1956–1979* (University of Brighton, unpublished PhD thesis, 2010), p. 15.

51 Rose, *Henry Moore in America*, p. 13.

52 Julian Trevelyan, *Indigo Days: The Art and Memoirs of Julian Trevelyan* (Aldershot: Scolar Press, 1996 [1957]), p. 55.

53 A full exploration of the use and effect of the work of Henry Moore in cultural relations would fill a book in itself. As just one of many examples of post-exhibition events, as a demonstration of his support for emerging democracies, Moore donated a sculpture, *Helmet Head 6*, to the National Gallery of Bulgaria after his British Council travelling exhibition visited Sofia in 1959. With thanks to British Council staff Jenny White and Krassimira Tancheva for this information.

54 Henry Meyric Hughes, 'The Promotion and Reception of British Sculpture Abroad, 1948–1960', op. cit.

55 Ibid.

56 Nancy Jachec, 'The "New British Sculpture" at the Venice Biennale: Europeanism and its limits', *British Art Journal*, Vol. 7, No. 1 (Spring/Summer 2006), pp. 25–32.

57 Fine Arts Committee minutes, 1 July 1952, p. 1.

58 Alfred Barr, Letter to the *Manchester Guardian*, 3 September 1952. Report on Progress to the 54th Meeting of the British Council's Fine Arts Committee, Tuesday, 9 December 1952 quoted in Henry Meyric Hughes, 'The Promotion and Reception of British Sculpture Abroad, 1948–1960', op. cit.

59 Fine Arts Committee minutes, 1 July 1952, p. 1.

60 *British Council Annual Report*, 1952–3, p. 45.

61 Kenneth Armitage interviewed by John McEwen and Tamsyn Woollcombe, National Life Stories: Artists' Lives C466/08, British Library, p. 106, <https://sounds.bl.uk/related-content/TRANSCRIPTS/021T-C0466X0008XX-ZZZZA0.pdf>, accessed 23 June 2019.

62 'British Council calls for another £55,000', *Guardian*, 23 October 1956, p. 2, quoted in Verity Clarkson, *The Organisation and Reception of Eastern Bloc Exhibitions*, op. cit., p. 54.

63 In 1948, the Council was instructed that the Foreign Secretary "'wished to concentrate as much as possible on those activities which were most likely to produce quick returns in the political field, for example, visits, courses, lectures and English lessons, rather than longer-term projects such as exhibitions of modern paintings'." Minute by C. Mayhew, 19 April 1948, in Foreign Office papers FO924/615, quoted in Diana Jane Eastman, *The Policies and Position of the British Council from the Outbreak of War to 1950*, PhD thesis, University of Leeds, 1982, p. 214.

64 'UK Tests 2nd H-Bomb in Christmas Is. Blast';

'Protest Demonstration at British Embassy', *Mainichi*, 2 June 1957, p. 1 and 'International Art Exhibition Prize Winners', *Mainichi*, 2 June 1957, p. 3.

65 *The Drogheda Report: Proposals for Reorganisation of British Council Work in Various Territories*, 1954. The National Archives, FO924/1034.

66 David Kelly, 'Some Impressions of the British Council at Work', *British Council Annual Report* 1955–6, 1956, p. 14.

67 Ibid., p. 2.

68 Ibid., p. 3.

69 Stanley Unwin quoted in A. J. S. White, *The British Council: The First 25 Years 1934–1959* (London: British Council, 1965), p. 46.

70 Harold Nicolson quoted in *The Beaverbrook Press and the British Council* (London: British Council Staff Association, 1954), p. 3.

71 Fine Arts Committee minutes, 31 January 1955, pp. 2–6.

72 Ibid., p. 4.

73 Fine Arts Committee minutes, 18 October 1955, p. 5

74 Fine Arts Committee minutes, 31 January 1955, p. 5.

75 Fine Arts Committee minutes, 31 January 1955, p. 3.

76 A. J. S. White, *The British Council: The First 25 Years 1934–1959* (London: British Council, 1965), p. 97.

77 Margaret Garlake, *New Art, New World: British Art in Postwar Society* (London and New Haven: Yale University Press, 1988), p. 17

Chapter 3

1 Fine Arts Committee minutes, 4 July 1957, p. 5

2 Lord Bridges, Countess of Albemarle, Noel Annan, and Sir George Barnes, *Help for the Arts: A Report to the Calouste Gulbenkian Foundation* (London: Calouste Gulbenkian Foundation, 1959), p. 45.

3 Lord Bridges, Countess of Albemarle, Noel Annan, and Sir George Barnes, *Help for the Arts*, op. cit., p. 60.

4 General Correspondence on Permanent Collection, Gulbenkian Collection of Modern British Art. TGA200317/6/4.

5 Sir Philip Hendy letter to W. Sanderson, secretary to the Trustees of the Gulbenkian Foundation, 29 May 1958. General Correspondence on Permanent Collection, Gulbenkian Collection of Modern British Art. TGA200317/6/4.

6 Ibid.

7 W. Sanderson letter to Sir Paul Sinker, director-general of the British Council, 28 October 1959. General Correspondence on Permanent Collection, Gulbenkian Collection of Modern British Art. TGA200317/6/4.

8 Draft report to the Executive Committee, 18 September 1970. General Correspondence on Permanent Collection, Gulbenkian Collection of Modern British Art. TGA200317/6/5

9 General Correspondence on Permanent Collection, Gulbenkian Collection of Modern British Art. TGA200317/6/4.

10 Correspondence from Fine Arts Committee to British Council Executive, 25 October 1960. TGA200317/6/4.

11 General Correspondence on Permanent Collection, Gulbenkian Collection of Modern British Art. TGA200317/6/4.

12 Ibid.

13 David Hockney, quoted in *Metamorphosis: British Art of the Sixties – Works from the Collections of the British Council and the Calouste Gulbenkian Foundation* (Lisbon: Basil and Elise Goulandris Foundation/ Museum of Contemporary Art, 2005), p. 65.

14 *British Council Annual Report 1960–1*, 1961, p. 50.

15 J. G. Ballard, *Miracle of Life: An Autobiography* (London: Fourth Estate, 2008) quoted in Andrea Rose, 'The British Council Collection: A Brief Overview', *British Council Collection: Passports* (London: British Council, 2009), p. 13.

16 Alexander Massouras, *Patronage, Professionalism and Youth: The Emerging Artist and London's Art Institutions 1949–1988*. Unpublished PhD thesis, Birkbeck College, University of London, 2013.

17 Report on Gulbenkian Foundation, 26 February 1969. General Correspondence on Permanent Collection. Gulbenkian Collection of Modern British Art. TGA200317/6/4.

18 *Metamorphosis: British Art of the Sixties*, <http://visualarts.britishcouncil.org/exhibitions/exhibition/metamorphosis-british-

arts-of-the-sixties-2005>; Post-Pop: Beyond the Commonplace, <http://visualarts.britishcouncil.org/exhibitions/exhibition/post-pop-beyond-the-commonplace-2018>, both accessed 7 November 2020.

19 Geoffrey Grigson, 'Introduction', *British Drawings and Watercolours of the 20th Century from the Collection of the British Council*, typed manuscript, TGA9712/2/74. Published as Geoffrey Grigson, *Aguarelas e desenhos ingleses do século vinte da colecção British Council* (Lisbon: Calouste Gulbenkian Foundation, 1955).

20 Leonor de Oliveira, 'Politics, Diplomatic Relations and Institutional Promotion through Modern Art – the *British Art of the Twentieth Century* Exhibition in Portugal, 1962', *RIHA Journal*, No. 72 (2013).

21 Ibid.

22 Amélia Fernandes, *A Exposição de Arte Portuguesa em Londres 1955/ 1956: 'A Personalidade Artística do País'*, Lisbon 2001, 263 quoted in Leonor de Oliveira, "Politics, Diplomatic Relations and Institutional Promotion through Modern Art – the *British Art of the Twentieth Century* Exhibition in Portugal, 1962", *RIHA Journal*, No. 72 (2013).

23 Hubert Dalwood letter to Lilian Somerville, 9 April 1961, Tate Archive, TGA 9712/2/209.

24 Bernard Meadows letter to Lilian Somerville, 19 June 1961, Tate Archive, TGA 9712/2/210.

25 Barbara Hepworth letter to Lilian Somerville, 21 March 1961, Tate Archive, TGA 9712/2/209.

26 Lilian Somerville letter to Barbara Hepworth, 15 May 1961, Tate Archive, TGA 9712/2/209.

27 'London Diary: Banbridge born sculptor takes a courageous step', *Northern Whig*, 22 November 1961, p. 1. Tate Archive, TGA 9712/2/208.

28 'Boycott', *Observer*, 29 October 1961, p. 13. Tate Archive, TGA 9712/2/208.

29 Leonor de Oliveira, 'Politics, Diplomatic Relations and Institutional Promotion through Modern Art – the *British Art of the Twentieth Century* Exhibition in Portugal, 1962', op. cit., p. 115.

30 John Hulton (Director, Fine Arts) to Assistant Controller, Arts and Sciences, 20 March 1962. Tate Archive, TGA 9712/2/208.

31 *British Council Annual Report*, 1965–66, 1966, p. 8.

32 John Harrison (Art and Exhibitions officer), 10 February 1949. Correspondence in relation to Jamaica. TGA200317/1/1.

33 See, for example, notes in Henry Moore Exhibitions of Drawings in Guadalajara, Jalisco, Mexico, Feb–March 1950, TGA9712/2/39; and Prints since 1970 – Norway 1977, TGA200317/3.

34 Correspondence from P. B. Naylor (representative) to Mr David Rogers, Asociacion Argentina de Cultura Britanica, Cordoba, 21 January 1974, Artists' Prints of the 60s. TGA 200317/2/1/140.

35 Richard Riley, 'Introduction', *As Is When: A Boom in British Printmaking 1961–1972* (London: British Council, 2003), p. 8.

36 Richard Riley, *David Hockney: Words and Pictures* (London: British Council Touring Collections, n.d. [c. 2015]), p. 5.

37 Mr C. P. Hope (British Embassy, Mexico) letter to C. G. B. Stewart (Cultural Relations Department), 5 June 1968, 'Place: Mexico City, Mexico Scope and Content: Cultural Events for Olympic Games', The National Archives, FCO 13/182.

38 Gerald Forty letter to D. Warren-Knott, 18 June 1968, The National Archives, FCO 13/182.

39 D. Warren-Knott letter to Mr. D. F. Duncan, 11 June 1968, The National Archives, FCO 13/182.

40 D. F. Duncan letter to D. Warren-Knott, 12 June 1968, The National Archives, FCO 13/182.

41 Mr C. P. Hope (British Embassy, Mexico), handwritten addition to letter to C. G. B. Stewart (Cultural Relations Department), 13 June 1968, The National Archives, FCO 13/182.

42 Neil MacGregor, *History of the World in 100 Objects* (London: Penguin, 2011).

43 *David Hockney: Words and Pictures*, <http://visualarts.britishcouncil.org/exhibitions/exhibition/david-hockney-words-and-pictures-2002>, accessed 7 November 2020.

44 *British Council Annual Report* 1969–70, 1970, p. 15.

Chapter 4

1 Fine Arts Committee Minutes, 27 November 1956, p. 2.
2 Norbert Lynton, 'Paris Biennale', *Guardian*, 7 October 1965, p. 8.
3 Fine Arts Committee minutes, 14 January 1969, p. 5
4 Fine Arts Committee minutes, 15 July 1969, p. 2
5 John Hulton, 'Gra Bretanha', *XI Bienal de São Paulo: Catálogo* (São Paulo: Fundação Bienal de São Paulo, 1971), p. 92.
6 Jon Wood, 'Apropos Moore: Observations on Moore's Legacies for Contemporary British Artists', *Henry Moore* (London: Tate, 2010) pp. 80–2.
7 Rosalind Krauss, 'Sculpture in the Expanded Field', *October*, Vol. 8. (Spring, 1979), pp. 30–44, p. 30.
8 Rudi Fuchs, 'More on The New Art', *Studio International*, December 1972, pp. 182–4, quoted in Michael Archer, 'Out of the Studio', in Clive Phillpot and Andrea Tarsia, *Live in Your Head: Concept and Experiment in Britain 1965–75* (London: Whitechapel Gallery, 2000), p. 28.
9 Michael Archer, 'Out of the Studio', op. cit., p. 28.
10 'The British Council and Western Europe', *British Council Annual Report* 1971–2, 1972, p. 8.
11 Ibid., p. 6.
12 Fine Arts Committee minutes, 16 May 1972, p. 2.
13 Fine Arts Advisory Committee minutes, 25 May 1971, p. 2.
14 Nikolaus Pevsner, *The Englishness of English Art* (London: Penguin, 1978 [1956]), p. 21.
15 Ibid., p. 23.
16 Ibid., p. 194.
17 'Typically English', *Deutsche Zeitung*, 14 December 1979, TGA200317/2/232.
18 A. M. Campoy, '"Veinticinco Exposiciones"', *ABC De Las Artes*, 1 July 1972, p. 1.
19 'British Council Exhibition', *Pioneer*, Ghana, 21 May 1971, pp. 1 and 4.
20 Chon Syng-boc, 'Vitality Goes Deeper than the Senses', Seoul press cutting. TGA200317/11/29.
21 Jacob Klintowitz, 'Digressions starting from Colour in British Painting', *Jornal da Tarde*, Brazil, 18 February 1978.
22 Francesco Ogliari and Gerald Forty, 'Foreword', *English Art Today 1960–76: Vol. 1* (Milan: Rizzoli, 1976), p. 1.
23 Guido Ballo and Franco Russoli, 'A Propos of the Exhibition', *English Art Today 1960–76: Vol. 1*, op. cit., p. 10.
24 Richard Cork, 'Alternative Developments', *English Art Today 1960–76: Vol. 2* (Milan: Rizzoli, 1976), p. 312.
25 These Keith Arnatt works appeared in British Council exhibitions but are not part of the British Council Collection.
26 Ted Little, 'Performance Art', *English Art Today 1960–76, Vol. 2*, op. cit., pp. 407–13.
27 Ted Little quoted in Simon Ford, *Wreckers of Civilisation: The Story of COUM Transmissions and Throbbing Gristle* (London: Black Dog, 1999), p. 6.9.
28 Ted Little, 'Performance Art', op. cit., p. 422.
29 Richard Cork quoted in Simon Ford, *Wreckers of Civilisation: The Story of COUM Transmissions and Throbbing Gristle*, op. cit., p. 6.5.
30 Fine Arts Committee minutes, 3 November 1976, p. 2.
31 *British Council Annual Report* 1976, 1976, p. 55.
32 Michael O'Flaherty, 'State Aid for 'Cosey' Travelling Sex Troup', *Daily Express*, 21 October 1976.
33 Nicholas de Jongh, 'British Council attacked for "porn subsidy"', *Guardian*, 21 October 1976.
34 Article quoted in 'The Orridge Furore', *Studio International*, Vol. 193, No. 895 (January/February 1977), p. 35.
35 Nicholas Fairbairn quoted in Michael O'Flaherty, 'State Aid for 'Cosey' Travelling Sex Troup', op. cit.
36 Fine Arts Committee minutes, 3 November 1976, p. 2.
37 Fine Arts Committee minutes, 3 November 1976, p. 3.
38 Simon Ford, *Wreckers of Civilisation: The Story of COUM Transmissions and Throbbing Gristle*, op. cit., p. 6.8.
39 Fine Arts Committee minutes, 25 January 1978, p. 6.
40 Ibid., p. 5–7.
41 Gerald Forty, *Un Certain Art Anglais ... Selection d'Artistes Britanniques 1970–1979* (Paris: ARC, 1979), p. 9.
42 Suzanne Pagé, *Un Certain Art Anglais ... Selection d'Artistes Britanniques 1970–1979*, op. cit., p. 6.
43 Anne Sington, 'British Art has Paris Exposure', *Daily Telegraph*, 6 March 1979.

44 Londoner's Diary, 'More Sex Please We're the British Council', *Evening Standard*, 6 March 1979.
45 Jackie Hatfield, interview with Kevin Atherton, 21 July 2005.
46 Londoner's Diary, 'More Sex Please We're the British Council', op. cit.
47 Fine Arts Committee minutes, 15 May 1979, p. 2.
48 Memories of the exhibition provided by Henry Meyric Hughes and Adrian Forty. Henry Meyric Hughes, interview with the author, 19 December 2018; Adrian Forty (son of the late Gerald Forty), interview with the author, 26 November 2018.
49 *Un Certain Art Anglais ... Selection d'Artistes Britanniques 1970–1979*, op. cit., pp. 38–9.
50 Sir Nicholas Henderson MP, quoted in John A. Walker, *Left Shift: Radical Art in 1970s Britain* (London: I. B. Tauris, 2002), p. 150.
51 Adrian Forty, interview with the author, 26 November 2018.
52 *British Council Annual Report 1978–9*, 1979, p. 7.
53 Fine Arts Committee minutes, 15 May 1979, pp. 3–4.
54 David Medalla and Rasheed Araeen, 'Open Letter to the British Council', *Art Monthly*, April 1979.
55 Naseem Khan, *The Arts Britain Ignores: The Arts of Ethnic Minorities in Britain* (London: Arts Council of Great Britain, Calouste Gulbenkian Foundation, and Community Relations Commission, 1976); Naseem Khan, 'The Arts of Ethnic Minorities In Britain', *Journal of the Royal Society of Arts*, Vol. 128, No. 5290 (September 1980), pp. 676–88.
56 David Medalla and Rasheed Araeen, 'Open Letter to the British Council', op. cit.
57 Ibid.
58 Elena Crippa, '1970s: Out of Sculpture', *British Art Studies*, No. 3 (July 2016), <https://www.britishartstudies.ac.uk/issues/issue-index/issue-3/1970s>, accessed 14 March 2023.
59 Emma Dexter, director of Visual Arts department, interview with the author, 28 January 2019.

Chapter 5

1 *British Council Annual Report 1979–80*, 1980, p. 5.
2 Ibid., p. 7.
3 Letter from Henry Moore to Margaret Thatcher, 10 November 1979, Foreign and Commonwealth Office papers, PCB 410/1, quoted in Frances Donaldson, *The British Council: The First Fifty Years* (London: Jonathan Cape, 1984), p. 311.
4 Lord Seebohm, *Independent Review of the British Council*, 1 January 1979–31 December 1980. The National Archives BW/172.
5 'History of the Collection', The British Council Collection 1938–1984 (London: British Council, 1984), p. 9.
6 Andrea Rose, interview with the author, 10 January 2019.
7 Andrea Rose, 'The British Council Collection: A Brief Overview', *British Council Collection: Passports* (London: British Council / Whitechapel Gallery, 2009), p. 16.
8 *British Council Annual Report 1970–1*, 1970, p. 101.
9 Keith Arnatt, 'Sausages and Food: A Reply to the Interview with Alan Bowness of the Tate Gallery', *Creative Camera*, No. 214 (October 1982), quoted in David Campany (ed.), *Art and Photography* (London and New York: Phaidon, 2007), pp. 228–9.
10 Brett Rogers, interview with the author, 23 November 2018.
11 Ian Jeffrey, 'Stories of Detection and Home-Made Majesty', *Inscriptions and Inventions: British Photography in the 1980s* (London: British Council, 1987), p. 8.
12 *Reality Check: Recent Developments in British Photography and Video* (London: British Council, 2002).
13 Mike Winter, 'Documentary Dilemmas', *Connect: British Council Staff Magazine*, No. 64 (August 1993), p. 4.
14 Julian Germain's engagement with Brazilian photographers and communities since his British Council-funded trip to São Paulo has been extensive; a full list of projects can be found at <http://www.juliangermain.com/projects.php>, accessed 13 May 2019.
15 Richard Hoggart, Michael Bootle, Peter Brook, Susan Castle, and Andrew Norris, *The British Council and the Arts*, Activity Review No. 5 (London: British Council, 1986), p. 5.
16 Ibid., p. 30.
17 Ibid., 'General Thoughts } on Guidelines', Annexe M.
18 Ibid., p. 33.

19 Ibid., p. 2.
20 Ibid., p. 25
21 Ibid., p. 27.
22 Ibid., p. 27–8.
23 Ibid., p. 34.
24 John Burgh, British Council 50th anniversary speech, Bonn, October 1984, quoted in ibid., p. 34.
25 Ibid., p. 114.
26 Henry Meyric Hughes, interview with the author, 18 December 2018.
27 Brett Rogers, interview with the author, 23 November 2018.
28 Patrick Heron, 'Lilian Somerville', *Home and Abroad: British Council Staff Journal*, No. 17 (December 1970), pp. 56–8.
29 Andrea Rose, interview with the author, 10 January 2019.
30 Adrian Forty (son of Gerald Forty), interview with the author, 26 November 2018; and Henry Meyric Hughes, interview with the author, 18 December 2018.
31 Michael Middleton, 'The British Council Collection', *Studio*, June 1959, p. 163.
32 Marina Vaizey, 'British Shows of Strength', unnamed source, *c.* 1988, press cutting, British Council Exhibition Files, Francis Bacon, GEN/641/608.
33 Fine Arts Advisory Committee minutes, 18 November 1986.
34 Grey Gowrie, "Francis Bacon", *Francis Bacon* (Moscow: The British Council, 1988), p. 19.
35 Grey Gowrie, 'Francis Bacon', *Francis Bacon* (Moscow: British Council, 1988), pp. 17–20.
36 Gill Hedley, interview with the author, 5 December 2018.
37 Henry Meyric Hughes, interview with the author, 18 December 2018.
38 'Profile: Francis Bacon, Confounder of Art Critics', *Independent*, 28 September 1988, press cutting, British Council Exhibition Files, Francis Bacon, GEN/641/608.
39 David Sylvester, quoted in 'Master of Ebullient Despair', *Independent*, 24 September 1988, press cutting, British Council Exhibition Files, Francis Bacon, GEN/641/608.
40 'The Bacon Exhibition in Moscow', Moscow Radio English Language Service transcript, 17 October 1988, p. 2.
41 Quoted in press cutting, *Art Monthly*, 6 January 1989, British Council Exhibition Files, Francis Bacon, GEN/641/608.
42 Tyumen Yakimenko, Visitors' Book, entry number 18, British Council Exhibition Files, Francis Bacon, GEN/641/608.
43 Inscribed as '3 illegible signatures, lecturers', Visitors' Book, entry number 143.
44 Visitors' Book, entry number 114.
45 Irene Tolstikh, actress, Visitors' Book, entry number 180.
46 *British Council Annual Report 1988–89*, 1989, p. 50.
47 David Kelly, 'Cultural Relations with Soviet Russia', *British Council Annual Report*, 1956–7, 1957, pp. 2–5.
48 Ibid. p. 3.
49 *British Council Annual Report*, 1959–60, 1960, pp. 40–1.
50 Verity Clarkson, *The Organisation and Reception of Eastern Bloc Exhibitions on the British Cold War 'Home Front' c.* 1956–1979 (University of Brighton, unpublished PhD thesis, 2010), p. 141.
51 Ibid., p. 48.
52 *USSR: Great Britain – An Historical Exhibition*, Moscow, 1968. Fine Art exhibition files, GEN/641/203.
53 Fine Arts Advisory Committee meeting minutes, 14 January 1969, p. 4.
54 Andrea Rose, interview with the author, 10 January 2019.
55 Visual Arts Advisory Committee meeting minutes, 30 October 1990, p. 10.
56 Andrea Rose, interview with the author, 10 January 2019.
57 *For a Wider World*, exhibition catalogue (London: British Council, 1990), p. 130.
58 Andrea Rose, 'Introduction', *The British Council Collection 1984–1994* (London: British Council, 1995), p. x.
59 Henry Meyric Hughes, interview with the author, 18 December 2018. The Foreign Office was renamed the Foreign and Commonwealth Office in 1968.
60 *British Council Annual Report 1984–5*.

Chapter 6

1 Richard Cork, 'Reflections on the British Art Show: 18 November 1995', *Breaking Down the Barriers: Art in the 1990s* (New Haven and New York: Yale University Press, 2003), p. 125.
2 Julian Stallabrass, *High Art Lite: The Rise and Fall of Young British Art* (London: Verso, 2006 [1999]), p. 237.
3 Gregor Muir, *Lucky Kunst: The Rise and Fall of Young*

British Art (London: Aurum Press, 2009), pp. 122–3.
4 Ann Gallagher letter to Brendan Griggs, 18 April 1995, Visual Arts Department Files: Young British Artists – Venice 95, GEN/641/735 I.
5 Andrea Rose, 'Foreword', *General Release* (London: British Council, 1995), p. 6.
6 Andrea Rose, 'The British Council Collection: General Policy Guidelines' 1993, Visual Arts Department Permanent Collection Policy folder, 1991–6, GEN/641/1; Visual Arts Advisory Committee minutes, 26 October 1993, p. 8.
7 James Roberts, 'Never Had it so Good ...', *General Release*, op. cit., p. 49.
8 'Young London: The Fog Lifts on a New Scene', *New York Times*, 20 December 1964, p. 23.
9 *Brilliant! New Art from London* (Minneapolis: Walker Art Center, 1995).
10 Keith Goetzman, 'London Calling', *Minnesota Monthly*, October 1995, p. 15.
11 Richard Flood, quoted in 'Show Curator accuses British Press of Hating Young Artists', *Star Tribune*, 20 October 1995, p. E19.
12 Patricia Bickers, *The Brit Pack: Contemporary British Art – The View from Abroad* (Manchester: Cornerhouse, 1995), p. 18.
13 Ibid.
14 The Chapman Brothers, 'Stop the Chatter', excerpted from an interview by Douglas Fogle, London, 27 February 1995, in *Brilliant! New Art from London*, op. cit., p. 22.
15 Fine Arts Advisory Committee minutes, 15 October 1995, p. 2.
16 Patricia Bickers, 'As Others See Us: Towards a History of Recent Art from Britain', in Bernice Murphy (ed.), *Pictura Britannica: Art From Britain* (Sydney: Museum of Contemporary Art, 1997), pp. 65–88.
17 Nikos Papastergiadis, 'Back to Basics: British Art and the Problems of a Global Frame?"' in ibid., pp. 128–46.
18 Andrea Rose, quoted in James Hall, 'Teapot Tempest', *Artforum*, January 1996, p. 20.
19 Richard Flood, letter to Andrea Rose, 8 November 1995, *Brilliant!* exhibition files, GEN641/740.
20 Andrea Rose, letter to James Hall, 5 December 1995, *Brilliant!* exhibition files, GEN641/740.
21 Emin, Collishaw, and the Chapmans quoted in Hall, 'Teapot Tempest', op. cit.
22 Ibid.
23 'Show Curator accuses British Press of Hating Young Artists', *Star Tribune*, op. cit., p. E19.
24 See, for example, Stallabrass, *High Art Lite*, op. cit.; Simon Ford, 'The Myth of the Young British Artist', in Duncan McCorquodale, Naomi Siderfin and Julian Stallabrass (eds.) *Occupational Hazard: Critical Writing on Recent British Art* (London: Black Dog, 1998).
25 Jeffrey Kastner, 'Brilliant?', *Art Monthly*, No. 192 (December/January 1996).
26 All quotes from Michael Landy, *Scrapheap Services* (London), 1996.
27 Andrea Rose, 'Foreword', *Dimensions Variable* (London: British Council, 1997), p. 5.
28 Ann Gallagher, 'Introduction', *Dimensions Variable*, pp. 7–10.
29 Richard Cork, 'Introduction', *Breaking Down the Barriers*, op. cit., p. 9.
30 *British Council*, 1934–2016, Appraisal Report, Paper Records (London: The National Archives, 2016), p. 43.
31 Mark Leonard, *Britain TM: Renewing our Identity* (London: Demos, 1997).
32 Kobena Mercer, 'Ethnicity and Internationality: New British Art and Diaspora-Based Blackness', *Third Text*, No. 49 (Winter 1999–2000), p. 59.
33 *British Council Annual Report 1997–98*, 1998, p. 34.
34 Mark Leonard, *Britain TM*, op. cit., p. 10.
35 Courtney Kidd, 'Pictura Britannica', *Art Monthly*, No. 211 (November 1997), pp. 33–5.
36 Visual Art Advisory Committee minutes, 26 April 1988, p. 7.
37 Julian Stallabrass, *High Art Lite*, op. cit., p. 138.
38 Ibid., p. 246.
39 Bernice Murphy, 'Pictura Britannica: Scenes, Fictions and Constructions in Contemporary British Art', in Bernice Murphy (ed.), *Pictura Britannica: Art from Britain* (Sydney: Museum of Contemporary Art, 1997), p. 14–64.
40 Kobena Mercer, 'Back to my Routes: A Postscript to the 80s', in Murphy (ed.), *Pictura Britannica: Art from Britain*, pp. 112–23.
41 Chris Ofili quoted in Virginia Button, *The Turner*

Prize: Twenty Years (London: Tate, 2003 [1997]), p. 144.
42 Ofili quoted in *Brilliant! New Art from London*, op. cit., p. 67.
43 Louise Pether, Clarrie Rudrum, Clare Rowe and Ian Rogers, 'Dung Clarification Needed. Urgent', *Observer Review*, 21 September 1997, p. 1.
44 Peter Elborn, 'Preface', *A Changed World* (London: The British Council, 1997), p. 4.
45 Undated email from Diana Eccles, Curator, British Council Collection, to Peter Elborn, Director, British Council Pakistan, *A Changed World* exhibition files, PAK/654/905.
46 Andrea Rose, 'The British Council Collection: General Policy Guidelines', 1993, op. cit.
47 Diana Eccles, 'Featured Touring Exhibitions: A Changed World', in Clive Phillpot (ed.), *British Art Abroad: A Guide to the Work of Visual Arts at the British Council*, unpublished manuscript, c. 1999. TGA200317/15/5-7.
48 Andrea Rose, 'The British Council Collection: General Policy Guidelines', 1993, op. cit.
49 British Council Pakistan Country Plan 1997–8, 4 September 1997, *A Changed World* exhibition files, PAK/654/905.
50 Tasneem Ahmad, Acting Director, Lahore, letter to Peter Elborn, 5 August 1996, *A Changed World* exhibition files, PAK/654/905.
51 Visual Arts Advisory Committee minutes, 20 April 1998, p. 7.
52 'A Changed World at Shish Mahal', *Dawn* (Lahore, Pakistan), 12 December 1997, press cuttings, *A Changed World* exhibition files, PAK/654/905.
53 Sultan J. Qureshi, 'A Changed World amid Tongas and Bullock Carts', *News* (Lahore, Pakistan), 13 December 1997, p. 2.
54 Elborn, 'Preface', *A Changed World*, op. cit., p. 4.
55 Andrea Rose email to Henry Moore Foundation, 23 April 1997, GEN/654/905.
56 Peter Elborn letter to David Mitchinson, Curator, Henry Moore Foundation, 16 June 1997, *A Changed World* exhibition files, PAK/654/905.
57 Hadrian Piggott, 'A Report on Exhibiting and Art School in Lahore, Pakistan', 1998, n.p. *A Changed World* exhibition files, PAK/654/905.
58 Ibid.
59 Ibid.
60 'The Arts: Britain's Visible Exports', *British Council Annual Report* 1984–5, 1985, p. 53.
61 *British Council Annual Report* 1989–90, 1990, p. 15.
62 *British Council Annual Report* 1996–7, 1997, p. 41.
63 Julian Stallabrass, *High Art Lite*, op. cit., p. 297.
64 Matthew Collings, *Art Crazy Nation: The Post-Blimey! Art World* (London: 21 Publishing, 2001), p. 11.

Chapter 7

1 'British Council: Arts for a Dangerous World', undated (c. 2003), n.p., *Turning Points* General Correspondence, 5221, British Council document collection (known internally as Iron Mountain).
2 Ibid.
3 Nigel Reynolds, 'British Council takes arts to Islamic world', *Daily Telegraph*, 18 January 2003, p. 10.
4 'British Council: Arts for a Dangerous World', op. cit.
5 Nigel Reynolds, 'British Council takes arts to Islamic world', op. cit., p. 10.
6 'Common Ground: Moslem Experience of Life in the UK [working title]', undated (c. 2002), n.p., *Turning Points* General Correspondence, 5221, British Council document collection (known internally as Iron Mountain).
7 Suki Dhanda in Brett Rogers and Andrea Rose (eds), *Common Ground: Aspects of Contemporary British Muslim Experience* (Manchester: Cornerhouse, 2003), n.p.
8 Suki Dhanda in conversation with Lalita Gupta, *Homelands: A 21st Century Story of Home, Away, and All the Places In Between* (London: British Council, 2013), p. 59.
9 Dhanda, *Common Ground: Aspects of Contemporary British Muslim Experience*, op. cit., n.p.
10 *Secure Borders, Safe Haven: Integration with Diversity in Modern Britain* (London: Home Office, 2002).
11 Arifa Akbar, 'Photo Exhibition Depicting the Lives of British Muslim Women Tours the Globe', *Independent*, 27 June 2006.
12 Ibid.
13 Andrea Rose quoted in Cheryl Chapman and Michaela Crimmin, 'Art across Borders', *RSA Journal*, No. 154: 5527 (February 2007), p. 46.

14 Eva Ulrike Pirker, 'Images of Muslim Britain go Global: A Reading of the British Council's Touring Exhibition *Common Ground*', in Lars Eckstein, Barbara Korte, Eva Ulrike Pirker, and Christoph Reinfandt (eds), *Multiethnic Britain 2000+: New Perspectives in Literature, Film and the Arts* (Amsterdam: Brill / Rodopi), pp. 187–225.

15 Martin Davidson, 'Constructive Engagement: The Art of Cultural Relations', House of Commons, 31 July 2008, n.p.

16 Ibid.

17 Foreign and Commonwealth Office Country Profiles: Iran, 12 January 2004, n.p., *Turning Points* General Correspondence, 5221, British Council document collection (known internally as Iron Mountain).

18 Andrea Rose, interview with the author, 10 January 2019.

19 Hamid Keshmirshekan, 'Modern and Contemporary Iranian Art: Developments and Challenges', in Hossein Amirsadeghi (ed.), *Different Sames: New Perspectives in Contemporary Iranian Art* (London: Thames and Hudson, 2009), p. 16.

20 Fereshteh Daftari, 'Another Modernism: An Iranian Perspective', in Shiva Balaghi and Lynn Gumpert (eds), *Picturing Iran: Art, Society and Revolution* (London: I. B. Tauris, 2002), p. 72.

21 Rose Issa, 'Borrowed Ware', in Rose Issa, Carol Brown, and Mark Sutcliffe (eds), *Iranian Contemporary Art* (London: Booth-Clibborn, 2001), p. 13.

22 Tallin Gregor, *Contemporary Iranian Art: From the Street to the Studio* (London: Reaktion, 2014), pp. 19–20.

23 Issa, 'Borrowed Ware', op. cit., p. 23.

24 Saeed Kamali Dehghan, 'Former Queen of Iran on assembling Tehran's art collection', *Guardian*, 1 August 2012.

25 Hamid Keshmirshekan, 'The Contemporary Art Scene of Iran: Cultural policy, infrastructure, dissemination and exchange', in Nick Wadham-Smith and Danny Whitehead (eds), *Didgah: New Perspectives on UK–Iran Cultural Relations* (London: British Council, 2015), p. 6.

26 Issa, 'Borrowed Ware', op. cit., p. 13.

27 'Turning Points: 20th Century British Sculpture', project outline, n.d. (*c.* 2002), n.p., *Turning Points* General Correspondence, 5221, British Council document collection (known internally as Iron Mountain).

28 'British Council, 1934–2016 [Paper Records]', *Draft Appraisal Report*, National Archives, 2016, p. 47.

29 Andrea Rose, interview with the author, 10 January 2019.

30 Michael Willson (director, British Council Iran) email to Andrea Rose, 4 August 2003. *Turning Points* General Correspondence, 5221, British Council document collection (known internally as Iron Mountain).

31 Michael Bracewell, 'Violent and Original in their Work', *Financial Times*, 15 October 2001, p. 8.

32 Michael Willson email to Andrea Rose, 4 August 2003, op. cit.

33 Richard Brooks, 'Hirst's 'crucifixion' will go to Iran', *Sunday Times*, 18 Jan 2004, p. 4.

34 Mark Irving and Raymond Whitaker, 'Damien Hirst leads Britart's diplomatic mission to Iran', *Independent on Sunday*, 18 January 2004, p. 9.

35 Fereshteh Daftari, 'Beyond Islamic Roots – Beyond Modernism', *RES: Anthropology and Aesthetics*, No. 43 (Spring 2003), p. 175.

36 Shirazeh Houshiary letter to Andrea Rose, 4 December 2003. *Turning Points* General Correspondence, 5221, British Council document collection (known internally as Iron Mountain).

37 Fereshteh Daftari email to Andrea Rose and Shirazeh Houshiary, 17 December 2003. *Turning Points* General Correspondence, 5221, British Council document collection (known internally as Iron Mountain).

38 Shirazeh Houshiary quoted in Lauren Hinkson, 'Shirazeh Houshiary: Presence', Guggenheim Museum, <https://www.guggenheim.org/artwork/23258>, accessed 22 June 2019.

39 Andrea Rose, *Turning Points: 20th Century British Sculpture* (Tehran: Tehran Museum of Contemporary Art, 2004), p. 8.

40 Barbara Reis, 'Khomeini, Khamenei and Damien Hirst's skeleton Christ', undated press cutting, unknown source, Andrea Rose collection.

41 Andrew Renton, 'The Tate Britain sell out?', *Evening Standard*, 27 January 2004;

Gavin Turk 'Diary', *Independent on Sunday*, 18 January 2004, p. 25.
42 Sami-Azar quoted in Mark Irving and Raymond Whitaker, 'Damien Hirst leads Britart's diplomatic mission to Iran', *Independent on Sunday*, 18 January 2004, p. 9.
43 Woodrow quoted in Barbara Reis, 'Khomeini, Khamenei and Damien Hirst's skeleton Christ'.
44 Bidoun, '20th Century Sculpture', *Bidoun East 1* (2004), <https://bidoun.org/issues/1-we-are-spatial>, accessed 22 June 2019.
45 Fereshteh Daftari, 'Redefining Modernism: Pluralist Art before the 1979 Revolution', in *Iran Modern* (New York: Asia Society, 2013), p. 41.
46 Anthony Downey, 'Diasporic Communities and Global Networks: The Contemporaneity of Iranian Art Today', in Rose Issa, Carol Brown, and Mark Sutcliffe (eds) *Iranian Contemporary Art*, op. cit., p. 49.
47 Jenny White, interview with the author, 6 December 2018.
48 'Teacher's Works Cause a Problem', *Tehran Journal*, 18 April 1971, p. 9.
49 Maryam Borjian, 'The Rise and Fall of a Partnership: The British Council and the Islamic Republic of Iran', *Iranian Studies*, Vol. 44, No. 4 (July 2011), p. 557.
50 Hamid Keshmirshekan, 'The Contemporary Art Scene of Iran', op. cit., p. 138.
51 Maryam Borjian, 'The Rise and Fall of a Partnership', op. cit., p. 559.
52 Angus McDowall, 'No sensation as Brit Art goes to Tehran with a show of tact and diplomacy', *Independent*, 25 February 2004.
53 Jennie King, interview with Anahita Rezvani for 'Visual Arts: The Long Story', British Council internal report, 2015–16.
54 Jennie King, interview with Payam Parishanzadeh for 'Visual Arts: The Long Story', British Council internal report, 2015–16.
55 'Critics and Criticism: Reflections on Iranian Contemporary Art', Iran Heritage Foundation, 2017, <https://www.iranheritage.org/icandc2017.html>, accessed 5 October 2019.
56 Andrea Rose, interview with the author, 10 January 2019.
57 Richard Dorment, 'British Council: These crass bureaucrats are placing the arts in real danger', *Telegraph*, 19 December 2007.
58 'Dismay at British Council Arts Cuts', *Guardian*, 12 January 2018.
59 British Council, *Action Plan for the Arts*, n.d. (c. 2008), p. 4.
60 *Action Plan for the Arts*, p. 3.
61 *Action Plan for the Arts*, p. 14.
62 *Flicker: A Visual Intervention into the Cityscape of Damascus*, <http://visualarts.britishcouncil.org/exhibitions/exhibition/flicker-a-visual-intervention-in-the-cityscape-of-damascus-2009>, accessed 23 June 2019].
63 *My Father's House*, <http://visualarts.britishcouncil.org/exhibitions/exhibition/my-fathers-house-2009>, accessed 23 June 2019.
64 Bernd and Hilla Becher were themselves funded by the British Council to undertake artistic research in Britain in 1966. 'Hilla Becher in conversation with Thomas Weaver', *AA Files*, No. 66 (2013), p. 26.
65 *British Council Annual Report, 1943–44*, 1944, p. 4.
66 Jenny White, interview with the author, 6 December 2018.
67 Gemma Hollington, interview with the author, 6 December 2018.
68 Martin Davidson, 'Cultural relations: Building networks to face twenty-first-century challenges', in *Engagement: Public diplomacy in a globalised world* (London: Foreign and Commonwealth Office, 2008), The National Archives.
69 Sultan Barakat, *Recreating trust in the Middle East* (London: Counterpoint, 2004), quoted in Martin Davidson, 'Cultural relations', op. cit.
70 Baroness Helena Kennedy, *British Council Annual Report 2003–4*, 2004, p. 2.
71 'British Council: Arts for a Dangerous World', op. cit.

Chapter 8

1 Michael Craig-Martin, 'Passports', *The British Council Collection: Passports* (London: British Council, 2009), p. 9.
2 'Worldwide Search for the Fifth Curator', e-flux, 8 July 2009, <https://www.e-flux.com/announcements/37892/the-fifth-curator-competition/>, accessed 1 July 2019.
3 Theodor Ringborg, 'Fall Out: War and Conflict

in the British Council Collection', Whitechapel Gallery exhibition leaflet, 2010, p. 2–3.

4 Tomoe Takagi, 'Re-Hang the Collection: Recent Curating in British Art Institutions', *Private Utopia: Contemporary Art from the British Council Collection* (Japan: Asahi Shimbun, 2014), p. 129.

5 Jenny White, interview with the author, 18 December 2018.

6 Richard Riley, correspondence with the author, 25 September 2019.

7 With thanks to former Visual Arts curators Diana Eccles and Richard Riley, for providing these reflections and details.

8 *British Council Annual Report 1965–66*, 1966, p. 10.

9 Lilian Somerville letter to the British Council representative, Norway, 16 March 1953. General Correspondence with Norway, TGA 200317/5/2.

10 P. B. de Jongh (Functional Officer for Representative, Greece) letter to Fine Arts Department, 12 October 1950, Henry Moore Exhibition, Greece, 1951, TGA9712/2/48.

11 *British Council Annual Report*, 1951–2, 1952, p. 11.

12 *Annual Report, Greece*, 1950–1, Henry Moore Exhibition, Greece, 1951, TGA9712/2/48.

13 N. A. R. Mackay (director, Latin America department), 30 September 1949, TGA 9712/5/3.

14 *Report on the Henry Moore Exhibition in Athens*, 4–22 *March* 1951, Henry Moore Exhibition, Greece, 1951, TGA9712/2/48.

15 For example, following the 1957 Drogheda Review, it was recommended that the organization focus more on cultural relations with 'undeveloped' countries. Fine Arts Committee minutes, 15 October 1957, p. 5.

16 Brett Rogers, interview with the author, 24 November 2018.

17 Andrea Rose, interview with the author, 10 January 2019.

18 Nicola Heald, interview with the author, 11 October 2018.

19 'To be Continued', British Council Visual Arts, <http://visualarts.britishcouncil.org/exhibitions/exhibition/to-be-continued-2005>, accessed 1 July 2019.

20 Andrea Rose, 'Introduction', *Homelands: A 21st Century Story of Home, Away, and All the Places In Between* (India: British Council, 2013), p. 10.

21 Latika Gupta, 'Homelands: A 21st Century Story of Home, Away, and All the Places In Between', ibid., pp. 87–8.

22 Salman Rushdie, *Imaginary Homelands* (London: Vintage, 2010), p. 12, quoted in ibid., p. 89.

23 'Anthony Haughey in conversation with Latika Gupta', *Homelands*, op. cit., p. 79.

24 Ibid., p. 83.

25 *British Council Annual Report 1949–50*, 1950, p. 7.

26 Jennie King interview with Latika Gupta for 'Visual Arts: The Long Story', British Council internal report, 2015–16.

27 Ibid.

28 Rattanamol Singh Johal, *Art India*, March 2013, quoted in Jennie King, 'Visual Arts: The Long Story', op. cit.

29 Rob Lynes, 'Foreword', *Homelands*, op. cit., p. 9.

30 Homi K. Bhaba, *The Location of Culture* (London: Routledge, 1994), pp. 1–2, quoted in Gupta, 'Homelands: A 21st Century Story of Home, Away, and All the Places In Between', op. cit., pp. 92–3.

31 *Art Connects Us: Our Strategy in the Arts* (London: British Council, 2016), p. 8.

32 *British Council Annual Report 1941–2*, 1942, p. 14.

33 *Henry Moore Comes Home* (London: British Council, 2015), p. 34.

34 Richard Hoggart, Michael Bootle, Peter Brook, Susan Castle, and Andrew Norris, *The British Council and the Arts*, Activity Review No. 5 (London: British Council, 1986), p. 30.

35 *Henry Moore Comes Home*, op. cit., pp. 30–1.

36 Examination of Witnesses, Funding of the Arts and Heritage, Culture, Media and Sport Committee, 2 November 2010, <https://publications.parliament.uk/pa/cm201011/cmselect/cmcumeds/464/10110201.htm>, accessed 1 July 2019.

37 Loveday Shewell, *A Review of the Arts Council Collection, British Council Collection and Government Art Collection* (London: Arts Council England, 2012), p. 6.

38 Peter Hennessey, *Muddling Through: Power, Politics and the Quality of Government in Post-War Britain* (London: Phoenix, 1997), pp. 163–5, quoted in Ian Black, 'Cultural Diplomacy: No Business like Show Business', *Guardian*, 4 August 1998, p. 13.

39 *British Council Annual Report 2017–18*, 2018.
40 Emma Dexter, interview with the author, 28 January 2019.
41 'Pristina: Burrneshat', <https://kosovo.britishcouncil.org/en/programmes/arts/perceptions/burrneshat>, accessed 1 July 2019.
42 'The Beauty of a Flower is in the Picking', <https://www.britishcouncil.me/en/programmes/arts/perceptions/banjaluka>, accessed 1 July 2019.
43 Emma Dexter, interview with the author, 28 January 2019.
44 'Pristina: Burrneshat', <https://kosovo.britishcouncil.org/en/programmes/arts/perceptions/burrneshat>, accessed 1 July 2019.
45 'About the Western Balkans Summit', <https://www.gov.uk/government/topical-events/western-balkans-summit-london-2018/about>, accessed 1 July 2019.
46 *British Council Annual Report 2010–11*, 2011, p. 15.
47 Katrina Schwarz (curator, Visual Arts, British Council), interview with the author, 11 October 2018.
48 'You Look Familiar: A Digital Exhibition', <https://www.britishcouncil.org.tr/en/programmes/arts/you-look-familiar>, accessed 1 July 2019.
49 'Dancing with Witches: A Digital Exhibition', <https://www.britishcouncil.org.tr/en/programmes/arts/dancing-with-witches>, accessed 1 July 2019.
50 Emma Dexter, interview with the author, 28 January 2019.
51 André Malraux, *Museum Without Walls* (London: Secker and Warburg, 1967).
52 Alan Kane in *The Art of Dissonance: Lubaina Himid, Alan Kane and Ed Hall on Art, Democracy and Protest* (film), 'The Art of Dissonance', <http://visualarts.britishcouncil.org/exhibitions/exhibition/the-art-of-dissonance-2017>, accessed 1 July 2019.
53 Ibid.
54 Ibid.
55 Ibid.
56 Siobhan Forshaw, 'Political Activism in Paint: An Interview with Lubaina Himid', *Corridor*, No. 8, 6 November 2017, <https://corridor8.co.uk/article/political-activism-paint-interview-lubaina-himid/>, accessed 1 July 2019.
57 HMA Charles Hay MVO, ambassador to Korea at the opening of *The Art of Dissonance*, September 2017, 'The Art of Dissonance', <http://visualarts.britishcouncil.org/exhibitions/exhibition/the-art-of-dissonance-2017>, accessed 1 July 2019.
58 *Art Connects Us: Our Strategy in the Arts* (London: British Council, 2016), p. 8.
59 'British Council Collection', <http://visualarts.britishcouncil.org/collection/collection-policy-30816>, accessed 1 July 2019.
60 Moira Lindsay, interview with the author, 26 June 2019.
61 Alun Evans, 'Where are All the British Asian Artists?', *Vice*, 23 September 2015, <https://www.vice.com/en_uk/article/exq5yw/where-are-all-the-british-asian-artists-623>, accessed 1 July 2019.
62 Moira Lindsay, interview with the author, 26 June 2019.
63 Ibid.
64 Geraldine Bedell, 'Best of British', *Observer*, 31 October 2004.
65 Darren K. Clarke, *The Politics of Partnership: Vanessa Bell and Duncan Grant, 1912–1961*, unpublished DPhil thesis, University of Sussex, 2012, p. 77.

Conclusion

1 Anthony Downey, 'Introduction: Global Culture and Political Engagement', *Art and Politics Now* (London: Thames & Hudson, 2014), p. 24.
2 Jacques Rancière, 'The Paradoxes of Political Art', *Dissensus: On Politics and Aesthetics* (London: Continuum, 2012), p. 149.

Patricia Bickers, *The Brit Pack: Contemporary British Art: The View from Abroad* (Manchester: Cornerhouse, 1995)

Lord Bridges, Countess of Albemarle, Noel Annan, and Sir George Barnes, *Help for the Arts: A Report to the Calouste Gulbenkian Foundation* (London: Calouste Gulbenkian Foundation, 1959)

The British Council Collection 1938–1984 (London: British Council, 1984)

The British Council Collection 1984–1994 (London: British Council, 1995)

Sophie Bowness and Clive Phillpot (eds), *Britain at the Venice Biennale 1895–1995* (London: British Council, 1995)

Darren K. Clarke, *The Politics of Partnership: Vanessa Bell and Duncan Grant, 1912–1961* (University of Sussex, DPhil thesis, 2012)

Verity Clarkson, *The Organisation and Reception of Eastern Bloc Exhibitions on the British Cold War 'Home Front' c. 1956–1979* (University of Brighton, PhD thesis, 2010)

Michael Craig-Martin and Andrea Rose, *British Council Collection: Passports* (London: British Council, 2009)

Elena Crippa, '1970s: Out of Sculpture', *British Art Studies*, No. 3 (July 2016)

Nicholas J. Cull, 'Overture to an Alliance: British Propaganda at the New York World's Fair, 1939–1940', *Journal of British Studies*, Vol. 36, No. 3 (July 1997), pp. 325–54

Martin Davidson, 'Cultural relations: Building Networks to Face Twenty-First-Century Challenges', in Jolyon Welsh and Daniel Fearn (eds), *Engagement: Public Diplomacy in a Globalised World* (London: Foreign and Commonwealth Office, 2008)

Frances Donaldson, *The British Council: The First Fifty Years* (London: Jonathan Cape, 1984)

Anthony Downey, *Art and Politics Now* (London: Thames & Hudson, 2014)

Diana Jane Eastman, *The Policies and Position of the British Council from the Outbreak of War to 1950* (PhD thesis, University of Leeds, 1982)

Lars Eckstein, Barbara Korte, Eva Ulrike Pirker, and Christoph Reinfandt (eds), *Multiethnic Britain 2000+: New Perspectives in Literature, Film and the Arts* (Amsterdam: Brill / Rodopi, 2008)

Simon Ford, *Wreckers of Civilisation: The Story of COUM Transmissions and Throbbing Gristle* (London: Black Dog, 1999)

Margaret Garlake, *New Art, New World: British Art in Postwar Society* (London and New Haven: Yale University Press, 1988)

Imogen Hart, 'Craft, War and Cultural Diplomacy: Modern British Crafts in the United States, 1942–45', *Winterthur Portfolio*, Vol. 53, No. 23 (Summer / Autumn 2019), pp. 95–196

Richard Hoggart, Michael Bootle, Peter Brook, Susan Castle, and Andrew Norris, *The British Council and the Arts, Activity Review No. 5* (London: British Council, 1986)

Nancy Jachec, 'The "New British Sculpture" at the Venice Biennale: Europeanism and its limits', *British Art Journal*, Vol. 7, No. 1 (Spring / Summer 2006)

Hamid Keshmirshekan, 'The Contemporary Art Scene of Iran: Cultural policy, infrastructure, dissemination and exchange', in Nick Wadham-Smith and Danny

Whitehead (eds), *Didgah: New Perspectives on UK–Iran Cultural Relations* (London: British Council, 2015)

Naseem Khan, *The Arts Britain Ignores: The Arts of Ethnic Minorities in Britain* (London: Arts Council of Great Britain, Calouste Gulbenkian Foundation, and Community Relations Commission, 1976)

Naseem Khan, 'The Arts of Ethnic Minorities in Britain', *Journal of the Royal Society of Arts*, Vol. 128, No. 5290 (September 1980), pp. 676–88

Rosalind Krauss, 'Sculpture in the Expanded Field', *October*, Vol. 8. (Spring 1979), pp. 30–44

Judith Legrove, *Diamond Lil: Lilian Somerville, The Woman Behind the Post-War British Art Boom* (London: Osborne Samuel Gallery, 2022)

Alexander Massouras, *Patronage, Professionalism and Youth: The Emerging Artist and London's Art Institutions 1949–1988* (PhD thesis, Birkbeck College, University of London, 2013)

Duncan McCorquodale, Naomi Siderfin, and Julian Stallabrass (eds), *Occupational Hazard: Critical Writing on Recent British Art* (London: Black Dog, 1998)

Kobena Mercer, 'Ethnicity and Internationality: New British Art and Diaspora-Based Blackness', *Third Text*, No. 49 (Winter 1999–2000), pp. 51–62

Henry Meyric Hughes, 'The Promotion and Reception of British Sculpture Abroad, 1948–1960: Herbert Read, Henry Moore, Barbara Hepworth, and the "Young British Sculptors"', *British Art Studies*, No. 3 (July 2016)

Gregor Muir, *Lucky Kunst: The Rise and Fall of Young British Art* (London: Aurum Press, 2009)

Leonor de Oliveira, 'Politics, Diplomatic Relations and Institutional Promotion through Modern Art: The British Art of the Twentieth Century Exhibition in Portugal, 1962', *RIHA Journal*, No. 72, 2013

Nikolaus Pevsner, *The Englishness of English Art* (London: Penguin, 1978 [1956])

Jacques Rancière, *Dissensus: On Politics and Aesthetics* (London: Continuum, 2012)

Pauline Rose, *Henry Moore in America: Art, Business and the Special Relationship* (London: I. B. Tauris, 2014)

Loveday Shewell, *A Review of the Arts Council Collection, British Council Collection and Government Art Collection* (London: Arts Council England, 2012)

Julian Stallabrass, *High Art Lite: The Rise and Fall of Young British Art* (London: Verso, 2006 [1999])

Andrew Stephenson, 'Fashioning a Post-War Reputation: Henry Moore as a Civic Sculptor c. 1943–58' in *Henry Moore: Sculptural Process and Public Identity*, Tate Research Publication, 2015

Philip M. Taylor, *The Projection of Britain: British Overseas Publicity and Propaganda 1919–1939* (Cambridge: Cambridge University Press, 1981)

John A. Walker, *Left Shift: Radical Art in 1970s Britain* (London: I. B. Tauris, 2002)

J. S. White, *The British Council: The First 25 Years 1934–1959* (London: British Council, 1965)

Every effort has been made to credit the copyright holders, photographers, and source of images in this book.

l = left, r = right, t = top, c = centre, b = bottom

6, 276, 277: © Suki Dhanda
14, 15l, 15r, 73l, 73r, 130, 352: National Portrait Gallery
24: © Martin, Tony and Richard Freeth
16, 98, 100, 109: © Archivio Storico della Biennale di Venezia – ASAC
28: © The Estate of Cyril Power. All Rights Reserved, 2023 / Bridgeman Images
29, 30: © The Estate of Blair Hughes-Stanton
35: From the papers of Muriel Rose at the Crafts Study Centre, University for the Creative Arts, MRA/1284
46: © Courtesy of the Estate of Michael Cardew / Estate and Crafts Study Centre, University for the Creative Arts
49: © Courtesy of the Estate of Michael Cardew
56, 76, 80r, 88, 89, 94, 106, 134, 135, 139, 146, 173, 179, 180, 183, 189, 203, 207, 219, 303: Tate
58: © Jill Crowley
59: © Ara Cardew
60t: © Edmund de Waal
60c: © The Maker. © Courtesy of Marsden Woo Gallery, London
60b: © The Artist
62–3, 65: © Alan Kane
66, 68, 98, 104: © Estate of Graham Sutherland
71, 83, 84, 87, 86b, 88, 89, 90, 92, 94, 302, 303: Reproduced by permission of The Henry Moore Foundation
74: © Estate of Duncan Grant. All Rights Reserved, DACS 2023
95, 96, 97, 137, 301: Barbara Hepworth © Bowness
101: © Trustees of the Paolozzi Foundation, Licensed by DACS 2020
102: © The Kenneth Armitage Foundation / Bridgeman Images
103, 109: © The Estate of Lynn Chadwick / Bridgeman Images
110: © The Estate of Jack Smith
113: © Julian Hartnoll / Bridgeman Images
114, 124: © Peter Blake. All Rights Reserved, DACS 2023
119: © David Hockney. Photo: Centro de Arte Moderna Gulbenkian, Lisbon
123, 145, 349: © David Hockney. Photo: Richard Schmidt
133: By permission of copyright owner
135: © Estate of Reg Butler
136: Digital image courtesy of Athayde de Barros, Fundaçao Bienal de São Paulo, Arquivo Histórico Wanda Svevo
138: © Estate of Hubert Dalwood
139: © The estate of Bernard Meadows
142t: © Richard Smith Foundation. All Rights Reserved, DACS 2023
142b: © The Estate of Patrick Caulfield. All Rights Reserved, DACS 2023
143: Photograph of a multiple made by Euan Duff, London. © The Estate of Richard Hamilton. All Rights Reserved, DACS 2023
146: © David Hockney. Tate Archive
151, 153: © Bridget Riley 2023. All Rights Reserved
154: © Bruce McLean / Bridgeman Images
161, 291, 321: © Gilbert & George
162: © Rita Donagh. All Rights Reserved, DACS 2023
163: © The Artist's Estate
165, 163: © the artists
171t: Photographed by Tina Tranter
171b: Photographed by Terry Moore
173, 174, 175, 176: © Richard Long. All Rights Reserved, DACS 2023
178, 196, 326: © Tim Head
179: © Michael Craig-Martin. Photo: Chris Davies
180: © Kevin Atherton. Photo: Chris Davies
181: © Stuart Brisley
187: © Rasheed Araeen
189, 203: © Peter Fraser. Photo © Tate
191, 192: © The Lucian Freud Archive / Bridgeman Images
195: © The British Library Board
197: © Sharon Kivland
200: © John Davies
201: © Julian Germain
202: © Richard Wentworth. All Rights Reserved, DACS 2023
204, 205: © Verdi Yahooda
206: © Martin Parr / Magnum Photos
211l: The Museum of Modern Art Archives, New York. IN607.24. Photograph by Soichi Sunami.

211r: Museum of Modern Art Archives, New York. IN607.36
213, 319: © The Estate of Richard Hamilton. All Rights Reserved, DACS 2023
214, 215: © Estate of Bruce Bernard (Virginia Verran)
217, 219: © The Estate of Francis Bacon. All rights reserved, DACS 2023.
223: © Estate of Victor Pasmore. All rights Reserved, DACS 2023
227: © The Estate of Helen Chadwick, Courtesy Richard Saltoun Gallery
228, 229: © Bill Woodrow
233, 255: © Chris Ofili
235: © Studio lost but found / DACS 2023
236, 237: © Fiona Banner
239: © Tracey Emin. All Rights Reserved, DACS 2023
244, 245: © Michael Landy
246, 247: © Vong Phaophanit. All Rights Reserved, DACS 2023
251: © The Artist
252, 253: © Estate of Maud Sulter. All Rights Reserved, DACS 2023
260, 261: © DACS 2023
262: © Richard Deacon
263, 288, 289: © Mona Hatoum
264: © Rachel Whiteread
265: © Damien Hirst and Science Ltd. All Rights Reserved, DACS 2023
266, 267: © The Artist
269, 298: © Anish Kapoor. All Rights Reserved, DACS 2023
273, 295, 296: © The artist and Thomas Dane Gallery, London
278, 279: © Anthony Lam. All Rights Reserved.
281: Courtesy of the Artist
284: Photo by Onish Aminelahi
285: Tehran Museum of Contemporary Art
286: Photo by Alain Nogues
292: Photo by Behrouz Mehri / AFP / Getty Images
293: © Damien Hirst and Science Ltd. All Rights Reserved, DACS 2023. Photo by Rick Jenkins and Donald Thompson
295: © Shirazeh Houshiary
309: © The Artists
310, 311, 338: © Tim Hetherington/IWM/ Magnum Photos
314, 354: © Courtesy the artist and Kooper Astner
318: © Sean Scully. Photo: courtesy the artist.
320: © © Damien Hirst and Science Ltd. All rights reserved, DACS 2023.
322: © Richard Woodward
323: © Jake and Dinos Chapman. All Rights Reserved, DACS 2023
325: © Stephen Dixon
334: © Danny Treacy
336: © Grayson Perry. Courtesy the artist and Victoria Miro
337: © The artist and Frith Street Gallery, London
339: © The Artist. Courtesy Wilkinson Gallery, London
340: © Anthony Haughey
341: © Jimmie Durham Estate
346–7: © Grayson Perry. Courtesy the artist and Victoria Miro
353: © The Artist, courtesy Sadie Coles HQ, London
355: © Courtesy the artist and Southard Reid
360: © Courtesy of the Estate of Paula Rego and Marlborough Fine Art
361: Courtesy of the Artist
363, endpapers: Banners made by Ed Hall
364, 365: © J Deller & A Kane
366, 367, 368: Photo by Sangtae Kim, © Seoul Museum of Art
369: © Photo Andy Keate, courtesy The Artist and Hollybush Gardens
370–1: © The artist, purchased jointly by British Council and Tate with assistance from the Art Fund 2014.
374: © Hardeep Pandhal
377: © Delaine Le Bas
378: Photograph Chin Yui Jasmine Lau

The writing of this book has been enriched by conversations, reflections, and support from many generous academics, archivists, and curators, alongside British Council staff, past and present: Harriet Atkinson, Jeremy Aynsley, Greta Bertram, Andrew Brown, Verity Clarkson, Rebekkah Deighton, Emma Dexter, Diana Eccles, Adrian Forty, Adrian Glew, Nicola Heald, Gill Hedley, Gemma Hollington, Henry Meyric Hughes, Jacky Klein, Chin Yui Jasmine Lau, Moira Lindsay, Emily Medd, Richard Riley, Brett Rogers, Andrea Rose, Katrina Schwarz, Miranda Stacey, Ying Tan, Charlie Walker, Jenny White, Sean Williams, and Stephen Witkowski. There have also been many others within the British Council, too numerous to mention here, who have made important contributions to the production of this book. My thanks go to all of them.

Brighton, June 2023

Numerals in *italics* indicate pages with illustrations

COU
CTIO